CONCERN FOR OTHERS

CONCEPTS IN DEVELOPMENTAL PSYCHOLOGY
Series editor: David Cohen

Also in this series

THE DEVELOPMENT OF PLAY
David Cohen

CONCERN FOR OTHERS

A New Psychology of Conscience and Morality

TOM KITWOOD

ROUTLEDGE
London and New York

First published 1990
by Routledge
11 New Fetter Lane, London EC4P 4EE

Simultaneously published in the USA and Canada
by Routledge
a division of Routledge, Chapman and Hall, Inc.
29 West 35th Street, New York, NY 10001

©1990 Tom Kitwood

Typeset by LaserScript Limited, Mitcham, Surrey.
Printed and bound in Great Britain by
Biddles Ltd, Guildford and King's Lynn

British Library Cataloguing in Publication Data

Kitwood, T. M. (Thomas Marris, *1937–)
Concern for others: a new psychology of conscience and morality.
1. Moral development
I. Title
155.2'5

Library of Congress Cataloging in Publication Data

Also available

ISBN 0-415-02338-6
0-415-04377-8 (pbk)

CONTENTS

SERIES FOREWORD

Since psychology became a 'scientific' discipline, one of its key areas has been developmental psychology. How children grow up remains one of the most important, and intriguing, of questions. For a long time, outside psychoanalysis, developmental psychology was dominated by studies of intelligence, but children don't just grow cognitively. In the last fifteen years, there have been a wealth of studies on different aspects of growing up – from how children begin to relate, to how they learn to speak, to how their sense of humour matures. Video recording techniques have helped to widen the scope of developmental psychology so it is now possible to observe children more accurately than ever before. The whole area of study is exciting and growing.

This series aims to reflect the growth of developmental psychology. Each volume will be written by an interesting psychologist whose brief is to write an account of a particular developmental patch. For some books that patch will be conventionally defined. Other books will take a wider than usual look at a particular area. Some will take a concept that is well accepted in everyday life, such as conscience, but which academic psychology has tended to ignore or, at best, to treat intellectually. Each book will offer a clear, readable, and authoritative account of the latest ideas and research in the area at a level which is both interesting to the specialist and accessible to the undergraduate.

David Cohen

ACKNOWLEDGEMENTS

The fact that I have managed to complete this book, during a very unsettled time for the British universities, is due in large measure to the help and encouragement I have received. Back in 1986, when I was hesitating, my son Andrew and daughter Lucy, then aged 14 and 12, 'advised' me to go ahead, and gave me detailed arguments to show that it was feasible. More recently, Lucy did the artwork. Mike Woodman and Pauline Speight prepared draft material for chapters 4 and 5 respectively, and I am happy to regard these as joint publications. I discussed the content of the book with a number of people, and am especially grateful to Jenny Aste, Matthew Plant, Chris Henry, Janet Watson, and Derek Wright for their criticisms and suggestions. David Cohen read most of the material in draft form, and made many valuable comments. Anne-Marie Robinson word-processed almost all the text, and was unfailingly patient and good-humoured despite my many additions and revisions. I have enjoyed sharing this project with all those whom I have mentioned, and a number more. I would like to say thank you to them all.

I also acknowledge permission from the editor of the *Journal of Moral Education* to draw on the three articles of mine that the journal has published recently. These are listed in the references.

INTRODUCTION

During the last few years I have taken part intensely in two very different communities of knowledge and action, two different social life-worlds, beyond my immediate personal ties and interests. Both of them have, I think, helped me to be more human; also to understand something of what 'morality' is about.

My professional work has been within a university, as an academic social psychologist. For some time I was a member of a group which we called MOSAIC, set up to explore aspects of morality, primarily on the border between philosophy and the social sciences. We formed this group at a conference in 1977, when Lawrence Kohlberg came to Britain to give an account of his work to his admirers and critics. His grasp of the field and his achievements in research were so impressive that for some time afterwards we seemed to be engaging primarily with an appraisal of his ideas; only gradually were we able to put them into perspective. At the conference Kohlberg said very little about his practical attempts to set up a 'just community' in a school setting, and I sense that this very human aspect of his work may have been undervalued.

My own research at this time involved an empirical enquiry into values, and the way these are woven into the texture of everyday life. While developing my method I experienced a kind of revulsion against some of the main approaches in social psychology as I had encountered it. Strongly influenced by behaviourism, these often seemed implicitly to depersonalize their 'subjects'; and I came to believe that the numerical data thus accumulated often gave little insight into their real lives as social and historical beings. I had strong feelings, in my own work, that I wanted to do research

1

'with' people rather than 'on' them. At the theoretical level I found a good deal of justification for this in the new psychological humanism that was growing in certain quarters. Its fundamental axiom, as I saw it, was 'for scientific purposes, [to] treat people as if they were human beings' (Harré and Secord 1972: 84); its hope was to create a psychology that would not be a 'natural science of behaviour' but a 'moral science of action' (Shotter 1975: 23). In this psychology the 'subjects', like the psychologists themselves, would be viewed and respected as responsible agents. This humanism, which has now produced a substantive body of theory, is still one of my main inspirations.

It is not only in an academic sense, however, that work in a British university during the last years has proved to be some kind of moral education. At its best a university is a 'community of scholars', able to transcend individualistic concern and to work co-operatively for the advancement of knowledge in the service of a broader social good. I have certainly experienced a form of academic life that comes close to this, and at times still do; it is not the norm now, but something to be achieved with considerable effort. Much more typical of the present state of affairs, when the life of the universities has been under severe threat, is the loss of the sense of common weal, and of commitment to some vision of a better world. Bonds of trust created over the years were severed almost overnight; people who had previously seemed to have moral integrity were found to be behaving with extraordinary ruthlessness and self-interest. New affiliations were created, not based on human values, but on money-grabbing and naked desire for self-preservation. In Britain, at least, the social fabric of the university proved to be exceedingly fragile, and concern for others among academics a labile species. Under pressure, organizational imperatives generally proved stronger than moral motives.

Secondly, however, I have been involved increasingly in the experiential domain of psychology: in counselling, psychotherapy, groupwork, bodywork. Before immersing myself in this, both as a recipient and (later) as a giver, I had of course gained a rudimentary knowledge of the theory of psychoanalysis and the therapies that developed from it. I could recite some of the axioms of Rogerian counselling, talk about the needs for nurturance, achievement, and affiliation, or discuss the 'neurotic personality of our time'. Now, however, I began to appreciate what some of these

2

ideas meant in my own experience, as I tried to come to terms with
certain deeply unresolved problems of my own, and then to share
my growing understanding with others. As I reflected upon what I
was learning in the therapeutic milieu I came to believe that in this
profound but confused area of practical psychology there were
many insights vital to a rounded understanding of our contemporary moral predicament, even though they sometimes eluded
clear conceptualization, and were impossible to ground in 'hard'
data. In my involvement with these two kinds of psychology, I
seemed to come across a striking contrast. Whereas the new
academic humanists tended to view the person as rational, whole,
and competent, therapists drew attention to widespread impair-
ment, alienation, and fragmentation. As the 1980s have continued,
more and more people seem to have come to the end of their
personal resources, suffering 'burn-out', anxiety, depression, and
a whole variety of stress-related illnesses. In many organizations a
greater output is demanded, with fewer opportunities for support.
As I began to develop my particular line in counselling work, I
came to characterize my main goal as that of facilitating the
enlargement of a person's experiential frame, primarily through
the recovery and acceptance of a wider range of feelings and
emotions, with their many conflicts and ambivalences. This would
be the basis for a fuller sense of agency, and a better capacity to
relate to others. In my experience, this was how my own life
seemed to have been developing.

The main foundations for this book were laid during the
summer of 1987, when I was granted a term of study leave from
Bradford University. My general practice was to continue with my
writing during the mornings, and to give some time during the
afternoons for counselling work. I very soon found that there was
a close relationship, almost a dialectical interchange, between the
two activities. Both, in their different ways, were concerned with
the psychology of the moral life. In the morning I would be
struggling to order my thoughts about personhood, the moral
agent, the foundations of concern for others, and so on. In the
afternoon I would be spending time with Bill, gradually coming to
terms with the failure of his marriage; with Jane, trying to extricate
herself from a near-suffocating relationship with her very needy
mother; with Richard, emotionally involved with both his wife and
his lover; with Brenda, a widow suffering the after-effects of a

marriage in which her own vitality was crushed; with Peter, a child grieving for his handicapped state, as he witnessed his younger brother overtaking him; with Carol, sensing that if she ends her present, and deeply unsatisfactory sexual relationship, she may be on her own for the rest of her life. (These are all real people, although their identities are disguised.)

During this time all those with whom I was involved in a counselling role were dealing with what might properly be regarded as moral questions. I wanted my own contribution to the psychology of moral development to engage directly with the kind of concerns they raised. Here one point is very striking. Something that professes to be a moral 'ought', when it arises as a topic in counselling and therapy, is almost always present as negative, destructive, life-denying – part of a system of explicit or hidden blackmail in which a person's own authentic life is stifled. In the well-known collection of essays on moral development edited by Lickona (1975) James Gilligan claimed, on psychoanalytic grounds, that morality was a force antagonistic to life. He wrote, 'I see morality as a necessary but immature stage of affective and cognitive development, so that fixation at the moral stage represents developmental retardation, or immaturity, and regression to it represents psychopathology, or neurosis' (p.145). In the most superficial sense, and only so, I agree with this. But what Gilligan seems not to have realized is that he also was advancing a moral point of view – one in which love had pre-eminence. In my own way I am developing this kind of thesis. For depth psychology, as I shall present it here, takes us to the very heart of what it means to be a person, and is profoundly moral in its concern for human relationship and well-being. The 'morality' to which it is opposed is simply that of the authoritarian, the obsessional moralist, and the hypocrite.

So I have called this book *Concern for Others*, because I wanted to make a definitive separation between what I am talking about and everyday ideas of morality, which have such strong connotations of 'doing what you don't want to do, not doing what you actually want to do – and feeling guilty if you fail'. This, of course, is merely a commonsensical notion, but its presence is pervasive for good reason. I believe it is this. Moral discourse in western culture has been corrupted by two pernicious ingredients. One is a kind of 'pure' intellectualism that ultimately derives from Plato, suggesting that we can know the good in some timeless, separate, and disembodied (psychoanalysts might say 'schizoid') way. The other is a conglomerate of deprecating and masochistic ideas about human nature, derived mainly from the Augustinian form of Christianity, and behind that, from parts of Judaism. In some of the traditions of the Orient, notably that of tantra within Hinduism and Buddhism, we find forms of moral discourse that are far more earth-bound, sensuous, and life-affirming. (To be fair to Christianity, here is something which some contemporary Christians also are trying to rediscover.)

In accepting an invitation to write a book that would give a new perspective on the topic of moral development, I knew, then, that I wanted to draw not only on my work as an empirical researcher and as an academic, but also on my knowledge and personal understanding of depth psychology. In so doing, I hope to contribute something towards the vision of morality as concerned primarily with life-affirmation and awareness, not respectability and restraint. This book presents no new data such as would be accepted as valid by psychologists strongly oriented towards measurement; but it does attempt to bring into the moral field a large body of work that has as yet been given only scanty recognition there. Also it is based on a great deal of raw data from my own experience, and my involvement with others, reflected upon and slowly being integrated into my academic work.

This book consists of eight chapters, which together cover a good deal of the field of moral psychology. However, it questions, in certain respects, the way in which the field is currently constituted. Primarily I am offering a standpoint, a new way of looking at familiar topics, by bringing work from existing moral psychology and psychotherapy together. It should be noted at the outset that these two areas are, in fact, quite closely related. For the greater part of psychotherapeutic work is concerned with the harm human beings have caused one another, often unwittingly: the failure to perceive their vulnerability, to heed their desires, to hear their grievances, to comprehend their distresses. Moreover, these interpersonal actions and inactions, which may be judged as morally wrong in their failure to give due respect for persons, often occur where there are inequalities of power, and are set in larger contexts of social injustice. Conversely, the therapeutic environment, at its best, may be seen as a microcosmic restoration of a moral world, a place in which a person's subjectivity is honoured, possibly for the first time ever.

In common with some of the academic humanists to whom I have referred, I hold that psychology is (or should be) fundamentally concerned with the enrichment of our understanding of the human-reality – a phrase adapted from Sartre to mean social life as it is experienced from within. Here psychology will not build up an esoteric jargon, but will clarify, enrich, and in some cases transform concepts and knowledge embedded in ordinary language. By means of careful research, it will develop insights and understandings that go far beyond the deceptive platitudes of common sense. In so doing, I believe that there is no reason for it to be founded on principles and methods which are commonly held to be those of natural science, although these may be valuable at times as additional resources. All this gives me a way of looking at morality, and the psychology of moral development. Ultimately I conclude that the project of mapping and promoting the moral development of individuals involves a mistaken emphasis. Moral development, I suggest, is a category more applicable to collective life; the notion of the moral needs to be recalled to the social domain, whence it originated. There are, however, forms of development whose proper referent is the individual person, which are conducive to moral development in the broader sense.

In Chapter 1 I attempt to characterize concern for others, and then go on to give a brief survey of the way in which moral discourse has developed, beginning with the primal form of social life – that of the hunter-gatherers. It is clear that the moral 'ought', as we know it in the western cultural tradition, is highly problematic, when its psychological 'adhesions' are considered. As societies have become more complex, there has been some divergence between the kinds of moral discourse taken to be relevant to interpersonal relations, and to the whole organization of society. Psychology needs to keep sight of both.

Chapter 2 lays the foundation for a psychological enquiry into concern for others, particularly through an examination of certain key concepts such as agency and personhood. If we take agency seriously, and give due account to the problem of 'weakness of will', we seem to be led immediately towards the kind of understanding of the person that depth psychology provides. In the light of this I attempt to characterize the project of psychology in a way that does justice both to its 'academic' and 'therapeutic' forms. Psychology is concerned with the interpretive under-standing of individuals in their uniqueness, against a background knowledge which is not commonsensical, but informed by many low-level generalizations; these, although often helpful and liberating, are partial and culture-bound, and do not meet the criteria of natural-scientific law.

In Chapter 3 I develop an image of the person as a sentient being, in contrast to two other images that are pervasive: the rational cognitive actor and the 'driven creature', the latter taken from those crude appropriations of Freud's ideas that are found in mainstream social science. The person thus portrayed is an agent. But he or she is less whole and rational than the academic humanists imply: divided in motive, impaired in experiential capability, damaged by failures in nurture, maimed by social injustice, distorted by stereotypical scripts concerning gender. We explore briefly what such a concept of the person means for a theory of social action, and for the understanding of morality. A crucial concept is explicated: that of 'moral space'.

Chapter 4 is an attempt to say something about the foundations of concern for others in infants and young children, long before they are able to engage in critical discourse about it. Here depth psychology comes to our aid, although the story that it tells is not always directly testable. The key point is that to be human is to be moral from the very first; morality is not something that is added on later, as a kind of overlay or injection. However, a person may be deeply and perhaps irrevocably damaged as a moral being, as a result of early privations or injuries.

Chapter 5 takes up the topic of moral judgement, which has had such a central place in the field during the last twenty years. The work of both Piaget and Kohlberg is examined, together with the crucial question of how moral judgement and moral action are related; here Piaget's approach may be the more illuminating. Also, we look briefly at the work of Carol Gilligan on the ethic of care. My conclusion on the work of the Kohlberg group is that, although it has told us a great deal about how one kind of 'theoretical morality' develops, its approach will not suffice as a linchpin for holding the whole edifice of moral psychology together.

Chapter 6 deals with the question of behaviour in the formal organizations that are typical of industrial society: those which have a hierarchical structure, and very clear role requirements for their members. These organizations seem to be an essential feature of contemporary life in both the capitalist and the state-planned economies. Their presence has brought certain very great benefits; but it also seems to be the care that they have induced some of the greatest atrocities in world history. We explore some possible reasons why this is the case. A new agenda item for the psychology of morality is thereby opened up.

Chapter 7 examines the topic the moral character. In common with a few other theorists in the field, I argue that it is one of crucial importance, and more encompassing than a person's stage of moral judgement. In the first part of the chapter we look at some of the relevant research and come to the conclusion that the topic of character was generally abandoned for insufficient reason. In the second part I offer an account of the process of psychotherapy as a praxis upon character; idealizing therapy to some extent, I try to exhibit it as a paradigm of moral restoration, in which deep-seated psychic wounds are healed.

Chapter 8 is a kind of postscript, in which I spell out briefly what I believe to be the broader implications of the position developed throughout the book. Whereas my own values are present but latent in the whole text, here they become explicit. My account leads us into the realm of 'the pathology of what is taken as normality', and I suggest the need for a form of social life in which certain therapeutic ideals can be realized. Psychology as I have characterized it in this book suggests that social fabric, whose essential feature is trust between persons, is primary; and that considerations of distributive justice are important secondarily, in that they are dealing with the conditions under which social fabric can be maintained. Contemporary society is caught up in a vicious circle of reproduction, in which both institutions and personalities are impaired. Despite many gloomy signs, there are grounds for believing that the circle can be, and slowly is being, broken.

We live now in an era that has aptly been described as postmodern. The great hope of the European Enlightenment – the reform of the world through the triumph of reason – has collapsed in disillusionment. The triumphant prospect held out by industrialization and advanced technology – the delivery to humankind of permanent safety and abundance – has proved to be a terrible deception. The postmodern condition, then, is typified by a resort to extreme cynicism and superficiality, a 'life on the surface'. At the same time fundamentalisms and sectarianisms are flourishing, feeding on widespread insecurity. In British politics it is becoming fashionable to exalt self-interest flagrantly, to devalue all serious expression of concern for others or aspirations for a just society. This book adds something to our psychological grounds for believing that all such reactions to past failure are deeply harmful. They are a gross denial, a 'manic defence', a warding off of awareness of our true predicament. To be human is to exist in relationship, and this involves a 'depth' dimension, difficult as it is and full of contradictions. In a society that does not provide the conditions conducive to the formation and strengthening of relationship, all manner of dire pathologies will ensue. Conversely, the good society is one which, above all else, allows relationship to flourish. Whatever may be its political form, this is its psychological desideratum.

Chapter One

THE CONSTRUCTION AND USE OF MORAL DISCOURSE

To have concern for another person is, above all else, to experience a feeling, a 'movement of the soul', in which that person's being is honoured and respected as if it were one's own. Often we construe the other as a means to our own ends, project on to the other the image of our own unfulfilled desires. Occasionally we transcend this selfishness to some degree, and see and value the other more truly; our desire for that person's protection from harm, and for the benign unfolding of life are for his or her sake, not our own. Concern for others emerges from fullness, flourishes in a climate of generosity and well-being; but easily withers away, and putrefies into egoism and hatred, under conditions of emotional threat or scarcity. In everyday life it is carried within such forms as greeting, holding, sharing, giving, carrying, and caressing. Ceremonially, it is celebrated in acts of blessing: the laying on of hands, the anointing of the body with perfumed oil, the bestowal of a garland of flowers; above all, perhaps, in some of those ancient forms of dance, in which a group of people celebrate their togetherness. It need hardly be said that none of these is necessarily or universally sincere; many outward expressions are no more than an empty shell. Concern for others is only one of a great variety of human propensities, and among them all it may be the most fragile.

The whole tenor of psychology is to suggest that concern for others begins, in the individual, in a special relationship with a very few significant persons; sometimes only one, and usually no more than seven. This concern arises as a necessary accompaniment of the formation of a self from the immensely complex and sensitive organism that is the new-born infant. For some persons this is the total extent of their concern, throughout the whole duration of life; and there may be a few who do not get even that far, in whom the first movements towards self-transcendence were aborted. Generally, however, the feeling that began in such a limited way is extended more widely, like the circular waves after a stone has been dropped into a pool. Perhaps it goes so far as to include some with whom there is no close relationship – simply on the grounds that they are persons, too. But, of course, once this step has been taken, and its implications understood, there is no reason for excluding any person in the world, and even those who are as yet unborn. This wider concern is, however, experienced in a mode that is primarily intellectual; for we seem to be constituted, by virtue of our biological inheritance, as fairly parochial beings, adapted best to groups of less than one hundred people; as such, we are limited in our capacities for knowing others well as individuals, and restricted in our natural sympathies.[1]

Many societies have existed, so anthropology seems to indicate, without ever developing systematic doctrines or theories that we would easily identify as moral. Concern for others is expressed in forms of practice, and if expressed verbally, largely through myth and fable. But when theories are created, the proponents have no option but to draw on the available resources of the culture, its familiar metaphors and preoccupations; at least these provide a starting point, even if they are modified in use. In the west, especially since the eighteenth-century cultural movement known as the Enlightenment (when the world was, supposedly, to be redeemed by reason), moral theory has been dominated by a few specially powerful ideas. In particular, widespread use has been made of the concepts of 'right' and 'duty', which might be regarded initially as metaphors. MacIntyre (1967, 1981) has traced the origins of these ideas, and the significance of his analysis is often overlooked. In the highly stratified societies of medieval feudalism, rights and duties referred to what was generally expected of the occupants of a particular role or class position, accompanied by such maxims as *'Noblesse oblige'*. The ideology, at its most generous, suggested that wherever there was privilege, there was also responsibility, and that where there was subservience, there was also security. Concomitantly, there arose the idea of a special kind of 'matter-that-was-owing', both upwards and downwards within the hierarchy: in a single word, an *ought*. Two

11

centuries or so later, what had been a specific, socially situated instruction became a kind of generalized and universalized command, freed from any particular social context. The matter-that-was-owing became a 'moral ought', and the idea of a community within which individuals might realize their social being became increasingly a disembodied dream.

Now, after a long period of philosophizing about the nature and content of the ought, its metaphorical status (as also that of its companion concepts) has been very largely forgotten. A special, 'moral' category has been created, and with it an immensely elaborate discourse; it is commonly held, within western philosophy, to be something apart, of its own kind, and reducible to no other – having an almost transcendent status.[2] There is a rich variety of opinions within the field that counts as moral, but the category itself has been largely uncontested. Philosophers sometimes overlook the fact that a lived concern for others is universal in a way that is not the case with what is often called morality; also, that for the greater part of the time that human beings have been upon the earth, no discourse has existed that would today be recognized as moral.

To elaborate this point a little, let us glance for a moment at the work of Immanuel Kant, who is justly considered to be the father of modern moral discourse in the west, and is certainly the figure who overarches psychological work in this field. Caputo (1986) points out that in his early writings Kant advanced a theory of moral sense or feeling, and (like his English contemporary Hume) grounded concern for others firmly in the naturally given inclinations. Later, when his vast project of critical philosophy had taken shape, he made what might be regarded now as a step away from psychological understanding. For he attempted to force an extreme separation between earthly desire and a pure will, the latter being taken by him to be the inspiration for all 'truly moral' endeavour. With this he postulated a moral law, somewhat similar to a divine command, but ultimately compelling only because of its rational appeal. In this way morality was separated from the fickleness of earthly desires.

This dissociation served a logical purpose, but left Kant with a problem in the area of motivation. It is true, of course, that we are 'motivated', or spurred to action, by reasons; but usually, and certainly for very significant action, those reasons are accompanied by feelings. Kant therefore suggested that the will is associated with a special kind of feeling, distinctively moral in quality, not subject to change and chance. Perhaps the truth is that Kant's idea of a moral law is but one particular, and highly culture-bound, rationalization of a feeling of respect for persons that is already present, at least to some degree, in most human beings. Kant exalted it to a special status, and treated it with reverence, partly because he experienced it with the utmost clarity and sensitivity. But it is questionable whether any 'moral law' alone could motivate concern for others; it is more likely that it simply gives expression to a motive that is already present, even if not fully conscious, and grounded in those dispositions which are part of our evolutionary heritage.

The idea of a transcendent moral 'ought' may satisfy a philosopher's desire for logical neatness, but it carries enormous practical difficulties, as most persons who have been involved in psychotherapeutic work will testify. For within real individuals motives are hardly ever single or unalloyed; most of our actions, and certainly most that come within the category of 'moral', seem to be carried out for a variety of reasons. So, even though it might be logically possible to distil the ought so as to obtain the purest essence of moral concern, this does not work psychologically. Moreover, there are many people who are, in their actual lives abundantly caring and compassionate, but who have little truck with moral ideas, and who actually find the idea of the moral ought incomprehensible.[3]

What is it, then, about the moral ought as we have inherited it, that makes it such a problematic way of focusing the meaning of concern for others? It is not, surely, that there is a fault in the core content, with its acknowledgement of the validity of persons as ends in themselves, and its unequivocal rejection of egoism as a basis for a truly human life. Nor is it to do with the actual form of moral utterance; in this case, a generalized, de-situated command. The difficulties are to be found, rather, in what might be called the psychological adhesions; connotations which have remained attached to the ought, as it is used in everyday life, associated with deeply entrenched ways of being and relating, and which derive from its context of origination.

In a highly stratified society, with very little opportunity for people to move out of their given social positions, there is usually

13

a code of rights and duties which at least serves to curb some excesses, and to mitigate the effects of domination. This was certainly the case in Europe, when the feudal social order was at its peak in the twelfth and thirteenth centuries. But the ethical system also served to maintain domination; there was very little possibility of going outside it, and raising the question of justice in a more fundamental way. It was inconceivable for a knight to challenge his baron about the conditions of his service, for a serf to negotiate with his lord concerning the ownership of land, or for a woman to have a full and equal say within the contract of marriage. The ought, then, often served to prevent the bringing of needs and interests into the open, and to keep people from engaging in honest and creative conflict. It functioned to maintain a *Gemeinschaft,* which is often no more than a semblance of community, with all its hidden agenda based on arrogance and resentment. When, in the fourteenth century, peasants began to revolt, and to ask such radical questions as 'When Adam delved and Eve span, who was then the gentleman?', they were often put down with violence. The moral ought, as we have inherited it, still carries marks of this ancestry. There seem to be many situations where people resort to moralistic considerations about what they ought to do in relation to others, when it would be perfectly possible to consult those others about what they actually want. Confrontation and open negotiation almost always threaten the status quo, and psychologically this is liable to be stressful and demanding. In a pure and ideal sense, the moral ought is absolutely opposed to privilege. The psychological reality is often the opposite of this, and privilege is subtle and pervasive.

There is another, but related, problem which arises when concern for others is conceptualized in moralistic terms, and attached to the category of ought. Psychologically, a whole range of feelings of personal inadequacy and unworthiness are often aroused, depriving a person of confidence and spontaneity. Here certain versions of Christianity, with their insistence that all human beings are desperately wicked and unworthy, living under divine condemnation, must surely have made a powerful contribution. But also, it is possible for people to be virtually crushed by a moral law, even if it carries no obvious religious meaning. This seems to reflect a failure to develop a sense of selfhood that is grounded in and sustained by optimistic and trustful feelings, leading to a lack of willingness to meet others on their own ground, to respect their selfhood as valid also. To misquote Nietzsche, whose original remark was about Christianity: 'Moralism either finds men sick or makes them so.' It easily becomes the basis for a life that is not lived, because such a life would be too risky.

Thus whatever may be said at a purely theoretical level, the moral ought in practice tends to obliterate the unique personhood of both the agent and those who might be the objects of concern. It is as if, in this way of framing the problem of how to regulate the way people treat one another, individual being has dwindled to a mere point, and an abstraction has come to take over the space that is thus vacated. At its most pernicious, moralism becomes part of a struggle for the maintenance of psychic reality by those who have little inkling of their own desires; they find themselves following imperatives which, however noble, are split off from their own selves. And then, at a 'higher' and more abstract level, moralism can become a kind of shadow-boxing engaged in by intellectuals, who have been known at times to take theories more seriously than persons. (It is noteworthy that Kant, the great theoretician, insisted that persons alone are worthy of respect.) In summary, then, the ought is exceedingly questionable as a motivator towards concern for others; in western culture, however, it may have some value as a rationalization. How the west acquired its particular tradition of moralism, with its emphasis on the ought, is a long and tortuous story. It will only be sketched out here, and in the most superficial way; but at least this will provide something of a context to the psychology with which this book is concerned.

THE EARLIEST FORMS OF HUMAN SOCIETY

So far as is known, our own species, *Homo* and *Mulier sapiens sapiens*, emerged through evolution as highly social, living in bands of around twenty to a hundred persons, their subsistence being based upon a combination of hunting and gathering. It is possible to say a good deal about their culture; partly on the basis of archaeological evidence, but principally from the anthropological study of certain peoples in Africa, Australia, and the Americas, whose way of life remained substantially unchanged right into the twentieth century. As a consequence of early migration their habitats varied from tropical rain forests and scorching deserts to the edge of the northern permafrost. Where the conditions of subsistence were relatively benign, there seem to have been certain very broad commonalities in the tenor of their mores: their customs, traditions, laws, and so on. However, there was great divergence in the mythological penumbra by which these were explained. Where scarcity had intervened, the differences between primal societies became very much wider.

In such societies there was a single social life-world, a single framework of shared meanings. All the social practices, both those which we might describe as having mainly instrumental functions (such as procuring food and shelter) or those which in our terms were primarily expressive (such as dance or story-telling) fitted together into a single pattern. The symbolic structure of myth and religion helped to make the fears, tensions, and contradictions of life acceptable. It appears that some hunter-gatherer peoples maintained the same way of life virtually unchanged for hundreds, even thousands of years. Modifications of culture came about in response to climatic variation, migration to a different kind of terrain, or the discovery and adoption of some new material technique like the making of pottery or woven fabric. In such societies the members generally took their human world to be on the same level as that of nature; it was immune from deep criticism or relativization – they could conceive of no other way of being. Their 'moralization' was no more, and no less, than their socialization.

Since the numbers in hunter-gatherer bands were small enough for each member to know all the others closely, and since there was virtually no privacy, the interpersonal and societal mores were identical. The way of life, under conditions of plenty, was markedly egalitarian, involving neither enduring forms of rule nor the domination of one sex by the other. Leadership was *ad hoc*, and no roles were sharply defined. The best hunters might organize the search for prey, the best healers care for illnesses of body or mind, the best story-tellers entertain. Skill and competence belonged to the whole group, bound together as an organic unit, rather than to individuals. There was a strong discouragement of any form of possessiveness, any tendency to accumulation, anything that might mark out one person above others. Even boastfulness or arrogance was firmly cut down. Among the Kung people of the Kalahari a hunter might come into a camp having killed a fine antelope, at a time when meat was scarce. Even if he modestly reported 'I have killed an animal', he might well be greeted with the joking, disparaging response 'Only one?' The explanation was simple. 'When a young man kills much meat he comes to think of the rest of us as his servants or inferiors. . . . Some day his pride will make him kill somebody' (Pfeiffer 1978: 325). Thus all forms of self-aggrandizement were condemned.

In such societies the members acquired the mores in the process of living; through observation of adults and practising under their instruction, through undergoing a succession of rites of passage, through learning the stories and myths. Of course, there were many transgressions. Typically, no individual took on the task of administering punishment; social control was a collective responsibility. It seems that the principal sanction was shame, a public loss of face. Probably there was no internalized sense of ought: a moral compulsion that applied whether or not others were present, and accompanied by feelings of guilt when norms or rules were violated.

Life in a hunter-gatherer society, under conditions of plenty, seems to have provided the members with a strong feeling of personal security and well-being. Each person was clearly demarcated, had a distinctive character. But the members were not individuals in the modern sense. They were conscious of being part of a collective; connectedness, rather than separateness, was the salient mode of awareness. But their social life was far from peaceful or idyllic. The anthropologists give us, rather, a sense of continual friction and tension; most of it dealt with fairly easily, but spasmodically erupting into deep antagonism and violence. This was generally acknowledged; custom allowed conflict to be dealt with quickly, and with the open expression of emotions.

These points are well illustrated by an anecdote concerning the Mbuti pygmies of the African rain forest, reported by Turnbull (1961). One man named Pepei was extremely lazy, and somewhat dishonest. His stealing from Bantu people who lived nearby was fully acceptable, and even minor thefts from his own group were often condoned. But one night he was caught taking food from an old woman's hut.

> The men ran out angrily and caught hold of Pepei while the youths broke off thorny branches and whipped him until he

managed to break away. He stayed in the forest for nearly
twenty-four hours, and when he came back the next night he
went straight to his hut, unseen, and lay down to sleep, crying
softly because even his brother wouldn't speak to him. . . .
The next day Pepei was his old self, and everyone was glad to
see him laughing; they were happy to be able to listen to his
jokes, and they all gave him so much food that he wouldn't
have to steal again (p. 112).

The behaviour of hunter-gatherers in relation to those who
were not of their own band, or at least of their own language group
('tribe'), is far less clear. It has become a matter of some controversy, especially since sociobiology claimed, on the flimsiest of
evidence, that a disposition to warfare was biologically given.[4]
Under benign environmental conditions the general pattern of
behaviour by one people towards another seems to have been one
of avoidance, of live and let live. Acts of 'war' were extremely rare,
and even then involved few killings, with much ritualized aggression. But in times of scarcity or perceived threat hunter-gatherers
have been known to engage in the most ruthless warfare against
their neighbours, even to the extent of what is virtually genocide.

What, we might ask, was the prime function of such mores?
Above all else, it was the preservation of social life, the maintenance of social fabric, a prevailing sense of trust and common
interest within the group. In a material sense, the continued
survival of a hunter-gatherer people required a very high level of
co-operation; it was under such conditions that the human species
actually evolved. In a psychological sense, the well-being of the
members depended on the continuity of social bonds, on a sense
of closeness to one another, on an accurate mutual understanding. Social life, even at an extremely egalitarian level, involves
a great deal of tension; social fabric is very easily destroyed. The
mores, then, provided a kind of 'container' for at least a minimal
concern for others, but mixed with a great deal that the western
tradition would not regard as quintessentially moral.

THE RISE OF MORAL TEACHING

So far as is known, developments from hunting and gathering led
in two main directions, from around 10,000 BC. One was towards

more or less permanent settlement, giving rise to a peasant way of life based largely on subsistence agriculture, with scattered villages of perhaps 500 to 1,000 persons. The other was towards pastoral nomadism, in which animals that had formerly been hunted were kept in herds, being moved across the country as grazing needs required. The developed and greatly modified descendants of these two early types are still to be found; in East Africa for example, in the Kikuyu and Baganda peoples on the one hand, and the Masai and the Karamajong on the other. In neither of these two types of society do we find clear evidence of a critique of the mores, but rather a more rigorous enforcement of them, and often punishment of greater severity, than with the hunter-gatherer peoples. In some of the more complex societies, particularly those which developed strong and authoritarian leadership, the beginnings of moral protest can be identified in rituals of 'symbolic inversion'. The clearest examples are to be found in rituals where a king was insulted, ridiculed, blamed, denounced, and (temporarily) rejected. Those who have studied such events claim that their main function, however, was not to promote radical change. They provided, rather, a kind of safety-valve, a temporary easing of tension; and so, paradoxically, emphasized and reinforced the social order.[5]

The first 'civilizations' came into being around the third millennium BC, in the so-called Age of Bronze. Some of these, as in Egypt, Babylon, the Indus Valley, and China, developed into large empires. One of the prototypes was a form of city state, in which an urban population was supported by agriculture in the periphery. How, precisely, civilization came into being, whether through internal development or through the incursion of one people on another, is still a matter of controversy. But it is clear that the first 'civilized' societies had far greater inequalities than most of their predecessors. Their typical social structure involved a small nobility living in great luxury, with the majority at the barest level of subsistence. Between these two classes there was a small tier of administrators, lawyers, and soldiers. These societies contained enormous social tensions, and were often controlled with great severity; but there is no clear evidence that they generated any coherent moral teaching.

It is only much later, in the more loosely stratified trading societies of the Iron Age, during the first millennium BC, that a critique of mores becomes visible in a form that we would recognize as moral discourse. Tentatively, it may be suggested that three conditions were necessary for this development. The first condition was by no means new. It was a deep feeling of unease and dissatisfaction with the existing conditions: a sense that in some way the meaning of what it was to be human was being violated by the prevailing social practices. The second was a broadening of cultural horizons as a result of trade, conquest, and exploration, with the accompanying realization that no social order is 'natural'; each is a human creation. The third condition was the existence, within the society, of sufficient *Lebensraum* for new thinking, for some degree of social criticism to be tolerated without it being felt as a threat to the social order. It is significant that the first known moral teachers typically came from the privileged sectors of society; their concern was based on a view from above, so to speak, rather than a protest from below. It is only in the civilizations of the Iron Age that all three conditions were present. Some authorities have talked of an axial era in world history, a period when a wave of moral consciousness moved across the Eurasian land mass. No such hypothesis is necessary, however, for we can explain the rise of moral teaching more directly, by reference to the material and social conditions.

To give three examples. In northern India the culture of the Iron Age had given rise to several powerful kingdoms, skilled in the techniques of war and carrying out vigorous trade. It was in one of these, during the sixth century BC, that Gautama, who came to be known as the Buddha, was born. After he lived, there was a long period when his teaching was preserved in an oral tradition, before any scriptures were written down.[6] But two of his central doctrines are plain. One is that of non-violence, and the other that of selflessness. The first may be understood as a moral protest against the ruthlessness and cruelty which pervaded these societies; the second, against the personal ambition and restless striving of the nobility and the trading classes.

In the middle east the Jewish people had occupied a tract of land that corresponds roughly with the modern state of Israel, by an invasion that had entailed virtual genocide of the existing inhabitants. There they established an elaborate patriarchal culture based on the worship of their God Jahweh. During the seventh and sixth centuries BC, at a point where the social order was in decay and the threat of invasion was increasing, various prophets taught that Jahweh was angry, and was calling the people to return to his ways.

> What to me is the multitude of your sacrifices?, says the Lord: I have had enough of the burnt offerings of rams and the fat of fed beasts . . . . Learn to do good; seek justice; correct oppression; defend the fatherless; plead for the widow. . . . If you are willing and obedient, you shall eat of the good of the land; but if you refuse and rebel, you shall be devoured by the sword.[7]

In Greece, too, there was an upsurge of moral enquiry at the same point in history. The earlier tribal society, celebrated in the Homeric corpus, had vanished, and in its place had developed a number of independent city states, each with its distinctive culture. The prevailing moral doctrine, advanced in various forms by the teachers known as the sophists, was that there are no absolute moral standards. 'You cannot ask or answer the question, what is justice? but only the questions, "What is justice-at-Athens?" and, "What is justice-at-Corinth?"' (MacIntyre 1967: 16). It was against such views that Socrates taught. It is hard to reconstruct his actual teaching, because the main source, Plato, frequently used Socrates as a mouthpiece for his own views. Evidently Socrates used a dialectical method, drawing out his opponents' arguments, and pointing the way to knowledge through admission of ignorance. According to Plato he challenged his hearers to get behind the flux of appearances and seek out the pure essence of virtue, known only in a world of intellectual understanding. Thus he believed that all the moral virtues were forms of knowledge. The chief drawback to moral excellence is ignorance; to know the good is to do it. In modern terms Socrates was the prototype of the moral philosopher, for he was the first to raise the problem of universal definition.

Clearly, in each of these three examples the mores that are being criticized are different. So also are the dissatisfactions, and the motives which support the moral teachings. The common ground is that in each case there is a critique of existing practices on the basis of considerations that claim to lie beyond the particular conditions of society – whether that basis is immediate awareness, or divine revelation, or the purity of thought. Thus the moral teacher makes a direct appeal, over the head of society, as if the individual self can have some kind of knowledge or intuition that is transcendent. And, typically, the societies in which moral teaching appeared had cultures of guilt, not shame: that is, some people at least had taken rules or principles of action into themselves, and when they violated these they felt devalued, not so much by society, as by God or their own selves.

Associated with these vast developments in human society in antiquity there occurred one of the most momentous of all transformations, one of outstanding but neglected moral significance. It is the rise and establishment of male domination. How, precisely, this came about is a matter of speculation; that it did come about is certain.[8] Some authorities see a crucial turning-point in the first territorial clashes, where male hunters, as the principal users of weapons, could declare that they were the powerful protectors of territory. Other authorities place their emphasis on the greater physical strength of men, and the relatively high prestige accorded to hunting as compared to gathering. Yet others associate male domination with the domestication of cattle and the beginning of stock-breeding. Here the role of the male in conception was clearly established. Woman could be viewed as a kind of domestic animal; men could proclaim themselves the true life-givers, and give glory to the phallus rather than to the womb.

So probably it was out of a combination of two factors – physically of male power, and psychologically of male insecurity – that sexual domination originated. This would have been enhanced in the division of labour that developed in both kinds of society derived from hunting and gathering. In the early agricultural societies women were the main cultivators, as well as the makers of cloth and pots; care of animals, and most of the hunting were in the hands of men. In the nomadic societies women were in charge of the camp and its crafts, while men tended the herds. A division of labour does not in itself entail domination. But in both cases this was coupled with a differential of power, and thus also of status and value. These changes had also another consequence, arguably of great significance for all later psychology. Both agriculture and pastoral nomadism involved new forms of child care, far less indulgent and easygoing than in the case of the hunter-gatherers; and the placing of responsibility for this almost exclusively upon the women.

The creation of civilization, in the generally accepted sense, was very largely a masculine project. The majority of the new crafts, in metallurgy and the use of money, in building and navigation, were in male control. The middle class of administrators, soldiers, and traders consisted virtually entirely of men. Thus by the time of the great Iron Age civilizations of antiquity, whether of China, India, Persia, Greece, or Rome, male domination was so firmly established as to have become part of the taken-for-granted world. All the notable moral teachers of this period, whose work remains, were men. Their teachings may be suspected of representing a masculine standpoint; certainly sexual domination was never brought forward as a major topic for moral consideration.

A DIVERGENCE OF EMPHASES

It is clear, even from the three examples we have glanced at, that moral teachings are most likely to be understood if their context is taken into account; and this is a point to which we shall return. But now it is necessary to make a very broad distinction between the way in which moral concern has developed in the oriental and occidental cultural traditions.

Western moralism is built, to a considerable extent, upon Greek and Judaeo-Christian foundations. From here arose the form of Christianity that became established as Catholicism. Later, from the eleventh century onwards, the influence of Greek thinking became even stronger. If there is a common core to the western moral tradition, it is its emphasis on *right doing*, and hence, upon prescriptions to guide actions. It is in this context that we can understand the ought with its massive condensation of meaning and persuasive power. Often in western moralism there seems to be a tacit assumption (rather like that attributed to Socrates) that, when intellectually convincing propositions can be found, many individuals will be disposed to live in a more praiseworthy way. (The trouble with the Ten Commandments, so to speak, was mainly that they were not sufficiently convincing.) Then, at the second-order level, there is a long history of strenuous attempts to identify coherent principles and criteria for morality, on the basis of which a logically satisfying and possibly timeless ethical code might be constructed. Here too the assumption seems to be that 'if only' a rigorous logical justification can be found, it will have the power to motivate right action.

In the east, however, and particularly within Hinduism and Buddhism (especially in the Zen tradition), the atmosphere is very different. Far less energy is spent on moral logic, and the main emphasis is upon *right being*. Here the assumption seems to be that if a person is, so to speak, properly situated in the world in a state of inner tranquillity, good actions will flow almost without effort. The main obstacles to right being are distractions; taking the form, for example, of inordinate desire for fame, possessions, or power. The essence of right being is immediate present awareness, free from regret about the past or fear about the future; part of that awareness consists of appreciating others more nearly 'as they are'. There are many paths to this, most of them involving some kind of meditation, and there have been many disputes about 'the way'. The west often seeks, so to speak, to create an ego with moral excellence as one of its attributes, even if that ego is a human shell that is indwelt by God. The east, however, seeks to cultivate a pure experiential self, without structure, without accretions, and so devoid of internal division. The western ego is easily crushed by moral failure, flattered by success; the east attempts to expose the ego as illusion, and thus suggests that the moral activism so strong in western culture is bound to fail. While the western moralist is distractedly trying to understand what he or she ought to do, the eastern adept will simply 'be there', trusting that compassion will spring from stillness and awareness.

This divergence is well illustrated by the following tantric precepts collected in India at least 4,000 years ago. The complete list contains over a hundred items, so what is given below is a very short extract:

> Radiant one, this experience may dawn between two breaths. After breath comes in and just before turning up – *the beneficence*. As breath turns from up to down – through both these turns – *realize*.

> When in worldly activity, keep attentive between the two breaths, and so practising, in a few days *be born anew*.

On joyously seeing a long-absent friend, *permeate this joy.*
At the start of sexual union, keep attentive on the fire *in the beginning,* and so continuing, avoid the embers in the end.
When in such embrace your senses are shaken as leaves, *enter the shaking.*

Wherever satisfaction is found, in whatever act, *actualize this.*

At the point of sleep when sleep has not yet come and external wakefulness vanishes, at this point *being is revealed.*

Feel the consciousness of each person as your own consciousness. So, leaving aside concern for self, *become each being.*

Wherever your attention alights, at this very point, *experience.*

As a hen mothers her chicks, mother particular knowings, particular doings, *in reality.*

(Reps 1957: 120ff.)

It is clear at once that we are on very different ground from that of western moralism. The east comes closest to the west in the principles of Kung Fu'Tze (Confucius), which are recognizably moralistic. Perhaps it is no coincidence that Confucianism flourished in a feudal empire, with constraints very similar to those of medieval Europe.

SOME DEVELOPMENTS IN MORAL THEORY IN THE WEST

During the first millennium AD western moral theory was overwhelmingly influenced by Christianity. The bureaucratized church produced a variety of doctrines; some more and some less life-denying. Perhaps the deepest stratum consists of the version of Christianity inaugurated by Paul of Tarsus, and continued in the fourth century by Augustine of Hippo. Here the influence of Plato, his rejection of the senses, and his ultimate unworldliness in all matters of knowledge, is particularly strong. According to Augustinian doctrine, all human faculties are totally depraved, due to original sin. No person is capable, in his or her own natural strength, of doing what is right. All of humanity stands under

25

God's condemnation, a mass headed for perdition. A few make the response of faith, receive forgiveness, and begin a new life, drawing on the strength God provides so that they can follow in his ways. The moral law, embodied in the Ten Commandments and its New Testament amplifications, serves primarily as a means of revealing to people their state of corruption. Even to believers it sets an unattainable standard. Their lives involve continual inner conflict. 'I can will what is right, but I cannot do it. For I do not do the good I want, but the evil I do not want is what I do.'[9] In this form Christianity provided some kind of critique of existing mores, although it had nothing to say about a good or just earthly society. To most moral philosophers doctrines of this kind are of little importance, because they seem to represent an extremely crude and narrow form of ethical thinking. To psychologists they may well be of greater significance. For a sense of inner division, of guilt and moral inadequacy, seems to lie deep in western culture; and it is striking how movements embodying Augustinian doctrines recur time and again, especially in periods of social upheaval, anxiety, or despair. The phenomenon of evangelist Fallwell, together with his dramatic 'fall', is a contemporary symptom.

In the eleventh and twelfth centuries, when feudal societies in Europe were at their most prosperous and stable, new and more positive forms of Christian moralism emerged. This was particularly the case with the work of Thomas Aquinas, who created a novel synthesis between the teachings of the church and some of the works of Aristotle. At first regarded as near-heretical, the doctrines of Aquinas eventually became official dogma; now, eight centuries later, they are still a key resource for Catholic social and moral theory. Aristotle had viewed humans as fundamentally social beings, in a way that was very different from that of Plato: they can only realize their *telos* (or, as Aquinas would say, carry out the purpose for which they were created) in accepting their ties to others, in being an integral part of a community. The basic concept of duty here is that of fulfilling the requirements of a particular position within a social order. Duty is intelligible and justifiable because its fulfilment works towards the fundamental goods of social harmony and individual well-being. For Aquinas there were natural virtues, and supernatural; a natural law, capable of discovery by observation and reason, and a supernatural law, given by divine revelation. Such an account of the right and the good fitted well with the dominant interests in a hierarchical social order, as we have already seen. A great deal of later moral theory, emphasizing egalitarian ideas, lost sight of the 'organicism' of Aristotle and Aquinas, and this is reflected in much of the moral psychology of the present day. Recently, however, there have been some notable attempts to shift to a more Aristotelian point of view.[10]

From the calamitous fourteenth century[11] onwards the relatively stable feudal order fell apart. Successive waves of famine and plague swept Europe; society was in a state of more or less continual chaos for three centuries; war and social unrest were endemic. This was a period of the most intense misogyny, when perhaps as many as two million women were burned or drowned as witches.[12] Slowly a new social order emerged, based much more on a market economy, and dependent on colonies overseas. The ascendant social class was that of (almost exclusively male) merchants, master-craftsmen, bankers, and independent farmers: the so-called bourgeoisie. Women in the more prosperous parts of society were increasingly confined to the home, as 'obedient wives' or aimless 'spinsters'. The new form of large social unit was the nation state.

One aspect of this period was an intense competition for the control of knowledge, following the collapse of ecclesiastical authority. Throughout the sixteenth and seventeenth centuries there were various movements whose aim was to integrate a fundamental reform of knowledge with the creation of a new and more beneficent society. Some of these were linked with the name of Paracelsus, the radical physician who had openly rejected the medical hegemony, inviting doctors to go direct to the evidence, and to learn from apothecaries and women healers. By the mid-seventeenth century, when the bourgeois social order was becoming established, virtually all these movements had been either crushed or marginalized, as if the rising class needed to destroy all epistemologies in rivalry to its own.[13] This is the context, and in part the explanation, of the witch craze. Now the most reliable form of knowledge was taken to be that of natural science; and here a 'rational mechanics', epitomized in Newton's work, was the norm. The fundamental picture of the world was one of particles of dead matter, in perpetual motion and collision. The domain of values had become, to say the least, intensely problematic.

As the new era was consolidated, moral philosophy rapidly developed and diversified. For virtually all the pioneers of moral theory from the seventeenth century onwards, divine revelation was irrelevant. If God existed at all, he was only in the background, leaving people largely to fend for themselves. Moralists looked, then, for totally secular ways of gounding their theories; whether (as in the case of Kant) on the basis of naked reason, or (as in that of Hume) on the careful understanding of such human dispositions as benevolence. 'Natural philosophy', gradually becoming 'science' as we would recognize it, had provided an outstandingly convincing example of the power of human beings to gain reliable knowledge about the world. Every moral theory from this time forward is marked in some way by its influence. If the domain of facts gave such assurance, what standing could be given to that of values?

Much greater emphasis was now placed upon the individual; the Aristotelian attention to the pattern of social life was largely forgotten. It is as if the (masculine) human of bourgeois common-sense, the owner of property, the possessor of legal rights, and self-determining through the rational pursuit of his own ends, has crept unrecognized into moral theory and become accepted as the criterion of a universal humanity. Defoe's Robinson Crusoe, complete in himself (but welcoming the services of Man Friday) defined the norm. Some theories were based on an analytical decomposition of society into its elements, followed by a demonstration of how it could be reconstructed on the basis of a shared agreement, allegedly following the scientific method of Galileo. The first and most famous example is the theory of Thomas Hobbes. In his account the 'state of nature' was one of self-seeking individuals, struggling against one another in pursuit of their own advantage and the avoidance of death. Rather than perpetuate this state of affairs, they agree to subject themselves to a powerful ruler, who will be their protector and the guarantor of social order. Hobbes' theory was not a critique; it was, rather, a legitimation of a monarchy verging on the absolute. His method was entirely ahistorical, and was intended as such. But it is worth pointing out that his presuppositions about human nature, which have been shared by many of the more conservative theorists of the bourgeois social order, are entirely at odds with anthropological evidence, where the social and co-operative aspects of primal society are pre-eminent.

Another feature of moral theory from this period onward is some degree of divergence between theories applying to the regulation of interpersonal relationships and those applying to society at large. Among the hunter-gatherer peoples, living in small bands, these two domains were completely co-extensive. In later small-scale societies such as those of European feudalism, they could at least be seen to cohere. But in the nation states and empires generated by capitalist expansion, the two domains were forced apart. Some moral theories had far more to say about how people should treat one another at, so to speak, a micro level; others had more to say about the structure of a just society.

Perhaps the most significant development of all, at least from the standpoint of psychology, is the emergence of the moral ought, to which we have already given some attention. It was Kant who, more than any other moral theorist, gave it a supremely important status, and his work now appears in context. Through natural science, so he believed, we can never know the world as it truly is. We bring our minds actively to bear, and it is as a result of our own structuring tendencies that we experience the world as if space, time, causation, and so on, were 'really there'. For Kant, empirical data derived from the senses were irrelevant as a foundation for ethics; the only reliable place to look is within ourselves. If a moral law is to be found, it will be one that is logically compelling, and the force of this logic will be our chief moral motivation. If I am acting morally, in Kant's terms, the basic principle under which my action falls must be one that I can accept as valid for all rational beings; I must 'will' that principle to be a universal law. Kant's account does not in itself provide us with a set of such principles, or categorical imperatives, but it provides a test by which to examine cases from particular moralities; promise-keeping, for example, meets his test. Kant's theory always sets up the *problematique* of morality as a potential conflict between duty and desire; and not, as in the moral tradition derived from Aristotle, the ordering of desires. A moral agent, in his terms, is one who exercises a special kind of freedom, acting out of sublime duty. That person is autonomous, not subject to any social code, but carrying the moral law in his or her innermost being.

Kant's treatment of morality may be regarded from two vantage-points. On the one hand – and this is a view that is widely accepted – he produced a convincing (although incomplete) criterion for identifying the form of what is truly moral; he completed the separation of morality from mores. In terms of a later vocabulary, Kant showed that moral judgements must be universalizable. 'Anyone who says, meaning it, that a certain action (or person, or state of affairs, etc.) is morally right or wrong, good or bad, ought or ought not to be done (or imitated, or pursued, etc.) is hereby committed to taking the same view about any other relevantly similar action (etc.)'. (Mackie 1977: 83). But on the other hand it may be argued that Kant's account, far from pointing towards genuinely transcendent criteria for morality, matches almost perfectly the bourgeois social order in its flux and instability. The idea of ought is merely formal, devoid of content, detached from any particular set of social arrangements, and from any conception of human needs. The notion of universalizability must always include a phrase such as 'relevantly similar'. But how is the relevance to be determined? At this point the theory is a slave of particular social values; with suitable criteria of relevance it can actually be used to justify almost any form of oppression. And Kant's moral agent is highly individualistic; having a remarkably uncomplicated psyche, free from all serious agony or conflict. For one who is rational and self-determining in all other spheres, it is no great problem to be so in the moral domain.

We have already touched on the divergence between moralities that are primarily interpersonal and those which are primarily societal in their subject-matter. In contrast to Kant, several theories were advanced with the main aim of giving principles for the ordering of a just society. Of these the most famous is that of utilitarianism. Its central thesis is that the rightness of an action is determined by its contribution to the well-being of everyone affected by it.[14] Here was an attempt to put moral theory on to a sound, no-nonsense basis; the simplicity of the initial assumptions and the use of quantification clearly relate to an empiricist understanding of the methods of classical physics. Utilitarianism was advanced by Bentham as a moral-legal theory that would come to terms with the vast social anomalies that accompanied the establishment of the bourgeois era. Among these were the residues of feudal privilege; the contrast between the life of the rich and the poor, the powerful and the powerless; the irrelevance and sterility of the older academic centres; the archaic and arbitrary character of much of the prevalent legal practice. The prime aim of the utilitarians was to bridge the gap between philosophy and law, and so contribute to the foundation of a new and more benign social order.

During the two centuries since Bentham's work utilitarian doctines have been developed in a variety of ways. In some versions it is not particular acts that are to be evaluated, but the rules under which those acts might be subsumed. Recently the theory has been extended to assert the global reference of a utilitarian calculus; and the obligation not only to carry out beneficent actions, but also to prevent what is harmful. All forms of utilitarianism are consequentialist in character, asserting that rightness is to be determined by results; thus in contrast to Kant's theory the conception of rightness is objective, in that it does not depend in any strong sense on the state of knowledge or the intentions of the moral agent.

One of the most revealing of all statements in utilitarianism comes from Bentham himself. 'The community is a fictitious *body*, composed of the individual persons who are considered as constituting as it were its *members*. The interest of the community then is – what? – the sum of the interests of the several members who compose it' (Burns and Hart 1970: 2). For here Bentham appears to deny the existence of any human community as an entity in itself, and to take a markedly 'undersocialized' conception of the human being. This doctrine had great pragmatic value in exposing bland generalizations about the national interest, or the welfare of the labouring classes, and in unmasking ideologies suggesting community where none existed. But in totally ignoring the importance of social fabric it entails an untenable psychology, one of individualism in its most extreme form.

Despite its power as an ethical theory utilitarianism has been much criticized, particularly on two accounts. First, it seems to be inadequate in dealing with motives, which must be central to all moral enquiry. Second, and paradoxically, in its concern with welfare – so to speak, in bulk – it is ineffective in dealing with the needs and circumstances of particular individuals. Two main alternatives have appeared in mid-twentieth century moral philosophy, advanced in part for the deliberate purpose of remedying these weaknesses.[15]

One is the theory of natural rights, whose chief modern exponent is Nozick (1974). This doctrine first made its appearance in the teaching of certain seventeenth-century radicals, demanding freedom from all residues of feudal ties and obligations. Later in the century it was fully explicated by John Locke; subsequently there were numerous popular expressions, as in the French Declaration of Rights of Citizens, of 1789, and the United Nations Declaration of Human Rights. Like the moral ought, as we have seen, the concept of natural rights is a descendant from an earlier idea within feudalism. 'Rights' originally consisted of certain socially given permissions to act, often attached to positions of privilege – as in the notorious case of the droit de seigneur. But theories of natural rights assert that certain permissions belong to all human beings; rights set an absolute constraint on how they are to be treated without their own consent. A concept of natural rights is a powerful instrument in criticizing mores that are experienced as unjust or oppressive, and in setting out principles for a new society. The main problem is knowing how such rights are to be identified in a way that genuinely transcends the conditions of all particular social orders. Can education, or the disposal of property, for example, be considered as natural rights, considering that for the greater part of human history neither the concept of education nor of property has existed?

The second main alternative, and one which brings some *rapprochement* between the ideas of Kant and the utilitarians, is that of Rawls (1972). Rawls makes use of the Hobbesian device of a fiction in which individuals come together to form a society; in this case, one which would meet rigorous logical criteria of justice. They must choose the social arrangements under conditions of ignorance: that is, they do not know how things will turn out for themselves, in relation to such aspects as class position, natural endowments, or the vicissitudes of life. In this way Rawls corrects for egoistic and particularistic bias; the veil of ignorance forces on the choosers a concern for people in all situations, in a manner not unlike Kant's categorical imperative. (It should be noted that the individuals who choose are not in a 'state of nature'; for the theory seems to imply that they must have a knowledge of politics, economics, sociology, and psychology at least equivalent to that of a secondary-school leaver who will go on to read for a degree.)

These considerations lead Rawls to two principles. The first is that all persons should have equal rights to the most extensive system of basic liberties compatible with similar liberty for all other members of the society. The second is that social and economic inequalities are to be arranged so that they are to the greatest benefit of the least advantaged; also, positions within social elites should be equally accessible to all. In this way Rawls realistically allows for the existence of those experts whose work carries high prestige, who are much needed in a modern technological society. Further, he corrects for one of the major difficulties in utilitarianism: that in some plan to maximize utility certain persons might fare extremely badly. According to Rawls, the worst case need only be one of tolerable hardship. As in the other theories we have touched on, the person here has already been formed as a modern bourgeois, in rational pursuit of self-interest; but compelled to do so under ingeniously devised logical constraints.

SOCIAL MOVEMENTS AS MORAL PROJECTS

The concern of moral theory as conventionally defined is the critique or evaluation of mores by external criteria. It is clear that most of what has commonly been accepted as belonging to this discourse has been based on a 'view from above', in relation both to class and gender. The project of western moralism proceeds on a general assumption about the power of thought, and its typical movement is from thought to action.

Moralism of this kind has proved to be only a weak force for change. History has shown again and again how easy it has been to assimilate into the status quo ideas which at first contained powerful critical insights. Christianity, avowing peace on earth and goodwill towards all humankind, has been associated with dogmatism, brutality, and war for two millennia; Islam has a history which is not dissimilar. The concept of natural rights, which at first provided at least a rhetoric against oppression, soon became a charter for *laissez-faire* capitalism, and now gives specious ground for yuppiedom. Utilitarianism, initially a radical doctrine against privilege, was incorporated in a grossly distorted form into crude welfare economics and such crass techniques as cost-benefit analysis, which often function in fact to preserve the interests of privileged groups such as owners of cars or houses. In the east, Buddhism and other doctrines less moralistic than those of the west, have continually served, not so much to restrain violence as to facilitate the consent of under-classes to gross oppression; a typical case might be the proletariat of Hong Kong.[16] These facts do not, of course, tell us anything about the logical validity of a particular moral theory, although they do suggest, psychologically, that theories are easily vulgarized in the light of human interests. Also, the conclusion must be that any moral theory without an 'action framework', some realistic project for positive change, is seriously deficient.

There is another aspect of morality, often not identified as such, and certainly much neglected by psychologists. It concerns the critique of mores, so to speak, from below: in the form not primarily of theory, but of withdrawal, refusal, protest and rebellion. Such 'practical morality' has been a recurrent theme in world history, at least from the period of the Bronze Age. In the latter days of the Persian and Roman empires insurrection was common, as soldiers and slaves could endure their conditions of service no longer. Monasticism, both eastern and western, was an attempt to create enclaves of mutual trust and care in a turbulent and ferocious world. The fourteenth to seventeenth centuries saw numerous revolutionary movements in Europe, during the collapse of feudalism and the rise of the bourgeois era: revolts of peasants, communitarian projects of Anabaptists, Rosicrucians, Levellers, Diggers. Later, with the rise of industrial capitalism, came the action of machine-wreckers, early trade-unionism, and the beginnings of a movement to secure the emancipation of women. In today's world there are many strong social movements that are morally motivated in the broad sense, clustered around such causes as socialism, environmentalism, feminism, peace, anti-racism and decolonization.

In this field of moral endeavour the *Zeitgeist* is very different from that of moral theory. Consider, for example, the last words that Nelson Mandela spoke in public before he was committed to life imprisonment:

> Africans want a just share in the whole of South Africa, we
> want security and a stake in society. Above all, we want equal

political rights, because without them our disabilities will be permanent. I know this sounds revolutionary to the whites in this country, because the majority of voters will be African. This makes the white man fear democracy. But his fear cannot be allowed to stand in the way of the only solution which will guarantee racial harmony and freedom for all. . . . Our struggle is a truly national one. It is a struggle with the African people, inspired by our own suffering and our own experience. It is a struggle for the right to live. During my lifetime I have dedicated myself to this struggle of the African people. I have fought against white domination and I have fought against black domination. I have cherished the ideal of a democratic and free society in which all persons live together in harmony and with equal opportunities. It is an ideal which I hope to live for and to achieve. But if needs be, it is an ideal for which I am prepared to die.

(Woods 1979: 42)

In contexts such as this the sense of unfairness, exploitation, or oppression is so strong that this is taken as sufficient reason for working towards change, without recourse to a fully articulated moral theory. There is always a heightened awareness, always a vision of some better future, even if only vaguely defined. The feelings typically involved are not shame or guilt, but anger and resentment as consciousness is raised, and expansiveness and celebration as objectives are gained. Where developed theory does exist its main emphases are likely to be upon careful analysis of the status quo, and on practical methods of achieving change. A fully fledged moral theory is, so to speak, an unnecessary luxury, or even a distraction from the task at hand. Indeed it is a characteristic of several modern social movements, particularly those that draw in some way on Marxism, to reject moralism as irredemably bourgeois, part of the web of deception that is to be broken apart.

At a popular level this rejection of moralism and its concern for universal criteria, this refusal to construct blueprints for a new society, may simply arise from the urgency and obvious importance of bringing about change. Theorizing is seen as merely vacuous, whereas pressing the cause further, or gaining a small victory in a historic struggle, appear to be indisputable necessities. But at least

35

within the tradition that derives from Marx, there is a carefully worked-out justification.[17] Marx was certainly inspired by a moral concern, in the broadest sense; for although he abstained from using the moral vocabulary of his day, his work was clearly meant to expose the injustices and hypocrisies of industrial capitalism. He wanted theory that would articulate with action, but never through the use of the moral ought. According to his historical materialism, it is necessary to enquire first into the economic base of society: that is, the way it provides for the material needs of its members, and the divisions of interest that surround production. History moves forward, so he believed, primarily through changes in this base, as new techniques are discovered and as social conflicts are worked out – especially those related to the ownership and control of the means of production. The leading system of ideas forms a superstructure strongly conditioned by the nature of this economic base, and serves mainly to legitimate the interests invested in it. Marx saw moral theory as part of this superstructure, and so as useless in promoting radical change. This applied both to the conventional moralism based on Christianity, justifying 'the rich man in his castle, the poor man at his gate', and to carefully worked-out moral doctrines such as those of the utilitarians. But there was a further point. Marx believed that people's mentalities were so formed by their present material and social circumstances that their power to transcend these in thought was strictly limited. To speculate in detail about the nature of the new society was, then, vacuous idealism. The important thing was to work towards the downfall of the existing social order, and to prepare for transformation. It would be for a new generation, uncorrupted by capitalism, its deficient social relations, and its false values, to create the just society.

Much later Habermas (1968), uniting the sociological traditions that derive from Marx and Weber, produced a new theory that also, in its own way, abstains from moralism. According to this, justice only has meaning in real historical situations. Although we cannot describe a just state of affairs in advance, we can specify the conditions under which that could be realized. This would be an 'ideal speech situation', one in which all persons and interest groups had equal access, and equal power, in open debate. The just outcome would be that which was then achieved, through extended negotiation. The condition of modernity has not yet produced such a situation; but as a result of the breakdown of tradition and the rise of rational enquiry it has begun to be possible for the first time ever.

The theories of Marx and Habermas are powerful, especially in the critique they give of moralism. But it may be argued that both do have the outlines of a moral theory, even if they have put the problem back from social justice in itself to the conditions under it might be achieved. Marx, in fact, went considerably further than this, and at least adumbrated what he conceived to be the just society that might emerge from capitalism: one in which there are no class divisions, and in which the means of production are owned and controlled collectively. A strong moral concern, in some ways echoing the Kantian emphasis on respect for persons, pervades both his work and that of Habermas. Thus we do not find here any reason for rejecting moral theory in entirety; but certainly there are grounds for looking very critically at moral theorizing that occurs, so to speak, *in vacuo*, and without an open acknowledgement of its relation to real social and historical conditions.

SOME PSYCHOLOGICAL IMPLICATIONS

This chapter, in its partial and extremely superficial survey of moral discourse, has not been intended as an exploration of the inner texture of philosophical theories, but rather to show something of the background against which the psychology of morality has emerged. If there is one main point, it is that the ought, which is often taken to be definitive of the moral dimension, does have a history, and one that makes the concept more problematic than it is often taken to be. This point, as a few theorists (such as MacIntyre) have noted, suggests that we would do well to sacrifice any neat demarcation of the moral domain, convenient though it may be for logical purposes. We are confronted by the possibility that the moral ought may be like that phenomenon in *Alice in Wonderland*, a 'grin without a cat'; a vestigial remain from Jahweh's commands in a world from which that kind of god has vanished, but in which the anxiety arising from transgression is very much alive. The guilt that accompanies moralism may, in part, be the guilt of the privileged.

In dealing with the primal societies of humankind, the main

37

function of the mores seemed to be the preservation of social fabric. If there was an interest in social justice in a modern sense, it was subservient to this; simply, social fabric is seriously threatened when there are gross inequalities of power or possessions. A concern with social fabric was present in some medieval theory, particularly where it was influenced by Aristotle and Aquinas. In most of 'liberal' moral theory, however, this topic has generally receded to insignificance; the main emphases have been on respect for persons as individuals, and on distributive justice, characterized in various ways. One of these theories, that of Rawls, has been specially influential in psychological work, as will become plain in Chapter 5.

The person as implicitly conceptualized in the greater part of liberal moral theory is, as we have seen, the (masculine) bourgeois: straightforward, unimaginative, without great inner anxiety or conflict, and with passions that are easily tamed: scarcely a biological being, and social in only an attenuated sense. Yet, paradoxically, this creature has been responsible, collectively, for some of the greatest monstrosities in world history: witch crazes, slave-trading, colonial conquest, genocide, holocausts, super-destructive wars, political terror, the rape of the natural environment, arms races, famine in the midst of plenty. How could such a mild and rational being accomplish evils such as these? Here it would appear that the liberal understanding of the person is disastrously inadequate, and that some view which allows for the existence of the demonic is required. In this book such a view is presented, derived both from academic psychology and from therapeutic work. And if there is one continuing theme, it is that moral psychology would be in a better position to confront the postmodern predicament if it took this kind of conception of the person into account.

Chapter Two

TOWARDS A PSYCHOLOGY OF THE MORAL LIFE

Psychology came into being as a distinctive field of enquiry during the sixteenth and seventeenth centuries. Its emergence was associated with those very changes towards a greater individualism and a reverence for natural science which we have touched on in Chapter 1. Almost from the very beginning there was controversy over the kind of knowledge that psychology would yield. Would this be similar in form to that being gained so rapidly about the physical world; or would it be different, privileged in some way, because we are in the unique position of knowing ourselves and our intersubjective 'human-reality' from within? Debate around this issue has continued right through to the present time, taking on a fresh aspect as each new school of psychology has come into being, and enriched by each new addition to the philosophy of science. Still, however, the basic question remains. Is psychology, or can it be, or should it be, a form of knowledge that resembles natural science, collecting data by similar methods, and producing comparable laws and theories? Alternatively, is it a distinctive form of knowledge, following its own methodological rules, and possibly having closer affinities to such areas of the humanities as history and literary criticism? There are some powerful arguments against the former view, at least in its simplistic and popular versions. Nevertheless, it still seems to hold great attraction for psychologists, especially in the conduct of research; and sometimes professional recognition actually requires it.

Much is at stake here, for psychology in all its different branches. Matters come to a crux, however, in relation to morality. For this topic cannot be studied in the same manner as, say, the speed of nerve conduction or the appearance of coloured spots in the visual field. Nor can it be subsumed within the category of behaviour: that is, of actions as observed merely from the outside. The study of morality takes us deeply into the areas of relatedness, trust, and responsibility; into the experience of value, the sense of freedom, the transcendence of social conditioning, the coming together of intellect and feeling in concern for others. We are compelled, then, to engage in some way with the problem of subjectivity.

This chapter looks briefly at this and related issues. In a small space we will cover large areas of territory in the borderland between philosophy, moral theory, and psychology; it is inevitable that we shall deal superficially with a number of highly complex and controversial questions. Our central concern will be with three issues that form a loosely connected sequence. First, what, broadly speaking, may be taken as the subject-matter for a psychological enquiry into morality? Second, what principles of method can guide us? Do these suggest some approaches that are suitable, and others that should be ruled out from the start? Third, among the various ways of viewing the person, each of which highlights particular aspects of the human-reality, is there any that especially commends itself?

Questions such as these cannot be avoided within psychology, in relation to this or any other topic. Those who do not face them openly – and regrettably the psychological literature is full of examples of those who apparently do not – have resolved nothing. All they have done is to deal with these questions implicitly, without awareness; and because of this they are the more likely to have come up with inadequate answers. This may be one reason why psychology sometimes appears to outsiders to be difficult, dull, inhuman, incoherent, or irrelevant. An enquiry into morality, then, provides a test case of what psychology should be.

THE HUMAN-REALITY

It need hardly be said that ours is an intensely social species. In this we are by no means unique, although (particularly because of what follows from our capacity to use language skilfully) our form of sociability, has many unique features. In evolutionary terms there is, clearly, a very close connection between our lack of natural means of self-protection, our sociability, and our highly developed intelligence – although the causal relations are uncertain. In developmental-psychological terms the roots of our social nature lie in the fact that the infant is born much further away from maturity than any other creature, and so needs a prolonged period of nurture and care. The individual self is relational from the outset.

Because of the fragmentation of life in the modern industrial societies, and their tendency to flood the individual with verbal outpourings, it is easy to forget the intensely social nature of our being, and the fact that it is embodied. Among many primal peoples living in fairly benign environments, it seems that breast-feeding was common until a child was three or four years old. Children under five might spend over half of their time in physical contact with another, and about a third of their time right through to the age of about fourteen.[1] This embodied sociability is manifested in many other ways; for example, in the fact that human beings have sexual desires far in excess of reproductive need; sexual activity is completely uncoupled from oestrus, the time of greatest fertility, and continues in many individuals long after the age when a new generation has come to maturity. The mores of hunter-gatherer peoples gave virtually no place for individualism or for prolonged privacy, as we have seen. The whole basis of a person's sense of identity was that of connectedness to others, and of performance with and for the group.

If any topic has been investigated really closely in psychology, it is that of attachment. It seems to be a near-universal feature of human life that intense and specific bonds develop between a young child and one or more main care-givers, although exclusive mothering is far less common. Studies in western societies show clearly that children who are not, for some external reason, able to form such attachments, or for whom important bonds are irrevocably broken in early years, are very likely to experience disturbance and distress around their relationships in later life.[2] More generally, in all societies and under virtually all conditions human beings show an overwhelming tendency to form bonds with one another, to seek out one another's company, to create affiliations. We seek integration into social groupings, and find rejection exceedingly painful. Deprived of company and personal affirmation over a long period, at whatever age, we tend to become anxious, depressed, and even to die.

The fabric of social life is exceedingly fragile, constantly in need of maintenance and repair. Its particular threads can be destroyed in the simplest of ways: through quarrels, betrayals, envy, neglect, individual arrogance – the direct effect of people acting upon one another. In almost all societies there is a tendency for some to remain only at its tattered edges: those who are chronically sick, crippled, blind, mad, or old. Human societies show a strong tendency to create out-groups, whether of strangers who live beyond the boundaries, or aliens within. More subtly and insidiously, the imposition of power by one social group over another, involving not only obvious conflict but also the unrecognized control of thought and desire, brings all manner of disturbances and distortions to personality and social being. The paradigm case is colonialism, breeding arrogance and cultural contempt in the colonizers, and self-devaluation in the colonized; and in some instances a terrible explosion of anger and violence accompanying its demise.

What kind of picture emerges, then, when features of the human-reality such as these are taken into account? We gain no flattering impression of 'man' as the lord of nature, set free from its constraints – as one main stream of western thought might suggest. Nor do we find confirmation of a view simplistically attributed to sociobiology, that social life is strongly structured by instinct-like patterns of behaviour. We gain a glimpse, rather, of an exceedingly variable and wayward creature; sensitive and vulnerable because so intelligently aware, and capable of carrying an inordinate burden of fear; needing others desperately, yet often finding their closeness a source of burden and tension. The very sense of self is precarious, being formed in the first place when the infant was powerless, and requiring continual validation and support from other persons. Each culture provides some degree of protection against the naked anguish of subjectivity, a refuge for a species that is not fully 'at home' in the natural world. And whenever individuals or cultures boast loudly about their achievements, power, or immortality, we may well suspect the presence of what psychoanalysts would call a defensive reaction – formed against existential truths too difficult to bear.

This, then, is the context of what has come to be called morality. Its psychology is concerned, fundamentally, with respect for persons, and hence with persons-in-relationship; beyond that, with the whole quality of social life within which persons have their being. In small-scale societies, as we have seen, the interpersonal and the political were virtually identical. In the more aggregated societies, including those of modern industrialism, they are not. So a psychology of the moral life must take as its subject-matter not only how people treat one another in their day-to-day interactions, but also the indirect and structural aspects, where no particular agents seem to be responsible. The paradigm case is the hierarchical organization, so pervasive in the contemporary world. Further, if people are crushed by poverty; if they are subjected to impossible strain through the obliteration of their future; if their self-esteem is damaged through the lack of any opportunity to contribute to the social good; if they are subtly forced into isolation, powerlessness, and despair – these too are questions relevant to moral psychology.

Human beings are great talkers, and they spend vast amounts of time discussing both their relationships with others and the social arrangements within which they conduct their lives. This kind of talk, too, is valid subject-matter for the psychology of the moral life. It should always be taken seriously, but it would be a mistake always to take it literally. It may indeed reveal genuine features of a person's moral outlook. However, it is often deceptive. People may use such talk to give plausible accounts of actions whose significance they are unable or unwilling to recognize. Groups may use such talk as rhetoric, not for its truth but for its instrumental potency in validating their claims; most insidiously, in legitimating a position of advantage. The study of moral verbiage alone, then, can tell us very little. Its significance becomes plain only when it is related to action, and to the context within which that action is embedded.

From time to time people do, of course, find themselves confronted by moral dilemmas. Some of these take the form of conflict between rival obligations (should I do this work for the Party, or go to visit that friend in hospital?). Some take the form of conflict between the prevailing norms and principled conviction (should I obey the law or violate it, by helping to sabotage this missile carrier?). Some take the classic form of conflict between duty and desire (should I stay in my marriage for the children's sake, or break free – for my own?). Dilemmas of these and other kinds are an important part of the subject-matter; both the way in which people reason about them, and how they actually resolve them in practice. Yet it would be a mistake either to exaggerate the frequency of dilemmas that are genuinely unavoidable, or to make them the touchstone of morality. Moreover, they cannot be separated from the background within which they took on their distinctive form. The dilemma made famous by Kohlberg, for example, involving the problem of whether a man should steal a drug for his dying wife, would only occur in a society where medicine was sold as a commodity at exorbitant prices.

A psychology of morality will be very much concerned with what people do to one another in the minutiae of everyday life, often without explicit awareness, and almost always without involving conscious moral dilemmas. Here we are not dealing with the product of blind conditioning, if ever that term could be applied appropriately to human beings. We are dealing, rather, with action that has become habituated, with skills which, once acquired, have passed below the level of conscious control, so setting the mind free for other matters – very much like the skilled playing of a musical instrument. Skills of this kind are available for conscious re-working, but generally do not need to be. They are, of course, the product of high intelligence and awareness, although those who have an academic prejudice in favour of static, reflective, spectator-knowledge tend to devalue them.

So we come to the concept of character, one which used to be considered central in moral theory, but which then fell out of favour; largely because certain studies seemed to imply that it did not exist. Now, however, it is gradually being reinstated. A person's character may be viewed as the residue left from many actions, a cluster of habits and tendencies. Its original base is, presumably, constitutional and temperamental, an endowment over which no one has a choice. Its social context of development, whether benign or oppressive, is not of the person's own making. But character grows and develops as a result of decisions, both trivial and momentous, and the habits that ensue; and in so far as a person was responsible for these, he or she may also be said to be responsible for the character that emerges. Linked to the idea of character are the traditional concepts of virtue and vice. Also, and of central importance in relating psychology and morality, there is the question of integration and integrity: that is, the extent to which a person is a unity, or fragmented into several self-like structures.

These, then, are some of the topics which together constitute a field for the psychology of morality: how people actually treat one another, both in their considered and their habituated actions; their moral ideas; their attempts at resolving moral dilemmas, both in theory and in practice; moral character and integrity; features of the larger social context, including the psychological consequences of social justice and injustice. If all these topics are important, then it would seem that the field as we presently know it is exceedingly lop-sided in its emphases. It has focused to an overwhelming degree on individuals, and then very largely on their theoretical morality – particularly their moral judgements. In part this has come about for reasons of method: once a particular paradigm, in the Kuhnian sense, has been established, it tends to attract further research. But also, perhaps, there is a reflection here of the more general tendency of psychology to abstract persons from their social settings. Thus, it may be argued, moral psychology as we currently know it tends to be pietistic, rather as Methodism was in the heyday of industrialization. Putting this in another way, it can easily be ideological (in the strong sense): that is, giving a specious or narrow account that is over-accepting of the status quo, and fitting in with dominant social interests.

PERSONHOOD: THE CENTRAL ISSUE

Clearly, the topic of morality presents a heavy agenda for psychology, and one with which it is not always well equipped to deal. The most crucial question of all is what we mean by a person; if empirical work failed to come to terms with this, for the sake of methodological convenience, or if the image of the human being were pared down so as to fit some *a priori* view of 'science', there would be the danger of trivializing the profoundest of all areas of psychological enquiry. The concept of the person has a long history, and its meaning has changed.[3] In most contemporary discussion, there are both descriptive and evaluative elements. That is to say, certain empirical requirements must be present for an object to qualify for the category; but also, built into the concept are certain ideas of actions and attitudes that are appropriate towards and by those who are to count as persons. Putting it differently, to use the category of person is not to talk about membership of a species, but to ascribe a status. We can appreciate this through such everyday utterances as 'The meeting felt to me to be totally impersonal' or 'Now at last I have found a teacher who treats me as a person'. In such usage evaluative notions are clearly present. A person is someone who is worthy of recognition; who legitimately belongs to a community of responsible agents; who merits treatment with respect. The category of the person as it exists today is inextricably bound up with ideas such as these. From the outset it carries moral, or at least proto-moral, implications.

It is difficult to specify a full set of empirical conditions that would be sufficient to guarantee membership of the category of persons. Intuitively we sense that computers, for all their 'intelligence', fall short. There are, however, some difficult borderline cases, such as chimpanzees that have been partially socialized into human ways, or old people fading into dementia. It is certainly possible to imagine extra-terrestrial beings whom humans would treat as persons; the literature of science fiction is full of them. Three human features are clearly necessary for personhood. They suggest in certain crucial ways the shape that a moral psychology might take.

1 The semiotic function

This is the English translation of the term used by Piaget to denote the capacity that a child acquires to use both symbols (which are like the objects they represent) and signs (which are not). Through the semiotic function we can represent the world to ourselves under many aspects; and we can juxtapose and rearrange our representations in purely intellectual activity, without any physical operations on the world. We do not simply exist in a given environment, but live in a social milieu where meanings are shared.

It has been pointed out by several commentators, such as Becker (1968), that a succession of stages in the evolution of mental capacity can be discerned, each one making the living creature less rigidly determined by what is occurring physically in the surroundings; and in that sense, more free. The first level is

that of direct response to environmental stimuli, whether attract-
ive or aversive. In this, and this alone so far as can be discerned,
consists the intelligence of the micro-organism. The second level
is that of the conditioned response. First there is a direct reaction
to a stimulus; and then, after a 'learning' period, to an associated
stimulus that is of no intrinsic interest, like the bell that causes the
Pavlovian dog to salivate. Or, first there are random behaviours;
and then, after some have been rewarded and some 'punished',
new patterns are established. The paradigm case here is that of rats
running in mazes at the behest of experimental psychologists,
administering their schedules of operant conditioning. The third
level is that at which a creature makes connections spontaneously
between events and conditions in the environment. Chimpanzees
have been observed to acquire rudimentary use of tools and
vessels, and to learn new ploys spontaneously, such as a male
enhancing his status by banging on an oil drum.[4] Here the animal
is making use of naturally occurring signs, and introducing a
genuine element of novelty into the situation. The higher primates
and other strongly social animals do not simply have repertoires of
instincts flexible enough to allow for considerable learning, but
also the capability of creating what might be considered as the
beginnings of culture. It is on this basis that we are able to induce
them to become so involved in our human world.

Finally, at the fourth level, use is made not only of symbols that
bear some likeness to their referent, but also of signs that are
arbitrary, whose meaning is validated only on the basis of
consensus. For creatures that can do this the environment is no
longer present under a 'natural' aspect, but is now fully a reality
subject to cultural definition. Language is, of course, the principal
semiotic system, although it is by no means the only one. Pictorial
art, sculpture, music, and dance, for example, must all be
considered; each, in its own way, adding meaning and richness to
the human-reality. But language is by far the most elaborate and
flexible semiotic system that our species employs. Its grammar is
exceedingly complex; and yet it is learned in an extraordinarily
short time – a fact that (among others) has led theorists such as
Chomsky to attribute to it an almost instinctual quality.[5] Moreover,
its most remarkable feature seems to be that it can allow ever new
meaningful combinations, perpetual novelty of expression.

So human beings are meaning-makers, and any creature that is not cannot be considered fully as a person. Persons do not only *behave*, in the sense of responding to stimuli at an almost purely physiological level. They *act*: that is, they construct what they do, in a matrix of meanings. Putting it in another way, they engage in what some sociologists term symbolic (or better, for our purposes, conscious-symbolic) interaction. Whatever human nature may have inherited as genetic tendency is never present in a pure form, but is fashioned distinctively in a culture. Each culture is unique. And as several anthropologists have made plain, two societies which occupy similar physical terrain may be markedly different in the meanings they give to the world, and even in the typical personalities that they produce.[6] Each culture tends to fill out the whole domain of experience with significance, creating myth and fantasy in those areas where it has not rigorously tested the evidence. All this stands testimony to a general human determination; nothing, ultimately, must seem to stand as meaningless or unrelated.

The semiotic function makes it possible to transcend mere 'conditioning', to go beyond the given. With that comes the possibility for human beings to behave towards one another with a cruelty and destructiveness that has no parallel in the animal world. But there is also the opportunity for them to understand one another in their uniqueness, and to develop ideas about what is good.

2 Sentience

If meaning-making and meaning-giving point to one distinctive aspect of personhood, these are related to another which is, in certain respects, even more fundamental. In order to grasp it in the English language we may bring the old word 'sentience' out of obscurity. Applied to the human-reality, it is the feeling, 'mooded' aspect of our subjectivity and intersubjectivity; present in all actions, relationships and understandings, even when not recognized, reflected upon, or explicitly conceptualized. An associated term is 'emotionality'. The emotions are commonly taken to be states of arousal, of deviation from some equilibrium; but the equilibria themselves are states of feeling, and possibly the more significant because they relate to a person's enduring attitudes, or stances taken towards and within the world. So sentience is the whole modality of which emotional arousal is but a small part. Some psychologists point to the same domain by means of the term 'affect'. This tends to have the connotation of a rather passive being, one who is acted upon, rather than a vital source of feeling and activity. In some recent discussions, however, the term 'affectivity' has been used in very much the same way as 'sentience' here.[7]

It is in their first year of life that human beings come to their most fundamental apprehension of the world, as a self is gradually formed, and begins to give meaning to a vast amount of information, both from within and without. These first meanings, it would seem, are primarily in the modality of feeling, and perhaps condensed in a world of private symbols. Later they are 're-worked' through the medium of language. Also, the young child is involved in action before he or she stops to consider what it is to be an agent. As we develop, it is in our capacity as sentient beings that the world continues to be disclosed to us directly. All our practical activity, all our relating to one another, involves our sentience. Even in the position favoured by intellectuals, and made famous by Descartes – a position of pure reflection – a person is still a sentient being; the state is simply one of passivity, quietness, and detachment.

Although it is often the practice to divide the mind into various faculties, this is a matter of convenience rather than representing anything fundamental in nature. There is no radical division between the domains of intellect, feeling, and willing. In the development of the individual the capacity for thinking in a way that is apparently separated off from all emotionality involves a long period of socialization, especially through school, where prolonged engagement with theoretical problems is given high priority. The whole process is specific to certain cultures, notably those in which the activities of the merchant, the scientist, the industrialist, and the bureaucrat are highly valued. Even there, in its extreme form, it is a way of being that pertains to a relatively small minority. If we look at intelligence in a more rounded way, and include the whole range of skilled practical activity, the division between thought and feeling largely disappears. For all persons the purely intellectual mode can only grow out of the sentient. In the case of a culture, too, the meanings which eventually crystallize have largely come out of action and relation; that is, from pre-reflective experience.

Sentience is a universal, but it shows wide cultural variety. At the most obvious level there are certain expressions of the emotions through face and gesture that seem to be widespread, possibly universal: these include fear, anger, surprise, and disgust. Beyond that, the culturally given rules for feeling and emotional expression seem to vary widely. Not only are some cultures more emotionally ambient than others, but also the range of emotions belonging to each cultural repertoire show marked differences.[8]

For at least some primal peoples, or so the evidence suggests, the whole modality of sentience was very different from our own. The sense of self was diffuse, centrifugal, permeating others and the whole environment. Sentience was a field of force outside each individual; a powerful person's anger might be a danger to a whole community; one person's sense of well-being might be a beneficence to all. Some psychoanalysts, particularly those influenced by the ideas of Melanie Klein, claim that this kind of apprehension ('projection' in various forms) is present in all young children, and that it is largely left behind in a process of healthy maturation. But for primal humanity, closely bonded into small groups, perhaps it was this that matched their adult, as well as their infantile, experience. The very idea of projection already implies a selfhood that is strongly individual and bounded; and if the self was not like this, the concept of projection largely disappears.

There is some ground for thinking that as cultural change took place there was a shift in the way sentience was experienced and conceptualized, consistent with changes in the apprehension of selfhood. As Leff (1973) has shown, many of the emotional terms used in feudal and peasant societies were somatic, referring more or less directly to bodily states. Residues of these remain to the present day; for example, there is in English an old set of phrases ('my heart was in my mouth', 'his presence made my flesh creep') which once were taken more or less literally, but now have been largely relegated to the level of cliché. In such societies it is as if the centrifugal self has long vanished, and there is not as yet a modern individual self, potentially the 'owner' of sentient states, to take its place. It is significant that people whose social life is in the transition from 'traditional' to 'modern' often seem to experience their psychological conflict in bodily expression, being particularly liable to affliction by hysteria.[9]

With the rise of the bourgeois era, to which the emergence of psychology itself roughly corresponded, sentience underwent yet further transformation. Madness was swept away, into the asylum, in what Foucault (1976) has called 'the great confinement'; folly was no longer valued as the counterpart of reason. Gender took on new forms, particularly with the idealization of the fragile, domesticated woman. In high culture, at least, there was a greater tendency to value logic and order, and science became the paradigm of intellectual accomplishment. The typical stance of merchant, and later industrial, capitalism, was one of instrumentality, of making use of people and things. Over many of the traditional forms of life, as Weber put it, 'rationalization' prevailed. The hierarchical, bureaucratic organization began to be pervasive. We may well suppose that with changes such as these people became less obviously emotional, less immediate, and generally found it harder to experience themselves as sentient beings. A new emotional vocabulary came into use, more abstract and interpretative; the term 'anxiety' was born. It was in this context that romanticism came into being, as a powerful reassertion of the feelings and sensibilities. So Blake asserted the value, the truth (as he saw it) of sensuousness, love, and spontaneity, and in many of his prophetic works deplored the reign of the false god Urizen (your reason).[10] Later, after many European poets and philosophers had asserted the importance of 'the unconscious', came psychoanalysis. Here we might see a systematic attempt, both in theory and in therapeutic practice, to undo what Whyte (1962) termed that 'facile disordering of experience', in which reason was separated from feeling, that was institutionalized around the time of Descartes.

Sentience is necessary to the concept of the person. For not only do we have knowledge of others, in the sense of having facts about them; we also know them in the deeper sense of having feelings for and with them. Our relationship to a purely cognitive being, however responsive, such as a computer of some future generation, could not be the same. All of this has a very direct bearing on our understanding of morality. Our most basic moral apprehensions are acquired, not as little moral philosophers, but as sentient beings, not yet capable of indirect, symbolic communication. The morality that is held by a mature and integrated person is not derived primarily from textbooks or instruction; but from the lived, felt experience of relationship – of care, support, respect, love, hatred, fear, rejection. Later, perhaps, it is reflected upon and incorporated into a personal world-view.

3 Self-hood

In all cultures, human beings are able to make symbolic representations of others. The clearest and simplest evidence is that, universally, people are given names, and there is no problem about knowing to whom the name refers. But further, human beings are able to represent themselves to themselves, in a sense as if they were another: to say 'I am', and to attach to that phrase any number of predicates. The new-born infant is no more than a proto-self; but gradually becomes, or acquires, a self as he or she enters the social world, aided by the intimate care and dialogue provided by some others. In many respects that world provides what the self becomes. Then, as awareness grows, the child learns how to articulate his or her actions skilfully in social life, and to observe these actions very much as if observing another. Furthermore, it is the sense of self that underlies concern for others.

Self-hood is a universal, but the experience of it, and the metaphors of being that accompany it, show great cross-cultural variety. Here, as in so many aspects, the primal experience of humanity seems to be far removed from that typical of the modern western person. Among some peoples, at least, the self was conceived, not as roughly co-extensive with the body, but as flowing out into the world; as being permeated by, and permeating, other selves. Even a person's clothing, shadow, or name were aspects of the self.[11] Those for whom self-hood took this form lived in a world that was intensely, almost totally, person-alized. The self belonged, so to speak, to a larger social matrix, there to be enhanced or damaged; it was not protected by the armour of the corporeal frame. Every event was liable to be interpreted as having a personal cause; there was virtually no place for accident or chance, and certainly no notion of objectivity.

In some cultures, so it seems, a highly social apprehension of self survived for millennia. Hsu (1985), for example, describes the traditional Chinese concept of Jen (roughly, the person). Here each individual is seen, not as an atomic entity, but rather as a locus in a social field involving relationships of varying degrees of intimacy and significance, ramifying into the larger society. Probably this was true also in traditional society in the west, until 'development' brought such dramatic changes. The elaboration of the idea of property led to a much sharper sense of the categories of 'mine' and 'yours'. Gradually, and perhaps associated with the widespread use of money, a clear notion of objectivity came into being. As the older 'natural philosophy' became transformed into modern science, the distinction between personal and non-personal causation became more clear. The world was, potentially, less a place of terror and superstition; but also it became depersonalized and disenchanted. The self shrank, until for many people it became more or less bounded by the body surface, clearly distinct from other selves. Thus with the decline of feudal and other enduring connections, and the rise of competition, capitalism, and science, the modern individual strode on to the stage of history, the 'subject' of modern psychology. The 'container' metaphor of mind came into common usage. It seems likely that a sense of loneliness and existential anguish became more common. If anything resembling the primal sense of self-hood remains in today's world, perhaps it is in the feeling of connectedness and expansiveness that accompanies deep emotional intimacy; and in certain kinds of mystical experience, in which the sense of being is enhanced and yet, paradoxically, the sense of individuality disappears.

It is the individual, rather than the centrifugal self that features in virtually all modern moral theory, and in the psychology which attaches to it. The primal self was concerned for others, but in a different way; there the life of the individual was, in a sense, the life of the whole. Self-hood in the modern form is fundamentally implicated in a certain kind of moral standpoint, as Nagel (1970) has shown. It is on the basis of an apprehension of my own self-hood that it is possible to take up a metaphysical standpoint in which I recognize that I am simply one person among others; they too have their personal reality, their desires and reasons, which have as much claim to validity as my own. Nagel's crucial point seems to be this. Unless this recognition is present to a considerable degree, for a good deal of the time, social life would be impossible; even the simplest of transactions, such as asking the way or buying a loaf of bread, would break down. A modest altruism, then, is logically built into the structure of practical reason. A fully moral standpoint would thus be one in which this sense of being 'one among others' was maintained consistently. In fact, however, we continually relapse into a form of solipsism, where we become insensitive to the self-hood of others, recognizing the validity of our own reasons only, and using others for our purposes. Seen in these terms, the crucial psychological question for today is to do with the conditions under which this moral standpoint can be developed and maintained, and those which are conducive to solipsistic dissociation.

AGENCY: ITS MEANING AND LIMITATIONS

As persons we live in the world of nature, but apprehend ourselves as being in some sense separate from it. We are creators of culture, inhabiting an intersubjective human-reality, and continually transforming the world. If this were not the case, if our species were fixed and sure in all its behaviours and social forms, there would be no moral questions. It is because of having a certain degree of freedom, the possibility of making choices and knowing that we are doing so, the capacity for critique and self-transcendence, that we are or can become, moral beings.

The sense of choice lies near to the core of what most people mean by morality. In particular, a person may choose (at least sometimes, and to some extent) to go beyond self-interest and take others into account. In the Kantian tradition, and even more strongly in the Augustinian Christianity that seems to underlie it, morality is often associated with doing the difficult thing, with the overriding of desire in obedience to some higher principle through the exercise of will. There are difficulties here, as we have seen. Nevertheless, the idea of will points towards three crucial aspects of human experience. First, we often seem to ourselves to be genuinely making choices, both in small matters and in large. We sense ourselves to be not like locomotives on a track, the points pre-set at every junction; but more like wayfarers, having to decide – and maybe to ask for help or guidance – at many branchings of the path. Second, there are times when we feel inwardly divided, as if pursuing incompatible goals, or torn between duty and desire.

Third, we hold others responsible; ask them to explain their actions, expecting intelligible answers; allocate praise or blame. This, in its most basic sense, is what agency means.

The concept of agency is not limited, however, to choices that are made deliberately and reflectively. Social life is extremely fluid, requiring a subtle and dynamic awareness. Each person occupies a distinctive position, and acts individually. Yet the actions all articulate together to produce the completed acts that form the continuing pattern of the culture. Here the participants are exercising a wonderful skill. Each person has to define and understand the social reality and interpret the actions of others in order to shape his or her own; moreover, to continue to do this as each act is accomplished. It is only rarely that social action breaks down through the failure of the participants to understand sufficient of one another's meanings – even though there may be much that is going on of which they are not consciously aware.

The sense of freedom is ineluctable; it is not extinguished totally, even in concentration camps or under conditions of starvation. Yet freedom is never absolute, and we may be seriously self-deceived about its extent. Presumably nature itself sets the ultimate limits, simply because of the properties of atoms and molecules. The social world within which we live and over which we have relatively little control, imposes many constraints not only on what actually can be done, but on what we conceive to be possible. A context of domination is liable, also, to transform every definition, emotion, and desire. The freedom of each individual is bounded by temperamental and constitutional endowments, derived from what was genetically inherited.

This is the outer context for another kind of limitation to agency: at the psychological level. We have touched on it already, in relation to the sense we sometimes have of being divided within ourselves. This matter is absolutely fundamental for all psychology, and in particular for the study of morality. Davidson (1982) argues that the general notion of intentionality suggests that a person's actions are to be explained by naming first a 'pro-attitude' (a desire, a goal, a value, and so on), and second, a belief that the action is such as would fulfil the desire, promote the goal, or actualize the value. Jane has half a grapefruit and a meagre salad for lunch, while others have prawn cocktail and lasagne. Why? She says she wants to slim, and believes that eating this kind of food will help her to do so. The reasons for an action may also be regarded as causes, although they do not fit into a framework of natural-scientific law. There is a tradition in the theory of action, going back to Plato, which claims that no intentional action can be irrational, since this would violate the very concept of rationality.

However, common experience suggests that there are many actions (as also beliefs and desires) that appear to be deeply irrational. Jane goes home in the evening, and has another frugal but nutritious meal; but she then eats three large bars of chocolate, and later says that it was almost as if another person had taken over. In moral theory such events are said to be instances of *akrasia,* or weakness of the will. How are they to be explained, if the core idea of intentionality is to stand? Here it seems as if normal rationality has broken down; as if mental causes are in operation that are not also reasons. Davidson's argument is that the only way to resolve the problem is by supposing that there is, within the person, more than one self-like structure, each of which is a more or less coherent centre of intentionality. Part of Jane holds the goal of being slim, and the belief about following a carefully planned diet to that end; but another part has the desire for a warm and comforting sense of fullness, and the belief that eating chocolate will bring that about. It should be noted that we are not talking of reason being overcome by desire or passion; but of one intentional centre influencing another, rather as one person might influence another in everyday life. Within the psyche, then, there are causes in operation which are not reasons (between the self-like structures) as well as those causes which are reasons (relating actions logically to intentions). In this way we arrive at a concept of the psyche strikingly similar to that postulated by psychoanalysis, and find that there is some justification for Freud's tendency to mix intentional and neurophysiological concepts in explaining human action. The flattering idea of the unitary self, which has underlain so much of European thought since the seventeenth century, is thus untenable; and a psychology that builds on this idea is inadequate both to direct experience and to the logic of action-explanation.

There is another aspect to the concept of agency, as has been shown, for example, by Taylor (1977, 1986). Beyond our immediate sense of freedom and choice in particular circumstances, there is the possibility of developing values: that is, we can step back from our desires, attitudes, and other motives, and evaluate them according to their worth as judged by some other criterion. For a social and moral being, the development of values is a matter of taking something of an objective stance towards the self, and considering the whole way and quality of life to which particular motives and actions might belong. Here, too, the idea of a unitary self is negated, although in a more positive way. From the point of view of the self that holds existing desires or attitudes, there is no reason for change. Thus the desire to change must come from another self-like centre, holding different motives. A person's values may become a vital part of the conscious frame of reference, intimately bound up with the sense of personal identity, and hence with the motivational structure of the self that occupies the seat of consciousness. Yet values are not settled once and for all; they, too, are subject to reappraisal in the light of new experience. Thus, Taylor suggests, a person who is open enough to reconsider his or her values is putting identity at risk, and being an agent in the profoundest sense. Anyone who can get as far as this, we might suppose, is well on the path towards psychic integration.

THE PSYCHOLOGY OF MORALITY: A DIVERSITY OF APPROACHES

The concepts of personhood and agency, roughly as characterized here, underpin our everyday experience; if these concepts and their entailments were to be abandoned (not only in theory but in practice) social life would break down. People would cease to take one another seriously, and even the most trivial of transactions would be in danger of dissolving into meaninglessness. Moreover, even natural science would be impossible.[12] For the scientist is one who actively searches for, and interprets, evidence, who takes responsibility for designing investigations and experiments, who belongs to a community of scientists with whom meanings are shared, and whose work is underpinned by certain values. The achievements of science – even those which appear to devalue persons – are not dead reflections, mechanically derived; they are the consequence of an active and personal engagement with the world.

This being the case, then, it would seem to follow that personhood and agency, and the principle of rational explanation that is their counterpart, should be fully acknowledged in psychological enquiry. At any rate, a study of human behaviour which ignored them, or which attempted to dispense with them, would be seriously impoverished. Some of the cruder forms of behaviourism, as exemplified by Watson's famous experiment in which he 'conditioned' fear of furry animals and cuddly toys into a two-year old boy,[13] clearly fall short in this respect. For they seem to be based on the erroneous view that human beings stand in relation to the environment as specified by only the first two stages in the sequence set out on page 46. Such a psychology is well suited to the amoeba or, in its more sophisticated versions, to the rat; it is inept for chimpanzees, and entirely unsuited for dealing with the special faculties of human beings, who grow into a world of shared meanings. In fact, it has proved useless in the study of morality; for the evidence strongly suggests that 'rewards' and 'punishments' are never taken in themselves, but always related to their context.[14]

Putting all this in another way, it is logical to demand that any psychological theory should be reflexive:[15] that is, the explanatory principles which are deployed in a theory about others should in principle be able to explain the psychologist's own activity, including the formulation of the theory. After all, the psychologist and the 'subjects' share in a common humanity. If this is a logical requirement, it is also, in a sense, a moral one: it implies respect for persons, and that equal cases should be treated in an equal way.

In practice, however, psychology has often fallen far short of this high ideal, largely for methodological reasons. Since its official recognition as an academic discipline, during the late nineteenth century, the psychological profession has tended to be extremely sensitive about the standing of its work, and to follow various examples taken from the natural sciences. In this process it has, at times, lost sight of debates going on within philosophy concerning the status of persons and the explanation of behaviour. Over the last twenty years, however, there has been something of a move to rectify matters, and to recreate a 'psychology of action', as we shall see in Chapter 3. Curiously, however, although this has strong moral implications, the psychology of morality has as yet remained relatively unaffected.

Over the whole field of moral psychology, as it has developed during the twentieth century, several different approaches can be discerned. Perhaps these might be called 'quasi-paradigms', in the sense that they go some way towards meeting the criteria of a Kuhnian paradigm in natural science. At any rate, each one brings some part of the field into focus, has its own distinctive assumptions, and typical methods of enquiry. Four of these have featured strongly in the psychology of morality.

The first of these, historically speaking, is psychoanalysis. Its practice required intense and prolonged encounters with individuals, usually those suffering some kind of mental distress. A great deal of *ad hoc* interpretation was involved, although Freud and his followers clearly believed that they were accumulating insights in a way that approximated to the method of natural science. The view of the person that emerged provided a powerful challenge to the western moralistic tradition, especially in its suggestion that human beings are, fundamentally, pleasure-seekers, searching above all else for self-gratification. What commonly passed as morality then appeared as little more than the result of a kind of blackmail, in which children were brought into conformity with parental damands, and later with the general mores of society, under the threat of loss of love. This was the doctrine of the superego. There were hints also of a more humanistic attitude, based on an ego ideal. In all of this the early psychoanalysts have mainly said something negative about the foundations of morality; most significantly, they may have uncovered in part the roots of certain pathologies of the moral life, in which a person suffers from irrational guilt and self-condemnation. But also, psychoanalysis did contain the germ of a positive morality, even if of a highly individualistic kind. For its project was to bring people towards a greater degree of integration, a more satisfactory compromise between conflicting elements within the psyche. As a result, it was believed, they might be able to negotiate their interests and desires more openly and creatively with others.

The Freudian scheme has provided the conceptual basis for several major empirical investigations, in which different types of moral character are delineated according to the strength of the ego and superego function. We should note, however, that later depth psychology has provided a far more sophisticated understanding of the relational – and, indeed, the moral – basis of human life. Thus far its insights have remained very largely outside mainstream moral psychology. This is a matter to which we shall return in Chapter 4.

The second main approach, more or less contemporary in its development with psychoanalysis, is that of learning theory; its origins lie in pure behaviourism and in experiments on animal behaviour, and its approach is still primarily experimental. The nature of the learning process is generally assumed to be the same throughout life: that is, little or no account is taken of psychological maturation. In some versions of learning theory the contribution of a person's constitutional or temperamental endowment is acknowledged: that is, the same process of 'moral conditioning' might have different effects on different persons; in relation, for example, to their liability to anxiety arousal.[16]

Learning theories usually place great emphasis on the way parents and other authority figures shape children's behaviour by rewards and punishments. The more sophisticated approach of social learning theory does acknowledge, to some degree, the importance of subjectivity. Imitation is taken to be the primary means by which behaviours are acquired; this is then followed by a process of 'internalization', so that what has been imitated gradually becomes, so to speak, part of the person. A typical experiment would be one in which children first see an adult mutilating a doll; then are subjected to frustration; then are given dolls like the one they had seen – in order to find out whether some will mutilate them in an imitative way. Social learning theory gives many insights into the general process of socialization, and the way people may acquire repertoires of action-schemata. Possibly it tells us less about what is distinctively moral; for here the crucial question is how those schemata are deployed. It is almost conceivable for there to be two individuals who had identical repertoires as a result of social learning; but for one to be callous, crass, and egoistic, and the other extremely sensitive and aware, as moral agents.

The third approach, which derives to some degree from learning theory, is that of psychometrics. Here the main research instrument is the questionnaire; and the answers are often taken, not so much as expressing meaningful content but as examples of verbal behaviour. On the basis of psychometrics it was hoped to build up a scientific analysis of personality, in terms of a small number of basic traits such as anxiety, excitability, tough-mindedness, dominance, and so on.[17] These might have a bearing on a person's moral responses. Psychometric methods have also been used in the direct study of morality. A typical early example was the set of fifty 'moral values items' of Crissman (1942), to be rated on a scale from 'least to most wrong'. In recent years psychometric methods have been used extensively in the attempt to study values; for example, through presenting the subject with a list of items to be placed in rank order.

Although enticing because of their methodological simplicity, psychometric tests are of extremely limited value in giving insights into morality. They often rely on self-report, in which people often unwittingly attempt a self-flattering presentation. They impose a frame on the 'subject', who has no option but to respond in the manner prescribed; thus many nuances of meaning are lost, and there is a near-total opacity to the problem of cognitive stage. Psychometric methods do have some use, in large, extensive surveys and in making broad comparisons between fairly homo-geneous groups – for example, in gaining some impression of prevailing moral attitudes. Here, perhaps, they can at least contri-bute to the first stage of some more detailed enquiry, in which the moral outlooks and judgements of individuals are explored.

This brings us, fourthly, to the approach or quasi-paradigm that has been the most in vogue of late in moral psychology: that of cognitive developmentalism, associated with the work of Piaget and, more recently, with that of Kohlberg. In marked contrast to the greater part of learning theory, here there is an uncom-promising mentalism, a determination to take seriously the subjectivity of all persons, regardless of their age, and however limited their cognitive frame. The assumption is that it is only by an act of understanding, and not merely by observation, that we can apprehend the morality of another. In the practice of research cognitive developmentalism has made great use of an extended interview, in which a person's utterance is carefully attended to, and his or her moral ideas and judgements pressed towards their limits. This has all led to a general developmental scheme; beginning in an outlook that is based on self-interest, and culminating in one where respect for the being of other persons, regardless of social convention, has pre-eminence.

Here, it may be argued, is the beginning of a moral psychology that comes much closer to a full acknowledgement of personhood and agency, and one that fully meets the criterion of reflexivity. It has certain limitations, as we shall see: notably its tendency to make moral judgement the corner-stone, and correspondingly its failure to deal adequately either with moral action or the question of character. Nevertheless, it is through the cognitive-developmental approach (and sometimes in reaction to it) that many of the real advances of recent years have been achieved.

PSYCHOLOGY AS ART AND SCIENCE

This brings us to what is perhaps the most important question of all about psychology, although it is one that seems very rarely to be asked or answered in the clear light of day. What is the purpose of the whole enterprise? Who is to benefit, and in what way?

The general answer, often stated by implication, would seem to be this. Science is a means towards human liberation, by delivering us from prejudice and tradition, and taking us some way nearer to the truth about the world. All truth is to be welcomed; and psychology generates a body of knowledge which, when well corroborated, contributes to that truth. How, precisely, the assured findings of science promote a general liberation is far from clear; but the assumption seems to be that professionals of many kinds – technologists, nurses, doctors, educators, and so on – will modify their practices in the light of new knowledge, with a general spirit of goodwill, and that the most important insights will gradually filter down to lay persons. Scientists can rest content with their project of building up an archive of sound knowledge, knowing that the truth will ultimately convince. If this idea underlies psychology in general, it also seems to inform the project of some of those who wish to recreate psychology in a way that is philosophically more coherent, acknowledging more fully the category of personhood.[18]

There is, however, another view about the purpose of psychology. Suppose we see it, first and foremost, as a practical activity: *the art of intersubjectivity*, of understanding persons in their uniqueness, of clearing up those failures of true meeting with which we are continually beset, and of rectifying their longer-term consequences. That art, in relation to morality, would focus on our capacity to experience concern for others, and be directed towards the enhancement of personhood, and the enlargement of the sense of agency. If psychology is primarily an art, we can see its rather heterogeneous empirical findings in a fresh light.

Whenever we attempt to understand other persons, to interpret their words, attend to their emotions, monitor their non-verbal signals, and so on, we do so in the light of certain background assumptions and expectations. For most people these are derived from common sense, which unfortunately is replete with falsehood: ideological distortions and mystifications, residues of prejudice that belonged to former times. Thus although a person might have considerable practical skill, he or she might still be limited by having inadequate assumptions. What psychological research can do is to provide a richer background resource, more sensitive, less prejudiced, and more surely grounded in evidence. These can enhance the art, although never replace it.

Psychology cannot produce laws in the natural-scientific sense: that is a set of timeless and culture-free empirical generalizations, which have resisted falsification. It does, however, produce a very wide range of more modest and culture-bound empirical findings. These are of several different kinds, such as the following:

- Among those with positions or characteristics $p_1 - p_n$, processes x, y, z are often at work (for example, most mothers and 6-month-old babies tend to interact thus . . .)

- When conditions $c_1 - c_n$ occur, outcome Y is likely to occur in about p per cent of the cases (for instance, people tend to conform, in certain situations of authority).

- Human beings when exposed to social processes $s_1 - s_n$ develop through the following stages (such as the Piagetian cognitive scheme, in western societies).

Generalizations such as these do, of course, go into an archive. But the point is that their diffusion into common knowledge comes primarily by good practice, rather than merely by the transmission of information. A person who has experienced the art of intersubjectivity, in the sense of being very well understood and validated, is more likely to begin to employ that art in daily life. And in general, the practical art is the really important thing; new knowledge has value primarily through its contribution to that art.

Does this, then, leave any place in psychology for description and explanation in a purely natural-scientific mode? Psychology covers a wide spectrum, from the minutiae of perception at one end through to the understanding of social life at the other. At its most physiological, psychology simply merges into natural science, and research can be carried on without any serious engagement with the problem of subjectivity. But the further we move away from this, the less and less appropriate does a purely natural-scientific frame become, and the more intentionality has to be considered. Even in the 'scientific' study of babies in psychology, attributions of intention are constantly being made. And when we come to the psychology of the moral life, concerned as it is with that which is most truly personal – our experience of relatedness and freedom – natural-science models have no legitimate place whatsoever.

In the most general sense, however (more familiar in the German and French than in the Anglo-Saxon tradition) psychology is a science as well as an art. For here we mean an organized domain of knowledge, with a set of methods appropriate to its subject-matter, and a very serious commitment to truth. If psychology uses an experimental method based on that of classical physics, or statistical tests derived from agricultural botany, or analogies from the high frontier of information technology, this in no way guarantees its epistemological standing. Persons are neither mechanisms, nor seeds, nor computers. It is important, rather, to articulate methods that acknowledge personhood as fully as possible, valid according to their own criteria.[18] Psychology, then, cannot remain a poor relation of natural science or a ward of prestigious technology, but has to take its stand as an art, informed by a critical discourse about action and experience, grounded as far as possible on empirical data. In terms of a famous German distinction, then, it is fundamentally a *Geistwissenschaft*: a human science, a science of meaning.

IMAGES OF THE PERSON

We come now to a question which is closely related to that of the different approaches, or quasi-paradigms, in psychology, but one which does not map neatly on to it. In the study of morality, as in any other field of the human sciences, it is necessary to choose how to view the person, and to take responsibility for that choice. 'The facts' will not do this on our behalf, nor would their accumulation lead us eventually to a conception of human nature as 'the crowning achievement of a completed science', to use a phrase of Sartre.[19] Wherever there are facts about persons, wherever there are observations and experiments, metaphors are already in use. It would be wise, therefore, to bring this matter out into the open, and to choose one's metaphorical resources for good reasons.

If we are to take personhood and agency into account we seem to be offered three species of image in western social science (see, for example, Hochschild 1975). The first two are well known; the third is only poorly and partially developed as yet in psychology, although it is one that might have much to offer to our subject.

The first species of image is that of the *rational, cognitive actor*: one who has clear wants and goals, and who carefully considers means to their achievement. The nature of the cognitions varies from one theorist to another, in their subject-matter, their complexity, and their integration; but the point is that the person is relatively straightforward, operating mainly as an instrumental thinker. This image occurs again and again in psychology and social psychology: for example, in Homans' exchange theory, in the theories of cognitive balance and of dissonance, and in all those frames modelled on micro-economics, which consider the person as one who attempts to maximize the product of value and probability. To some degree this is the image latent in much of symbolic interactionism, and in some of the recent attempts by academic humanists to develop a psychology of action rather than behaviour. As Hochschild points out, the rational cognitive actor is present even in the work of Goffman, where social life is viewed as a kind of drama; for here the person presents a self in public, and cunningly manages the impressions made on others, with a great deal of cool calculation behind the scenes.

The pervasive presence of this image in western social science need come as no surprise. For it is a simple reflection of the view of the person, or at least of the male, that underlies the bourgeois social order; the image is about as old as psychology itself. The arrival of that image was clearly echoed in Descartes' famous *cogito, ergo sum*, a proposition he put forward in his quest for the certain foundations of knowledge. Both the nature of the search and the answer that was given are highly revealing. For it is clear that a unitary self is being confidently asserted, despite Descartes' dualistic metaphysics; and that a cool and passionless rationality is upheld as the royal road to truth.

The second species of image might be named as that of the *driven creature*: one who, while going about the business of daily life, is subject to psychic forces largely unrecognized and beyond the realm of voluntary control. The obsessional neurotic, whose own version of rationality seems to others to spring from some deep inner disturbance, is the paradigm case for all humanity. This, of course, is the person as conceived within the more mechanistic versions of psychoanalytic theory, and the simplistic stereotype taken by social scientists who have drawn on psycho-analysis as a resource when their images of 'rational man' have broken down.

Psychoanalysis seems to reveal the person as having great 'depth' and complexity, and is far less complimentary to human-kind than the forms of psychology we have just considered. It was obvious, by the turn of the twentieth century, that many features of human life were inexplicable on the basis of an image of 'rational man'; hysterical affliction, melancholia, mania, multiple personality, masochism, delusion, together with all the facts concerning hypnosis, required a different view of the psyche. Moreover the First World War, coming after a century and more of incredible advancement in western civilization, seemed to reveal liberal humanism as trivial, and its hopes of unlimited progress as facile. At precisely the time when the arts were breaking with convention and realism in their rediscovery of the primitive, psychoanalysis was attempting to create an understanding of the person more adequate to the full range of phenomena, one that would take cognizance of the 'dark forces of the soul'. Freud conceived the human being as having a strong endowment from the evolutionary past, largely anti-social in character; and often as carrying into adult life all manner of incapacitating or destructive resultants from past injury, as well as the unresolved conflicts of childhood. The psyche was irrevocably consigned to a state of inner conflict and compromise, in dealing with the competing demands of appetite, conscience, and social reality.

Freud himself had a training in neurology and medicine, and was captivated by the ideals of natural science. It seems that he hoped at first to integrate all his findings into a wholly mechanistic framework. Gradually he came to believe that, at least in his day, this was impracticable, and that he would have to operate, at least in part, on psychological terrain. In fact, however, Freud never developed a purely psychological theory, valid in its own terms and complementary to neurophysiology. Instead he created a hybrid system, bringing into it a number of concepts of highly problematic status. The crucial example here is mental energy, viewed as undergoing transformation and conservation according to some principle resembling the first law of thermodynamics. When Freud was translated into English many of his allusions were lost, and his language was scientized and sterilized.[20] Nevertheless, the tendency to confound the mental and neurophysiological levels does remain. Freud, then, was correct in recognizing the existence of mental causes that are not reasons (cf. page 56), but incorrect in failing to distinguish clearly between the properties of mental and neurophysiological descriptions. In the words of Gellner's (1985) critique, which is in some respects grossly unfair and misleading, the framework is psychohydraulic or hydrohermeneutic. What Gellner completely fails to acknowledge, however, is the great development of depth psychology since the work of Freud.

This brings us, then, to the third species of image: the *sentient being*. Here the person is viewed in the full sense as an agent, whose actions are to be accounted for according to the principles of rational explanation; but who is inwardly divided, and whose psyche may at times be properly considered as consisting of, or containing, multiple selves. Moreover, the feelings, emotions, and moods are no longer in a residual category, perhaps being viewed as mere epiphenomena, but have the same kind of centrality as they do in psychoanalytic theory. This image, like that conveyed by psychoanalysis, is radical and unflattering, jarring in many respects with the cultural tradition of the west, so deeply committed to the idea of a unitary and rational 'man', and the view that progress comes easily. It is also fundamentally at odds with the prevailing tendencies in cognitive psychology, which model psychic functioning by analogy with the computer.[21]

To develop an image of the sentient being is a considerable task. For it involves not only taking account of what academic psychology has discovered concerning the feelings and emotions; but also bringing in of certain key ideas from psychoanalysis and psychotherapy, so creating a coherent frame of social science. In particular, this requires a re-working so that the last traces of mechanism are removed, and the anticipatory and relational character of social existence are taken more fully into account. If the arguments of this chapter are valid, the image of the sentient being might radically transform the psychology of the moral life.

Chapter Three

SENTIENT BEING, MORAL AGENT

I am a personal terrorist. . . . I use terror tactics to scare myself and so sabotage my progress. So by being a 'terrorist' I often never attain the goals I want to reach and can do easily. So what form of personal terrorism do I practise? I am afraid of failure and yet I am an extremely efficient person, when it comes to solving other problems in the office, when I do voluntary work in strange, dangerous places. But when it comes to taking time for myself – to plan for my future, get out of a bad relationship, finish my books and plays, I just can't do it . . . I terrorize myself by constantly letting other people's feelings and anticipated feelings come first. Am I a martyr because I have always lived for others and therefore avoiding painful situations and am seen by others as a 'good person'? I don't go out and enjoy myself, never left the house or office in case I was needed. Now I go away *but* I leave my phone number where I can be contacted – 'in case I'm needed'. I tend to feel selfish if I do something I want to do, and then bottle up the resentment.

Once upon a time there was a little boy. By the time he was six or seven he had lost something very important. He did not know he had lost it, nor did he know what it was, and it was a very long time before he knew. But what he had lost was his mother. He didn't know he had lost her because she was still there. But he had lost her because she had stopped being his mother, and had become his daughter whom he had to look after and be responsible for. This meant that the little boy had to be very old, almost as old as King Lear, who also had

69

daughters. And the old little boy had to look after the young little boy as well. Of course he didn't want to be an old man because it made him very anxious. But he became two people in one, a young little boy who wanted his mother, and an old little boy looking after his mother/daughter.

May this book help me to be clearer in spirit, simpler in thought, greater in love, more confiding in hope, more ablaze with faith, more humble in spirit.

The first of these passages was written by a woman who was slowly coming to terms with an oppressive feeling of personal inadequacy, and her failure, in some deep sense, to be 'good', despite her obvious appearance of morality. The second was written by a man during the course of psychotherapy, pondering on the way in which his relationship with his mother had in many respects set the pattern for his way of being in the world, and indeed given him his fundamental sense of who he was. The third was written by Joseph Goebbels, who became Hitler's Minister of Propaganda. The words form the opening of his diary of 2,000 and more pages,[1] in which he reveals the intensity of his hatred for all whom he took to be weaklings and inferiors, especially the Jewish people; his idolization of the Führer; and the incredible extent both of his small-mindedness and his delusions of grandeur.

Here we have three pointers to what may be the central issue in developing an adequate psychology of the moral life. Each of us is, to some degree, inwardly divided and disorganized. There is an important sense in which we are anticipators, and constructors of our actions, as we share minutely in the world of conscious-symbolic interaction; but also we may be living out larger patterns of which we have but little awareness, and sometimes we are even 'lived by' processes that we do not understand. Much of what passes as morality and piety, and much that is, intellectually, extremely sophisticated, is caught up in this web of self-deception.

'Academic' psychology, with its strongly natural-scientific emphasis, can help us to some extent in grasping this complexity. Particularly important here are those approaches which empha-size behaviour as human activity, rather than as a set of responses to stimuli; some of these tend, however, to view the person as a processor of information, and most say little about the feelings and emotions. 'Therapeutic' psychology stands in something of a contrast. Its concern is, primarily, with the relief of distress and the remedying of incompetence, rather than with adding to an archive of neutral knowledge. Here it is almost inevitably committed to engage with the person as a sentient being; for all the commonly presented forms of mental malaise, whether anxiety, depression, depersonalization, phobia, or despair, are sentient states, and of these the therapist is bound to have at least a commonsensical theory. In this kind of psychology the data base is extemely rich, for it is grounded in a close and serious involvement with persons. However, the 'samples' may be biased, and theory often rests rather lightly on evidence; also there is sometimes ground for doubting whether what actually goes on during therapy bears much resemblance to the official accounts, be they Freudian, Jungian, Kleinian, or whatever. Although there are problems such as these, therapeutic psychology has much to offer to the understanding of morality. Perhaps, by making a synthesis between parts of it and parts of 'academic' psychology, we can create an image of the person that is adequate for our purposes, and thus envisage forms of praxis that work towards moral development.

The account of the person contained in this chapter is culture-bound, in a double sense. On the one hand it is created from the categories of western culture, including psychology in both its 'academic' and 'therapeutic' branches. On the other hand, its subject-matter is, primarily, the person as formed within the advanced industrial societies of the west: that person for whom indirect, symbolic knowing has come to have so large a place in comparison to knowledge through lived experience, and who often moves quickly from one social life-world to another. It may be, however, that this image is, to some degree, of a wider relevance; or could be made to be so, with a little modification. Potentially it seems to offer a way of looking at certain features of the person, and hence of moral development, in different cultures, at least without the blatant chauvinism for which western psychology is sometimes at fault. This is a possibility that we shall briefly explore.

THE SENTIENT BEING

Our talk of mind inevitably uses metaphors, which should never be taken as literal truth. Here, in common with psychoanalytic theory, especially in its earlier forms, we shall speak of three 'levels' of psychic activity, going on concurrently during the waking life of the adult person: conscious, pre-conscious, and unconscious. Conscious activity is rational, in the minimal sense of 'understanding reasons', and closely bound to the conventions of language. Pre-conscious activity is less highly differentiated, less logically integrated; its conceptual elements carry a strong emotional toning. Its content, to use a phrase of Epstein (1985), is an 'experiential theory of reality', unwittingly constructed by the person in dealing with events and situations of high emotional significance. Clearly there is a great difference between knowledge held at these levels. A person with agoraphobic tendencies, for example, might 'know', in the first sense, that open places are not intrinsically dangerous; but might 'know', in the second sense, that they are very dangerous indeed. The third level, that of unconscious psychic activity, corresponds closely to the idea of 'unconscious fantasy' as explicated by Klein and the object-relations school – themselves developing Freud's idea of 'the unconscious'.[2] Its subject-matter, when it passes directly into consciousness, consists of images with very powerful emotional associations. Its process is not logical, nor is it subject to the ordinary categories of causality, space, and time.

In this model conscious and pre-conscious psychic activity may be viewed as standing in relation to each other as figure to ground; and unconscious psychic activity as lying behind that ground, in a slow but continual interchange of content with it. As the (pre-conscious) ground changes, so does the consciously apprehended figure that is embedded in it. A predicament which on one day is defined, cognitively, as hopeless, on another day looks full of promise – even when nothing, objectively, has changed. What has changed is the person's mood, and with it the pre-conscious construal. It seems likely that within western culture, which gives such a high place to theory and reflection, there is often a large disjunction between the three levels of psychic activity; but this may not be a necessary or universal aspect of mental functioning.

This view of mind makes good sense in developmental terms,

and is, *prima facie*, reconcilable with a Piagetian understanding. For the unconscious level approximates to a continuing of the very earliest mode of conscious thought: that of the infant, whose experience is pre-linguistic and at first very largely passive. If depth psychology is at least a guide to the truth, it is at this stage that a person acquires the most fundamental apprehension of the human-reality, which forms the background to every later stage setting in life. Its content, we may suppose, consists of certain overarching feelings about whether the world is safe and welcoming, or dangerous and hostile; whether the body is a locus of pleasure and fullness, or emptiness and pain; whether people are trustworthy and caring, or fickle and cruel. Some of these feelings are 'carried' by symbols of an extremely private form, and solipsistic in their focus: a 'guardian angel', perhaps, protecting from all harm, or a horrendous toad-like figure with a bird's beak, waiting to destroy.[3] The work of Klein and those who followed her suggests that unconscious mental life bears the consequences of the first intense ambivalences between love and hatred, archaic feelings of omnipotence and destructive rage. Possibly it carries the most basic flaws of personality; related to the failure to develop a coherent centre of experience in which the different poles of ambivalence are accepted and reconciled, the failure to come to realistic terms with a too painful and frustrating reality.

The pre-conscious level in the adult roughly corresponds to a continuation of the conscious psychic activity of the child who has not yet attained operational thinking; but who, possessing the use of language, can engage in everyday symbolic interaction, even if still in highly idiosyncratic terms. The child is emotionally vulnerable, and is far from a clear and objective understanding, but yet is required to undergo many new experiences. It is at this time that life-scripts are formed, and the key elements of the experiential theory of reality are acquired, a theory which will be elaborated in later life as further powerful events are dealt with.

'You must learn to keep your mouth shut', said my father harshly. I was astonished. 'But, Daddy, I *always* keep my mouth shut! Why must I keep it shut?'

'There you go again! Just when I have told you not to!' This defeated me. I was about to ask him another question, when I found myself crying instead. I thought it time to run away; he did not like it when I was a silly little cry-baby.'

(From Wilfred Bion's autobiographical sketch, *Long Week-End*, 1986: 24).

A child, equipped with the powers of pre-operational thought, can easily make incorrect inferences from experiential data; and yet these inferences have a compelling, self-evident quality about them. They are often not checked against reality; rather, reality is then set up so as to provide apparent confirmations. Sometimes the data are contradictory, implying different 'facts' about who the child is, and is to be. All this is hidden away in a private and half-forgotten world.

The conscious level of psychic activity is, primarily, that of concrete-operational thought, where the person knows and understands in a more obviously rational, although not very flexible, way. At this level there is a much greater degree of objectivity about the material world, and a more coherent form of interaction with others. Rules are followed and roles taken on, with an understanding of the prescriptions which constitute them. There is a greater separation of cognition from emotion; although each culture allows some degree of emotionality, through its gender-specific rules of feeling and rules of expression. For some persons, there is a further elaboration of conscious thought in formal operations. This mode of thinking is more abstract, further away from action; and here the separation of cognition from emotion is virtually complete.

Mind does not exist as a 'thing' in the world, and we can only speak of it in metaphors. That of levels is no exception; we would not expect to find them in the nervous tissue, on slicing through the brain. Nevertheless, this metaphor does seem to make neurophysiological sense.[4] The brain consists of interconnecting webs of neurons, with complexes of connections being formed as a result of different inputs, each performing different functions. The more enduring connections, so it is believed, involve not merely patterns of electrical and biochemical activity, but also structural changes at a molecular level. All neurons of the same type have the same properties; the chemical transmitters are of certain definite kinds; and some, at least, of the types of connective network are genetically determined. Nevertheless, the systematic properties of the brain come to be unique to each individual; and hence the mentality of each person is also unique. The unconscious, pre-conscious, and conscious levels, then, may correspond to different neural patterns or arrangements, in the order of their appearance. The earlier patterns remain (probably well established at a chemical level) and 'underlying' the successively later sets of connections. At certain points in the whole system, different functions may share the same connective networks. Thus what is later is always liable to be affected by what is more archaic.

Although this view of mind is like that held by some cognitive-developmentalists, it differs from it in certain crucial respects. For a strict Piagetian an earlier form of thinking is totally and irreversibly superseded when stage change takes place; it is on this ground, for example, that an explanation is given of the scarcity of childhood memories.[5] Here, however, it is postulated that earlier forms of thinking remain in the adult, although modified in the light of later experience. In a typical modern, western adult the three levels of psychic activity become somewhat separate from one another, and there tends to be an identification with what is focally conscious. It is for this reason that it often appears that the earlier forms of thought have disappeared. Piaget himself virtually acknowledged this, when in old age he recalled his six months as a recipient of psychoanalysis with Sabina Spielrein;[6] a brief phase when his world became again more magical, intense, and coloured. A person who limits his or her self-understanding to conscious, rational thought is, in a sense, alienated, because out of touch with the 'deeper' levels of psychic life. And when they irrupt into consciousness, perhaps in the form of a sudden attack of anxiety or an unaccountable sense of depression, it is almost as if an alien force has taken possession; such are among the experiences that commonly bring people to psychotherapy.

This general view of the psyche, while giving a full place to cognitive function, is well able to incorporate the emotions and feelings. Katz (1984), in his discussion of the origins of an individual's personal construct system, postulates the existence of certain 'primitive constructs', given genetically to our species. Glimpses of these are to be seen in Freud's notion of the id, in Jung's archetypes, and in the 'hereditary pattern-reactions' identified by some behaviourists. We may understand the primitive constructs as providing a kind of 'feeling-knowing'; perhaps the most archaic of all is a raw division of experience into pleasure and pain. The primitive constructs are elaborated during the individual's unique developmental experience, which itself takes place within a cultural frame. In this process a repertoire of emotions and feelings is acquired, with culturally given meanings. It is thus possible to account for both the universality of certain behavioural expressions of emotion, and the way in which the content of sentient experience varies from one culture to another.

Broadly speaking, the image we are building up is depth-psychological, even if not specifically psychoanalytic. Clearly, it does not entail any kind of general psychic determinism. The person is not a mechanism, a creature driven by mysterious and ontologically dubious forces, but an active and sentient being, even if inwardly divided. Also, there is far more emphasis than psychoanalytic theory on the pre-conscious level of psychic activity, or at least the pre-conscious is seen in a different way. In this respect we come close to some forms of humanistic psychology, with their insistence that a person should 'get in touch with feelings', 'in the here and now' (read, approximately: 'become aware of pre-conscious experiential construals'). Moreover, classical psychoanalysis has generally taken conscious psychic activity as the prime interface between the adult person and the world, with the pre-conscious as an intermediate territory, so to speak, *en route* to and from the unconscious. Here, however, pre-conscious, experiential construing is seen as the most powerful mode in which a person encounters the world, and the one which carries the strongest motives, including those which are embedded in unconscious mental life.

In a sense, then, the postulate of pre-conscious, experiential construing is the cornerstone for building an account of the person as a sentient being. In fact its presence is particularly well supported, by evidence of several different kinds. For example, there is now a considerable body of experimental work which shows a discrepancy between people's reports of what they apprehend consciously, and what they appear to 'know' at some other level, as judged by their physiological responses, or their actual behaviour.[7] All of this falls immediately into place if we accept the idea of pre-conscious construal. Another line of evidence is that from the study of non-verbal interaction.[8] This work shows that body language often contradicts what is being communicated verbally; people can 'give themselves away', or 'show what they are really feeling', by posture or gesture, or even by movements so subtle as the flickering of the eyes. Further support for the postulate of pre-conscious construal comes, although in a less precise way, from work in psychotherapy. A therapeutic interaction is commonly seen as one in which two or more people encounter one another at a level that is 'deeper', and 'more real' than is usually the case in everyday life. The training of a therapist or counsellor involves the cultivation of a variety of sensitivities and awarenesses in the domain of feeling and intuition that are relatively undeveloped in most persons. All of this can be understood readily in relation to the three-level scheme. Therapy involves an engagement at the pre-conscious, as well as at the conscious level. If it works on the unconscious level also, it does so via the pre-conscious, as a person's way of being in the world is destabilized and then re-founded. In effective therapeutic work it is necessary to be 'congruent', to use the term coined by Rogers (1961). That is, there should be a close correspondence between what the therapist is feeling and what he or she presents to the other. Where this is the case, it seems that the other can become more congruent too.

The idea of trying to bring psychoanalytic and cognitive-developmental theories together is by no means new, although the most successful ventures seem to have been those focusing on the first three or so years of life.[9] One of the more ambitious of recent attempts is that of Malerstein and Ahern (1982). This grew out of clinical and psychotherapeutic work, where they found that the energy concepts of conventional psychodynamics seemed far too crude to encompass the phenomena with which they were dealing. In their understanding, like that of many psychoanalysts, the basic structure of personality tends to 'set' around the age of seven or eight. This can be related, however, not to the progress and fixations of libido, but to one of three basic and enduring styles of 'social cognition', typical of the child of about three, five or seven years old respectively; whether this is conscious or pre-conscious, they do not make clear. The scheme they present is subtle, and puts several developmental issues in a new light. However, what this and other syntheses do not do well is to display clearly how a person engages with the world, relates to others, or acts in a social context. There is still something of that isolationism which is a common weakness in both Freudian and Piagetian theory. The scheme outlined in this chapter, however, which does lead to an account of social action, is an attempt to rectify this fault.

The whole view of the psyche presented here, with its imagery of levels, is based on modern, western experience. Let us return for a moment to the question of whether it has any cross-cultural validity. Some studies by anthropologists and cognitive-developmental psychologists suggest that primal peoples mainly use a form of thinking similar to the pre-operational, in which myth and magic are inextricably mixed with their practical concerns. On this basis, incidentally, they can operate very effectively in their world. Many peasant peoples, and those who live in fairly non-industrial mercantile societies, develop modes of concrete-operational thought, particularly in their commercial calculations.[10] It would appear, however, that formal-operational thought only became widespread in the advanced industrial societies, and here it is particularly associated with the development of natural science. Thus the levels correspond very roughly to different stages of historical change, in which cognition and sentience become increasingly dissociated. Piaget himself made a similar point in relation to his scheme, seeing the development unambivalently as the path of progress that led to modern scientific civilization. This view, however, is highly problematic, especially for the psychology of morality. It is arguable that for every one of us, whether or not an intellectual, our mode of being in the world involves us fundamentally in a kind of feeling-knowing or affectivity, and we neglect it at our peril.

Here, then, are the rudiments of a view of the psyche which mediates between 'academic' psychology (particularly some of the cognitive approaches) on the one hand, and 'therapeutic' psychology on the other. Although a few of the connections made here are speculative, the whole stands on a rather strong empirical base. It meets well the philosophical requirement that social-scientific theory should take the human being as a person and as an agent. It has a developmental slant, and gives a basis for understanding both character and cognition. On all these grounds it is well suited to a psychological enquiry into morality.

DEVELOPMENT AND ALIENATION

Thus far we have taken the adult as an already-existing being, and only caught glimpses of how this state of affairs might come about, in which thought is so separate from feeling, and different levels of psychic activity have become divorced from one another. An account can, however, be given in developmental terms, applying not only to the relatively well-charted transitions from infancy to adulthood, but also to the whole span of life. Here it is possible only to give the barest outline, focusing on aspects that are of special relevance to the acquisition and growth of concern for others, and the obstacles to this process.

The new-born child enters the world relatively far weaker and less formed than any of the animals we resemble closely. In line with the discoveries of Piaget and his successors, we may well suppose that the infant's experiential field is, initially, an incoherent and unstable flux of raw sense data from both inside and outside the body, out of which patterns are slowly formed. The new-born infant is not yet a sentient being, in the true sense; yet while having no capacities for symbolic interaction with others, and no self that belongs to an intersubjective human-reality, he or she is evidently a rich and powerful centre of feelings of some kind. Emotions are expressed with an immediacy unknown to adults in most cultures; we tend to take the cry of pain, the smile of recognition, the sleep of contentment, absolutely at face value – at least until the sense dawns that the infant is beginning to discover how to manipulate and struggle in a battle of wills. In certain respects, then, the very young human is the most morally straight-forward being imaginable, whose psychic and somatic life exist in unity: a person, or at least a proto-person, of complete integrity. Soon, however, compromises must be made. From the second half of the first year, as specific attachments grow, the infant is clearly acquiring a sense of self, and recognizing the fact of existence in a world that is peopled by other (imperfect) selves. Virtually all the main traditions in psychology converge in their belief that the formation of self is, fundamentally, relational; to be a person is to be that-which-exists-in-relationship. Psychoanalysis suggests that this journey is a perilous one, not a simple path of trouble-free development.

During the second year of life the child begins to acquire the semiotic function, and enters the domain of pre-operational thinking. It is now possible to use some of the socially shared signs and symbols, even though the world is still full of magical transitions. Now it is open to the child to gain a new and richer grasp of experience: to name and to begin to understand the joys and fears that hitherto have existed only in a private and unstable theatre of fantasy. Now the child can take bearings a little more clearly and objectively, gaining glimpses of the world as it is known in the culture. Potentially now the child can share his or her experience with others, and begin to occupy a place in a community of persons.

Let us be unashamedly Utopian for a moment, and try to envisage what might be the case if a child were to grow up into a world in which the moral principle of respect for persons were applied very rigorously from the beginning, by people to whom that same principle had been consistently applied: who therefore sensed themselves to be capable and well-cared-for, who were in touch with their own nature as sentient beings, at ease with their own embodiment and sexuality. Here, we might suppose, the child would have the sense of being a uniquely valuable person; both self and body would be affirmed, and there would be a feeling of fullness arising from the continuance of love and nurture. The ambivalent feelings that accompany the first privations would not be too intense. The child's own experience would be validated: that is, understood, accepted, and named. As cognitive development continued the child would elaborate conceptual knowledge that was in accord with feelings and emotions; and so, remain an integrated and sentient being. Primal fantasy would remain as a rich, dark ground for creative intuition and imagination.

As the child developed, he or she would be confident in the truth-value of his or her own experience, and so be able easily to empathize, to understand and share the emotions and feelings of others. Some respect and trust towards others would be 'natural'; or, to be more precise, it would be a construction from the immediate social world. There would be relatively little psychic defence, because the child's relational experience would be sufficiently benign for it not to require defending against. We cannot say what the self-apprehension of such a person would be, although it is unlikely that it would be that of the highly localized and bounded subjectivity typical in the industrial societies of today. All of this would not, of course, bring freedom from the pain, anguish, and conflict that are endemic to the human condition. Probably these things would be felt the more acutely; the self, however, would be strong enough not to avoid or deny such experiences, but to pass through them and assimilate them.

The general truth about socialization, however, is very different from this. It is beginning to be clear from historical studies,[11] particularly of northern Europe, that we carry the accumulated consequences of centuries of appallingly bad child care: children in medieval society often being treated virtually like domestic animals; infants in the Industrial Revolution being drugged with opium while their care-givers went out to work – later to join the ranks of overworked and malnourished child labour. Families and schools often had irrationally harsh and uncaring disciplinary regimes during the nineteenth century; this continued in some sectors of society virtually through to the present day, where, with boys at least, the cane and the strap were taken as a remedy for all ills. In contemporary industrial societies, with their much greater leisure and their heightened awareness of children as persons, matters may be very much better. There is still, however, a disturbing story of widespread violence and abuse towards children, which is probably no more than the outcrop of a more pervasive lack of respect – this derived, in part, from the incredibly stressed lives of some of their care-givers.[12] Bowlby (1979), whose criteria were minimal rather than optimal, has committed himself to the view that only about half of the children in Britain are receiving adequate nurture and care. Respect for his opinion on this point does not entail accepting his theory of exclusive mothering. At least there is an indication here of a failure that may have very severe moral consequences.

When the child's own subjectivity is not accepted and validated, there begins to develop a crucial dissociation between experience and understanding. The child learns to value the opinion of others, whether adults or children of a slightly older age, and to give less heed to his or her own immediate experience. In being taken into the social world the child is 'taken in' in another sense, having no option at this stage but to accept the meanings that are provided. It is difficult, perhaps impossible, to attend to delicate 'internal' signals which the culture does not acknowledge; or to give due weight to experience which is not validated by those others upon whom life depends, and from whom the sense of well-being, such as it is, derives. So comes about an adaptation to the existing reality, with all its attendant insensitivities, distortions, and vested interests. There is a disturbance in subjectivity which the child is in no position to understand.

Following to some extent the phenomenologies offered by Rogers (1965) and by Laing (1960), the position in later childhood and beyond may be described by means of a diagram, which shows the 'total field of experience' (see Figure 3.1).

Area 1 represents the whole experience of the embodied organ-

Figure 3.1

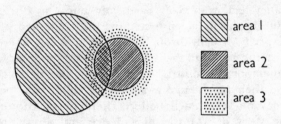

ism: that which a person is, in some sense undergoing (through taking in and processing sense data), whether or not this is registered in consciousness by means of symbols or words. Area 2 represents what is 'known' in consciousness, whether or not it corresponds accurately to what the person has actually undergone. Area 3 represents the pre-conscious apprehensions, which are in relation to consciousness as ground to figure. That part of 'genuine' experience which is available to consciousness at any one time is indicated by the overlap between areas 1 and 2.

A portrayal of the field of experience in this kind of way makes a good deal of therapeutic sense, without involving that difficulty which we noted in relation to Freud's original work: the use of physical or neurophysiological concepts when working at a psychological level. Immediately two aspects of the psychological predicament of the growing child are brought into focus. First, there is a vast amount that he or she has genuinely undergone, but without an adequate representation through the semiotic function. Some of this may have been too difficult or painful for the psyche to bear, and is (in Freud's terms) repressed. For example, some psychosomatic illness is explained by therapists on the assumption that anguish or conflict which a person has indeed experienced at some level, and yet been unwilling or unable to symbolize, makes its protest directly through bodily reactions. Second, part of what is 'known', in the sense of being represented by symbols to consciousness through the semiotic function, does not correspond accurately to the child's own lived, felt, experience; this consists of ideas, beliefs, precepts, injunctions, fantasies transmitted by others through the means of language – and not necessarily based on their own experience either. Thus the diagram points to two difficulties for the child, as the process of 'socialization' proceeds: the presence of what we might term 'unacknowledged experience', and of 'pseudo-experience'. In all of this language plays a highly ambivalent role. Potentially it can enable the child to gain a grasp of situations, to understand what is happening and what has happened, to interpret his or her feelings and emotions. However, it also creates the possibility for all manner of confusion and unwitting self-deception; not least because it is mainly through linguistic means that a person becomes subject to the moral authority of others.

How is it that a single human organism comes to be, or to 'have', several self-like structures that are in conflict? Experimental social psychologists often focus on three aspects of self-conception: social feedback, social comparison, and direct inference.[15] Social feedback refers to that process in which a person learns through the messages conveyed by others, and the messages are significant in so far as those others are to be taken seriously. Social comparison refers to the monitoring of one's own performance in relation to that of others who are seen, in some way, as appropriate or similar. Direct inference means drawing conclusions from one's own behaviour or subjective states without direct reference to others. When these processes are explored a little, their ramifications become complex. The point for our purposes here, however, is a simple one. The child is often not addressed consistently, has to face a bewildering variety of models for comparison, and is often seduced out of an awareness of his or her own subjectivity. This is particularly the case as he or she acquires a broader range of social experience, through school, peer-groups, clubs, churches, and so on. Each embryonic self is formed in the child's attempt to adapt appropriately to a particular social milieu, to be a person and an agent within it. For most people this is manageable; it is possible to maintain some semblance of overall consistency, and some basic sense of well-being. The transition from one 'self' to another brings no great disturbance, and is largely pre-conscious. In those very rare cases of 'grand hysteria', of which a few are well documented,[14] the child becomes, almost literally, two or more individuals, each with an identity and chain of memories; and each is bewildered by the apparent gaps in biography, when another self took over. Figure 3.1, then, is an attempt to describe the position at any particular point in time. We may envisage the pattern as being dynamic through time, as one 'self' recedes into the background and another comes to 'occupy the seat of consciousness'.

THE SCHIZOID DISTURBANCE

The state which is shown in Figure 3.1 might be termed that of 'common alienation', and to some extent it may be simply the price of being human, of having cultural patterns in place of instincts. But there is a further degree of alienation, which is found in its most acute form in the condition which psychoanalysts and others term 'schizoid'. From the outside the schizoid personality is often typified as being cold and unemotional, aloof and detached, unable to make warm and intimate relationships, tending to intellectualizations and technicalities, often involved with theory to the exclusion of people. Not surprisingly, some therapists have come to the conclusion that this disturbance is endemic in the modern industrial societies, and particularly prevalent within such occupational groups as artists, scientists, and academics.[15]

Although conceptualized in a variety of ways, the schizoid disturbance is generally assumed to be the most fundamental of all 'personality disorders', because it comes from a basic failure to develop a coherent sense of self, buoyant with good feelings, and confident in engagement with the world. Its essence is represented in Figure 3.2.

Figure 3.2

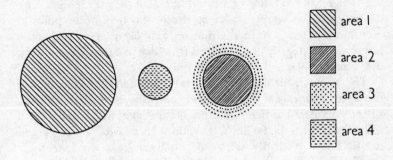

area 1

area 2

area 3

area 4

Those who have tried to understand the schizoid experience, through therapeutic work, all suggest that the typical apprehensions are those of not belonging, of being out of touch or isolated in some way.[16] The schizoid person keeps an intensely private self (area 4), often separated in fantasy from the body, and thereby immune from all violation by the world; it is with this that he or she makes the primary identification. Action is carried out in terms of one or more 'false selves', corresponding to area 2 and its pre-conscious penumbra; it is, in a sense, mechanical, devoid of feeling or emotion. To be schizoid is to live primarily by intellect and will.

The secret 'inner' self which the schizoid person maintains is never nourished by the closeness and validation of others. It is impotent, whatever illusions of power, invulnerability, and freedom it may possess. Of course, the more defended it is against the impact of external reality, the more unreal it becomes. Typically, then, the schizoid state is one of profound ontological insecurity; there may at times be a dreadful sense that the 'I am' is in danger of collapse or disintegration. The consequences of this divorce of the core self both from the body and the world, as Laing (1960) has pointed out, is that experience is meaningless and action is futile. Depth psychology gives some indications as to how this state may arise, even if there is also a genetic contribution; it is a way of dealing with a reality that a child feels to be unliveable, in which experience was continually discounted and undermined, and where the validity of his or her actions was denied. The defence can be adopted also by those who live under political conditions of terror or totalitarianism, as a way of preserving some last sense of integrity. 'I go around from day to day as if I am living in a glass bubble; and I protect myself by jokes.'[17]

There are disturbing parallels between the schizoid state and the style of moralism that has been pervasive in western culture, where goodness has been so strongly associated with intellect and will, so little with the feelings. It would seem possible that a person might be profoundly schizoid, and yet have an extremely sophisticated theoretical morality. In terms of Figure 3.2, this would be entirely within area 2. Such a 'morality' would be, primarily, part of the apparatus of the false self; and an expression, not of felt concern for others, but of self-protection against involvement, conflict, and negotiation. Also, ironically, it would be of little value to the one who held it, for it precludes those very contacts by which personhood would be nourished, sustained, and made real. At some level the schizoid person knows this, and intense moralism may express a kind of yearning; meanwhile, the hidden self is 'kept in cold storage', in the hope that one day it might be brought out, and allowed to grow strong in a climate of love.

MASCULINE, FEMININE

This general development picture is hardly open to dispute, whatever may be said of its details. Much more tentatively, because the evidence is far less robust, we can add some account of the acquisition of gender. A person's sex is given biologically (even though there are cases in which this is problematic). Gender, however, is a social construction, consisting of the meanings and evaluations that are attached to being male and female; it varies considerably from culture to culture.

At the level of conscious-symbolic interaction it is clear how young children acquire their resources for performing competently as members of a particular gender category.[18] The child is addressed as a boy or girl, mixes with other children who know whether they are boys or girls; is pointed towards older examples, both in real life and in media presentations; is given particular kinds of clothes and toys; is plied with numerous cues to indicate whether his or her social performance is acceptable. It appears that most children are aware of their gender identity by the age of three; but it is not until considerably later, around the time of concrete-operational thought, that they can give clear reasons to support their belief. Schooling confirms the gender identity in many ways. Childhood peer-groups, which in some respects are intensely conservative, may well be an even more powerful influence. Through experiences such as these a boy or girl develops resources for social action; not necessarily an authentic expression of his or her own being, but distorted according to the prevailing stereotypes. In terms of Figure 3.1, the area of pseudo-experience is strongly gendered.

Some rather speculative work based on psychoanalysis and psychotherapy, which we shall examine in greater detail in Chapter 4, suggests a 'deeper' aspect to the acquisition of gender. The story that emerges is of a divergence in the relational experience of boys and girls from a very early age; the consequence, not primarily of the fact that the biological mother is a woman, but of the gender arrangements in which men are dominant and often remote from their children, while child care is very largely in female hands. This divergence, it is claimed, underlies some of the most crucial features of adult personality, and in particular the capacities of men and women for autonomy and intimacy. If any generalization can be made, it is that the former is easier for men and the latter for women. These differences, in our terms, belong to unacknowledged experience, and for many people are never brought to symbolic representation.

TOWARDS ADULTHOOD AND OLD AGE

By the end of childhood most persons have become to some extent divided and alienated. The self as it is known in consciousness is only partially grounded in authentic personal experience, and involves a great deal of adaptation to the prescriptions and seductions held out by others through the use of language. At puberty powerful new processes are at work and the body undergoes dramatic changes. It is difficult for the growing person to deal with these developmentally, because of being out of touch with the experiential matrix into which they might be assimilated. How, for example, can a person integrate feelings of adult sexuality, if the body is not known already as a locus of sensuous pleasure? Moreover, adolescent cultures and subcultures tend to impose very strict role requirements upon their members, often with a strong basis in gender.[19] To be a competent performer requires a hyper-awareness to what is going on externally; to be in touch with the emotions and feelings might be a serious disadvantage.

Entry into adult life carries with it many possibilities for an even further degree of alienation. Generally the number of well-defined roles that a person takes on increases. Formal organizations, in particular, often require a person to make massive adaptations. Some of the roles which have been, traditionally, masculine, require a degree of ruthlessness and self-seeking that is incompatible with the development of the person as a sentient being. Some of the traditionally feminine roles – including, of course, that of 'housewife' – require those who occupy them to give unstinting service and nurture to others, while often remaining unaware of their own desires and needs. Looking after those who are handicapped or disabled, or those who are mentally or physically infirm in old age, can bring about an almost total loss of personal identity in the care-giver; and in Britain now this involves almost one household in five.[20] In these and other ways, then, life in the contemporary industrial societies fosters a very high degree of alienation and adaptation as people move through the first two decades of adulthood.

There is little, moreover, in middle or later life positively to engender a person's restoration as a sentient being. It is not surprising that Jung and others found many people suffering from mid-life crises, as if a shadow existed, of unacknowledged experience and potentiality that were waiting to be discovered.[21] Their clients (as indeed, in the greater part of psychotherapy) were mostly from the middle classes, with enough leisure to be aware of a deficiency and enough money to enable them to take steps to rectify it. But there is no ground for supposing that the problem is specifically located here. Those who have low wages or who are unemployed in middle and later life are often taken up with the sheer struggle for survival, and with maintaining self-respect when society provides them with so little. Many women have severe constraints put on them to continue in their roles as care-givers and providers. The division of the psyche is perpetuated, and the person still remains undeveloped as a sentient being. In old age, when many roles are withdrawn and the amount of social interaction diminished, self-hood itself becomes fragile, especially in so far as it is founded upon adaptation rather than personal experience, authentically symbolized. Is it possible that in some cases the alienation of a lifetime provides one of the psychological conditions for dementia, a final and irreversible loss of self-hood in old age? At any rate, this tragic predicament cannot be accounted for in terms of neuropathology alone.[22]

In giving this sketch of life-history we are indeed on the ground of depth psychology, but a considerable way away from orthodox psychoanalytic theory, with its heavy emphasis on the formative influence of early childhood. Biography appears, rather, as a succession of adjustments, in which some resources are increased, some diminished or extinguished; some defences are enhanced, some lowered, and some new defences are established. For many people, there is a tendency for an increasing disjuncture between the three levels of psychic functioning; and in extreme cases, the image of the 'driven creature' is entirely appropriate. One of the most telling descriptions of the tragic trajectory of contemporary life is given by Horney (1946), herself an analyst who had deviated from Freud. As she saw it, the neurotic tendencies, of which all partake to some degree, are the result of a succession of anxieties and attempted resolutions; from the early experience of the child, facing indifference, erratic treatment, loneliness, and pain, through to those broader anxieties that are societally engendered–associated (in her analysis) with the individualism, hypocrisy, and competitiveness of modern capitalism. To use one of her most powerful analogies: a neurotic person is like someone with a shady background, who keeps travelling on to new places, trying to avoid the past, and even bribing potential informers to keep quiet. There is, however, no rest or equilibrium. In each new place the past catches up inexorably, and the contradictions grow, until the person feels compelled to move again. Thus a neurotic life-pattern (to some extent that of every person) is seen as a succession of inadequate solutions to the problems and conflicts endemic to social existence. At any one time a person only has certain paths subjectively available out of all those that are objectively possible. People tend to remain with familiar, although ultimately unsatisfactory, ways of coping with life, for in the short term these are the least anxiety-provoking. This, then, is the life-course of a person who remains in the state of typical alienation; whose experience is not well integrated, and who is to that extent impaired as a moral agent.

EXPLAINING SOCIAL ACTION

The view of the person which we have been examining has radical implications for the way we understand all forms of behaviour, and particularly those that fall within the category of the moral. There is no possibility, for example, of giving a cogent account in terms parallel to those of bourgeois economic theory, where each individual is viewed as attempting to maximize PV, the product of probability and value. This kind of view is insufficiently social, and gives no place to motives of which a person may be unaware.

Following the phenomenological tradition in microsociology, and the work of those theorists who have drawn on this to create a more humanistic social psychology, we may consider everyday life as a succession of episodes, or miniature dramatic scenes. An episode might be as short as a greeting in the corridor, or as long as a transcontinental flight. Each episode provides what might be called a 'situation', and this is defined in some way, consciously, by the participants. Their agreed conscious definition – a neighbourly visit, a seminar, a reconciliation, a mugging – together with its implied prescriptions for action, can often be identified fairly easily. As Harré and Secord (1972) put it: 'Why not ask them?' (This often works, but there are times when more oblique approaches are advisable; for in sensitive situations to 'ask them' can lead to a re-definition of the situation as an interrogation, and the appropriate response is to reveal nothing.)[23]

An account such as this is still within the framework of the rational cognitive actor. The story is more complete if we also accommodate the possibility that each person may be defining the situation more privately and experientially, in terms provided by systems of construal that are pre-conscious. Here the participants' definitions may or may not be in agreement, but are more likely not to be. Thus each person acts, and responds to the others' actions, in a way that accords with his or her pre-conscious construals, but which is also generally acceptable within the agreed conscious definition. It is only in extreme cases that the situation 'breaks down', and it seems that there are very strong motives against this happening; the prospect of chaos is exceedingly threatening.

As soon as we allow the existence, within each individual, of three somewhat independent levels of psychic activity, the drama is more complex than any simple rational framework implies. A great deal is going on besides the transactions that are so readily available to the consciousness of the participants. Most obviously, human beings are actors and dramatizers, capable of cunning imitation and dissimulation. Thus in everyday life people often present themselves in ways that do not correspond even to those emotions and feelings of which they have some awareness. Wearing a mask, they hide what is unacceptable, such as feelings of grief or gloom, and feign what might be pleasing to others, such as cheerfulness or courage. But also – and possibly of greater importance for benefit or harm – people are responding to one another through their pre-conscious apprehensions; there is a secret drama going on of which they are not focally aware. An anxious teacher apprehends a child, pre-consciously, as a sack of potatoes that she wishes to kick into life. The child apprehends the teacher as a cruel and gigantic monster, eager to devour and destroy. Yet all that happened overtly was that the teacher made a rather tense request that the child hurry up in taking off her coat, in a typical brief episode between the playground and the classroom.

There have been various attempts to describe this secret drama, which underlies the ordinary and often humdrum episodes of everyday life. Most notably Laing (1969) reconstructed the Kleinian concept of unconscious fantasy, putting it into a more social and interactive context. For example, he developed the idea of collusion: people can, so to speak, unwittingly conspire together in maintaining psychological falsehood, in keeping up each other's defences. In a very different way Berne (1970) produced his theory of 'games', or patterns of behaviour that have hidden and non-productive payoffs, and which prevent people from really meeting each other. There is, for example, the famous 'rescue game', for two players. One person is victim, and the other is rescuer; all goes well for a while, until either the rescuer becomes resentful or the victim feels humiliated – and one of them now becomes a persecutor. Ultimately, nobody 'wins'.

All of this cannot simply be explained on the basis that a person is managing some kind of compromise between various motives, as a unitary self. In some instances at least it may be that there is a kind of inner struggle between different self-like structures, each being a centre of motivation. When a person is asked to justify or explain an action, however, the answer is likely to be largely in terms of the consciously held system of construal, with which he or she is primarily identified. In so far as the role of other motives is powerful but not acknowledged, the action may be said to be rationalized, in the psychoanalytic sense (that is, explained by specious reasons). A man often claims that he is unavoidably delayed at work, on the very days when his wife is due to go out to an evening class; a woman finds that she gets emotionally involved with a succession of men who are, in reality, inaccessible. Reasons for action, as we saw in chapter 2, can have the logical status of causes. But for this view to make psychological sense, the 'primary reasons' that count as causal must include those that lie below or behind consciousness, and which a person perhaps only comes to avow in a therapeutic context.

It follows, then, that in the conduct of everyday life, especially in the more intellectualized and formal settings, the relation between action and sentience has often become seriously disjointed. There are some episodes where the true drama of emotion and feeling is integrated and completed; as, for example, a free and mutual act of love-making, or a quarrel that goes through its full dramatic cycle, leaving no residues of unresolved hostility. These, however, seem to be relatively rare. Perhaps it is more typical not to complete the emotional experience associated with each episode, in part because of being alienated from pre-conscious construals; it is quite common, for example, for a person to feel the anger 'appropriate' to an episode only after it is over. Psychologically, this means carrying over to the next episode a certain degree of distraction, diminishing the attention available to meet its demands. Physiologically, this means that the body is continually being prepared for action that does not, in fact, take place; here may be one of the major components of the state of stress, which possibly underlies such typically modern afflictions as certain heart disorders and cancers.[24] Some therapies, notably the *Gestalt* approach developed by Perls (1969), are designed to help people 'complete' the emotions associated with significant episodes in the past. A person who has benefited from such therapy typically reports feeling 'unblocked', both in body and in mind; one aspect of this, in our terms, is that there is less of a disjuncture between the different psychic levels. The person is more of a whole, embodied, organism; experience and under-standing are beginning to come together.

So action often occurs in relation to motives of which an individual is not aware, and social life involves a great deal of subterfuge in relation to the feelings and emotions; some deliberately contrived, but much of it right outside any conscious awareness or control. The moral agent is far from being a unitary, rational self; and the day-to-day arena of moral action is one of profound incompetence and inauthenticity in relation to our capacities as sentient beings. If the image of the person we have been considering here has a basic validity, these are facts with which the psychology of the moral life must fundamentally come to terms.

We have looked briefly at the complexity of social life itself. But what competences does each person bring, individually, to it? This is a subset of the larger question of personality, of what a person has become through dealing with many episodes, going right back to infancy, granted a temperamental endowment which is genetic. In terms of a psychology that respects human agency, it can be conceptualized as a set of resources for action. We shall look at this in some detail in Chapter 7, but it is worth making a preliminary point here. Schon (1983) has made a close study of skilled practice, and come to the conclusion that it functions in a very different way from those forms of rational decision-making in which theory precedes action. It seems that the skilled prac-titioner, working under the tutelage of experts, gradually builds up a repertoire of standard solutions to problems in the field; these solutions exist as wholes, or as ready-made modules that can be assembled into wholes. When faced with a new situation, he or she pre-consciously 'searches the files' to find a solution that has an approximate fit, and from time to time produces a creative modification. Through this process, in reflection afterwards, and in discussion with those who are already experts, the repertoire of standard solutions is increased. In all of this Schon is quite close to some recent developments in social learning theory.[25] His ideas can be taken more generally into our understanding of social action, and moral action in particular. The moral agent is also a skilled practitioner. Some people are highly resourceful, and therefore flexible – having a large repertoire of standard solutions available; others are not, and perhaps their very defensiveness has restricted their opportunity for social learning. Standing back and deliberating, while obviously appropriate in some situations, can also be a sign of a serious lack of practical knowledge. Excessive pondering on what 'ought' to be done can be a standard solution that gets a person nowhere.

SOME IMPLICATIONS FOR MORAL KNOWLEDGE

The image presented in this chapter is one that makes psycho-therapeutic sense, while being consistent with many of the accepted findings of academic psychology. However, although empirically well-grounded, neither the image, nor the view of social action derived from it, has a standing analogous to corroborated knowledge in the field of natural science. They should be seen simply as constructs that have been chosen so as to highlight certain features of the problem-domain. There can be many other images and theories; none of them will deliver 'the truth'.

The kind of evidence on which we have drawn, even if tangentially, seems to suggest that we live in a culture that is often disastrously incompetent at dealing with our nature as sentient beings. Much of social life is charade, non-meeting, games-playing, status-seeking, often covered over by a pretentious mask of rationality. In relation to individuals, it suggests that below or behind many a robust and confident public presentation, many an assertion of love and concern for others, there may be a very different reality: persons who are fragile, frightened, frozen, alienated, damaged by the privations to which they have been subjected for the greater part of life, and with which they unknowingly collude. The destructive patterns of behaviour that so many people engage in, even doing so in the name of morality, involve motives of which they are often unaware; these patterns are locked into centuries, if not millennia, of structural injustice: created within patterns of domination, and tending to cause their perpetuation. This is a truly momentous challenge for a practical moral psychology.

To see the person, fundamentally, as a sentient being, rather than as an intellectual who may or may not have made the grade, implies a very unorthodox view of what constitutes moral knowledge. For this involves, clearly, much more than a person's conscious construals, of which one aspect is the sophistication of his or her moral judgements. The pre-conscious and unconscious aspects of psychic life need to be taken into account also, for it is here that so much lies which is crucially relevant to what is known 'experientially'. According to the tradition derived from Plato, the knowledge of the good can be obtained by the intellect alone; it is a kind of pure, unalloyed, timeless knowledge, that stands apart from the flux of embodied life. Following Plato, moral judgement has generally been placed beyond the reach of all affect, whether in the form of physical desires, intuitions, emotions, or sympathetic feelings; all these, so it is said, must ultimately be brought to the court of reason for appraisal.[26] A minority of theorists, on the other hand, whose emphasis has been closer to that of Aristotle, have been more earthy, arguing that moral understanding, if it means anything at all, is not a purely intellectual matter. We cannot be said to have understood a moral concept unless we know it in our full capacity as sentient beings, and follow it through in our commitments.[27] There might even be moral concepts which 'we know, but cannot tell'.

Now this is not a purely logical issue, but a psychological one as well. The view of the person we have been examining suggests a possible resolution. Moral judgements are made through the use of conscious intellectual processes, and the attempt to find valid criteria for morality must come, necessarily, through the use of reason, using formal operations. Moral discourse actually came into being when the mores of particular societies were subjected to critique; this new feature of human life can be associated with a development from the pre-operational thinking that seems to be characteristic of primal peoples. But it would be a mistake to suppose that knowledge in that purely intellectual sense is of any great moral significance. Much of it may be still dissociated from felt, embodied life and relationships. Returning to Figure 3.1 on p. 82, it may well belong largely to the area of pseudo-experience.

Thus a person with an enormously elaborated moral understanding on the purely intellectual level might still be deeply
alienated; and, living without an understanding of the hidden
sources of motivation, be disastrously self-deceived and ineffica-
cious as a moral agent. At the worst, to have a sophisticated
theoretical morality while having lost contact with the emotions
and feelings would be to be a partaker of the schizoid disturbance
endemic to the culture, and to baptize that disturbance with a
good name.

It would seem, then, that moral knowledge which is 'true' in a
psychological sense is that which is held in a kind of feeling-
knowing, and which is derived from lived experience; in terms of
the diagram, it comes from area 1. The causal order, then, would
seem to be: first, a form of life and a pattern of social relations;
next, a personal response which is largely pre-conscious; and then
a 'conscious realization' of what is, in a sense, already there. What
the intellect can do, on its own, is to extrapolate beyond
experience, exploring the broader implications of what is already
known. But there is a crucial sense in which knowing through the
intellect can never be a substitute for knowing through
experience. All this is very close to Piaget's account of moral
knowledge, as will become plain in Chapter 5. Piaget, however, was
a true son of the Enlightenment, and saw only a unitary psyche,
free from conflict or deep disturbance. His was a view from an
Alpine meadow; not from the street of town or city, where the
greater part of humanity is to be found.

FREE ATTENTION AND MORAL SPACE

Therapeutic psychology, with its emphasis on the person as a
sentient and relating being, suggests a way of looking at morality
that is very different from the greater part of accepted theory. In
the latter the core problem is often taken to be that of how a
person comes to his or her conscious moral understanding, and
then applies it in practice. Moral development is usually seen as a
movement towards the possession of sound, universalistic moral
principles, and living by them with greater consistency. From the
standpoint of this chapter, however, the core problem is different.
How is it possible for a person to see, to meet, to respect the being
of others, to treat their subjectivity as of equal value with his or her

own – and from this beginning with real, known persons, perhaps go forward to a broader concern?

In therapeutic terms, it is a matter of 'free attention', of being able to be close to another with a kind of caring objectivity, in which those distortions, judgements, projections, and distractions that normally get in the way of real meeting are minimized. Free attention seems to be possible in so far as a person is not beset by unacknowledged conflicts and fears, against which defences have been constructed. (Difficulties and painful feelings which are recognized in consciousness are a different matter, for they can be deliberately accepted and then, temporarily, laid aside.) Typically, a person with very little free attention almost immediately re-frames another's experience as a gloss on his or her own, as the following vignette illustrates.

> A young woman, evidently in very great pain, one foot bare and her ankle grossly swollen, is hobbling, with the aid of two helpers, into the casualty department of a hospital.
>
> MALE STRANGER (*to the woman*): What has happened to you, then?
>
> WOMAN (*between gasps*): We're moving house, and I fell down the stairs. I think I may have broken my ankle.
>
> STRANGER: Oh, that's bad luck. Now I've just brought my wife in. She's had a nasty burn. You see, it happened like this. She was . . .

This is a very understandable example, in its context, but it is a paradigm case of lack of free attention. In effect, the stranger treated the woman's pain and inconvenience as of no significance, other than as an example to himself of 'another woman in difficulty'. He was, at this point, almost totally caught up in his own concerns.

Another great barrier to free attention is being seduced into forms of discourse that are grounded very largely in pseudo-experience. Even the discussion of moral issues can function in this way. There is an intense theoretical interchange, and the illusion can be created that some of the world's problems have come a little nearer to being solved. Sometimes those involved have gratified their egos, but they may also have been caught up in

97

a process of collusive defence, and so unwittingly enhanced their alienation.

To put it very crudely, then, there are two great obstacles to free attention, and they are often related. These are anxiety and bullshit.

There is a great deal of variation between individuals in the amount of free attention that they can bring to bear, and this does not seem to have a close relationship to intellectual attainment. Indeed, there are academics, including some working in the moral field, who have a typical attention span of well under two minutes for the subjectivity of others, even though they may be able to concentrate on their own intellectual projects for several hours.[28] It also seems to be the case that an individual may fluctuate in the free attention that he or she has available. The key factor here is not so much those preoccupations or problems which are known in consciousness, but those which have not, as yet, been assimilated in experience. Indeed, a person might be under very great stress and still have free attention, because the source and nature of the stress are validly acknowledged.

When one person is able to give high-quality free attention and another is not, there is a moral situation, but only in a limited sense. It would be entirely appropriate in the case of a parent with a young child, or perhaps in dealing with an elderly person who is facing very upsetting life-changes. However, these one-sided situations do not provide an interpersonal space with moral quality. It is when two or more individuals have free attention jointly that something radically new comes into being. A simple equation sums it up:

$$\text{free attention} + \text{free attention} = \text{moral space}$$

Here each person is able to take the other's subjectivity seriously, with feeling and understanding, while also being very much in contact with his or her own. A focused awareness is given to a figure, and a diffuse awareness to the ground, at the same time. Relating this to the idea of the 'total field of experience', the situation can be roughly represented as in Figure 3.3.

The moral space so created is the very antithesis of distance, for it is something shared, into which both (or all) persons involved may enter freely. There are other types of interpersonal space too,

Figure 3.3

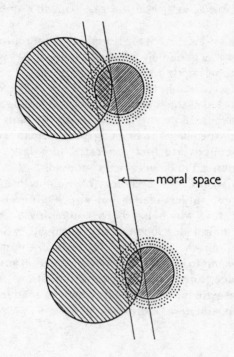

←——— moral space

with their own special characteristics, such as those of skilled co-operative work, of play, and of sexuality. But of all such spaces, the moral one is the most formative and fundamental.

According to this view, then, the heartland of morality is a complete particularism; a person is taken and accepted as nearly as possible exactly as he or she is, and not made an instance of anything else, be it a social category, a moral principle, or whatever. Also, moral space involves no prescription at all; no one 'ought' to do anything, for it is a place of being, relating, and discovery. Furthermore, what takes place there cannot be expressed adequately in terms of propositions, or captured in the relatively crude instruments of social science research. For much is only at the threshold of consciousness; its quality is lost when expressed in words, as is also the case with the ambience of a dream.

This space, however, is but the beginning of morality. The point is that without it, a genuinely felt concern for others is extremely unlikely, whatever impostors may be present, such as a compulsive superego or a set of well-honed intellectual principles. Moral space might be regarded as the source of those good feelings which give a sense of inner freedom and of agency, on the basis of which a person can face the many and exacting moral demands of everyday life. Those feelings are first generated in infancy and early childhood, but need to be sustained continually.

Seen in this light, the psychology of morality has not only a rather different subject-matter but also a different practical agenda from that which has been commonly accepted – to promote the moral development of individuals, whether their cognition or their character. Now, in contrast, the most crucial agenda item seems to be to bring about the creation and extension of moral space, and to change those situations where it is diminished or extinguished. Here it is always a matter of persons in relationship, and never individuals alone.

Chapter Four

THE ORIGINS OF CONCERN FOR OTHERS

There is a tendency within our culture, steeped as it is in moralism, to put the question of the very beginning of moral awareness in the human being in terms such as these: 'How is it that a child (initially self-centred, non-moral) comes to transcend naïve egoism and to be sensitive to social values, acquiring a sense of respect for other; eventually becoming able, in at least some contexts and with at least some persons, to envisage their standpoint and recognize their validity?' Freud, it seems, had a frame of this kind, as he made clear in his doctrine of the superego; the voice of parents and other authority figures is 'internalized' through a complex process, whose essence looks distinctly like a form of blackmail, under threat of the loss of love. As he put it in *The Ego and the Id*: 'Here we have that higher nature, in this ego-ideal or superego, the replica of our relations to our parents. When we were little children we knew these higher natures, we admired and feared them; and later we took them into ourselves' (1962: 26).

When we take full account of the relational nature of human life, however, and the way both personhood and agency develop in a relational context, it soon becomes plain that the idea of 'moralizing' an infant or child who is fundamentally egoistic is mistaken. As Wright (1986) has aptly pointed out, the very idea that morality is something that can be 'put into' a person is contradictory, since it violates one of the most fundamental criteria for regarding a process as moral. Morality entails a deep respect for the integrity of the being of another. Therefore, a moral standpoint cannot be taught according to the pedagogic model of putting water into a bucket, and far less can it be imposed by authority; it is something that each person must be allowed to construct on his or her own behalf.

So, to ask the question of origins in this 'moralizing' kind of way is to make a false start. In trying to answer it on those terms, we might find out a good deal about 'socialization' and similar matters, and we might discover in great detail how various processes of social learning operate, but we would not learn very much about the beginnings of that 'true morality' whose essence is a feeling of concern for others. The common notion that a person is first egoistic, then a mere follower of social conventions, and then (perhaps) 'truly moral' is mistaken. Rather, we might see the actual formation of a person from the new-born infant as the quintessentially moral process. The requirements of a moral standpoint, such as those Wright identifies (respect, fairness, honesty, and promise-keeping) are among the necessary conditions for bringing a person into being.

This conceptual point can be approached in another way, via what is now a very substantial body of research with young children. Here it has been shown clearly, for example, that even around the age of three many children can speak clearly about their awareness of a distinction between moral issues (such as those to do with lying, stealing, and violence), and those that are merely conventional (such as styles of dressing or eating). Even with limited conceptual powers they can grasp the point that moral issues do not depend on the nature of social rules; their moral awareness, however, is fairly restricted in range.[1] Some psychological studies of 'behaviour' (regardless of words) take the matter back rather earlier, to around two years old or eighteen months. At this age children seem to be well able to comfort others in distress, to be kind and helpful, and to give nurturance and care; at any rate, if their 'behaviours' are actions, this is the obvious interpretation;[2] and it is hard to attribute all they do merely to 'social learning'. It is possible, however, to trace the first evidences of morality back even further, into the second half of the first year of life, the very time when attachments are being formed and the self is coming into being. One sign of it is the way an infant, in a new situation, will continually look towards a known care-giver, as if asking for assurance that the situation is safe. 'Is it all right to experiment with this new object?' 'Is this intriguing stranger, to whom I want to reach out, reliable?' Here it seems that the infant already has a foundation of trust in another human being, and wants to build upon it.[3] Another very early sign of concern for others is in small acts of generosity:

> A few weeks ago I spent some time on the floor with our secretary's ll-month-old baby girl. When she picked up a toy, I held out my hand. After a pause she would give it to me. Then she picked up her favourite toy. When I held my hand out, she held it closer to herself, then smiled at me, reached with the other hand for another toy, and gave that to me.[4]

If we look at the question of origins in this kind of way, it is clear that methods of enquiry which rely mainly on verbal material (as is the case with the many studies of moral judgement) will not get us far. Methods are needed which are very sensitive to the fragile and delicate moral competences of infants and young children; which relate, in terms of Figure 3.1 on page 82, to area 1 – the totality of what the person is undergoing. We have, of necessity, to venture into the much less well-charted territory of pre-verbal, pre-conceptual experience; and try to discover something about that relational matrix within which personhood and agency are actually attained. Here mainstream child psychology, with its emphasis on careful, accurate, and testable observation, has revealed a great deal. However, if it is to be true to its method, it can say very little about the infant's subjective life. Depth psychology does, to some extent, fill this gap, engaging in something rather like an archaeological investigation. Interestingly, Freud himself used this metaphor; he likened the earliest years of life to the Minoan–Mycenian civilization whose remains were being discovered below those of ancient Greece.[5] There was an excavation, so to speak, to which he pointed, but which he himself never undertook; the subtleties of relationship were opaque to him, and in any case the backward trail of his enquiries petered out around the age of three years old. In archaeological work there are fragments of evidence, here and there. A full picture has to be built up gradually, using imagination and guesswork. Depth psychology does this too.

DEPTH PSYCHOLOGY AND METHOD

There is a paradox in all depth-psychological enquiry. Its prime subject-matter purports to be the experience of infancy and early childhood – and yet this is inaccessible through the ordinary channels of speech, since verbal meanings only become consolidated at the stage of concrete-operational thought. As soon as early experience is rendered in adult categories, a translation or re-formulation is necessarily involved. Freud, who in many respects was the pioneer, attempted to solve this problem by drawing primarily on material presented by adults during their psychoanalysis; he gave surprisingly little attention, either as analyst or observer, to young children. His work may indeed be called depth-psychological; but it is not, in any methodologically coherent sense, a psychology of early childhood. 'Deep' is not equivalent to 'early'; this is an important distinction.

The material elicited by psychoanalysis is of two main kinds. First, and most obviously, there is the verbal production of the analysand: both in ordinary discourse and specifically that derived from free association, where he or she speaks out anything that comes to mind, however incoherent, bizarre, disgusting, or seemingly irrelevant. Of course memories are re-called, but they have already been reconstructed; and sometimes people are quite unable to distinguish between recollections of real events and those which refer to what they have been told about themselves. Second, and possibly more important, there is evidence from the phenomena of transference. The kind of relationship that develops during analysis is analogous to some of the analysand's typical modes of relating, and as the process goes forward, those belonging to early life may be recaptured. In the transference, feelings of intense dependency, fears of abandonment, griefs over long-forgotten losses, anxieties about separation and ending, violent reactions of hatred or aggression, may emerge. The therapeutic hope is that these can be worked through creatively, and some 'unfinished business' brought to a conclusion. Evidence from transference is, of course, only partially dependent on words, and is more directly related to the sentient experience of both parties, as they develop an awareness of their relationship. Thus it is that analytic therapists attempt to reconstruct the unfolding drama of psychic life.

All this is what might be termed the 'classical' method of depth psychology, as devised by Freud and his immediate followers, such as Abraham and Ferenczi. Some later analysts, however, became much more directly involved with children, and in so doing brought the notions of 'deep' and 'early' into closer conjunction. Melanie Klein, for example, devoted much of her time as an analyst to work with children from the age of about three years upwards. She developed a technique in which the problems and fantasies of children could be interpreted by means of their play with dolls and toys, their drawings, and their behaviour towards herself (Mitchell 1986). Her work has remained highly contro-versial, particularly because of the apparent weakness of its empirical base. Other analysts, with a closer eye to the imitation of natural science, have collected data on children very system-atically. Bowlby and his colleagues such as Mary Ainsworth, for example, studied the attachment that develops between a child and the main care-taker, and their work was extended and refined in many later studies.[6] Winnicott, during his long career as paediatrician and psychoanalyst, is reported to have collected 20,000 case histories;[7] although he never articulated a systematic method for drawing inferences from his data, and frequently adopted an almost poetic style, his work has a far stronger grounding in real life than many studies that superficially meet the canons of 'behavioural science'.

The term 'deep' thus carries a greater richness than 'early', but also a much greater ambiguity. 'Early' can be taken literally; 'deep' is always a metaphor. That which is more deep is more constitutive of a person's subjective reality, and the greater part of it is inaccessible to everyday consciousness. Generally that which is very deep is also early, although not necessarily or exclusively. It may well be the case that some people, in coming to terms with exceedingly painful or traumatic events, or unresolved personal conflicts, attribute them in fantasy to very early life; thereby putting these at a safe distance, and perhaps for a while using this as a way to avoid having to take responsibility. Sometimes also, as Winnicott pointed out, material is presented which makes very good sense psychoanalytically, but which is incompatible with child psychology; its validity lies in the dimension of 'depth'.

There is another aspect to the contrast between 'deep' and 'early'. When a person gives a report about his or her own psychic reality, there is a great deal of material which is never made explicit, in part because it never impinged upon consciousness. More likely, attention will be focused on those disturbances and disruptions of which there is a growing and often painful realization. When an infant is being held well, both literally and metaphorically, he or she is unlikely to be aware of it. But when the holding fails or falters, then the fear of falling or abandonment manifests itself. Thus it is often the analyst who must, through the use of an imagination guided by other knowledge, such as that gained through observation, supply the background against which the material brought forward by the analysand makes sense. A parallel problem arises in dealing with accounts given in everyday settings; what is said gains significance when it is seen in relation to what is assumed, and this has to be reconstructed by the researcher.[8]

So the depth-psychological method can be characterized as one which attempts to grasp the unfolding of a person's psychic reality in terms of its significance, through a process of looking backwards and 'inwards'. In archaeology, as also in history and literary criticism, an interpretive element is always present; it is impossible to discover how things *really* were, or what an author *really* meant. There is always an interaction between the material and the investigator, who brings his or her own assumptions and experience to bear. All this is a long way from the method of natural science, although it has its own criteria of validity; further, no depth-psychological assertions are worth holding on to if they clearly contradict the findings of more 'scientific' approaches. In dealing with the human-reality we are bound to find ourselves telling stories, and in this we have a choice. On the one hand we can tell impoverished ones, almost threadbare in meaning, but legitimated by t-tests and significance levels. On the other hand, we can tell stories that have a rich tapestry of meaning; compatible with, but not slavishly bound to, the data. For a morally valuable account of the origins of concern for others, there is no option but to choose.

BECOMING A PERSON

The infant in the womb, we may suppose, has virtually no apprehension of self, since there is no ground in experience from which to infer its existence. The infant and the environment are indeed one, and the supply of basic physiological need is continuous. Possibly it is birth itself that gives the first jolt towards self-hood. For at this point the continuous and ultra-reliable supply of all needs comes to an end, never to be restored again; the cutting of the umbilical cord is a symbol of all that is to follow. The infant, now, is a separate being; but as yet there is no psychological self to grasp the fact of separateness.

Research that stays strictly within the Piagetian tradition focuses very largely on the infant's grasp of the physical world; other human beings are present, so to speak as laboratory assistants. The story has been told in great detail about how a baby begins to turn reflex movements into small action schemata; discovers the body and realizes that the limbs belong to it; co-ordinates vision and touch; and so on. Something is missing here. For, as Spitz (1965) and others have shown, there is powerful evidence that babies first develop knowledge in relation to persons, and only afterwards in relation to physical things. The first act of searching is for the nipple; one of the earliest patterns to be recognized is that of a human face. Also (although this is harder to show experimentally), it seems highly likely that the 'schema of the permanent object' is first acquired in relation to the mother or some other care-giver. The supply of food, comfort, and stimulation continually recur, even if that person is absent for a little while; but more than that, it seems as if the infant actually craves for closeness, and constructs the permanence of persons out of the permanence of relationship.

By analogy with what seems to be the case with external sense data, it may be the case that the infant is particularly sensitive to differences, of which the most obvious is that between satisfaction and fullness on the one hand, and emptiness and pain on the other. Here Klein has offered a suggestion which makes sense imaginatively, although it cannot, of course, be validated directly.[9] She invites us to imagine that the infant, not having (or being) as yet a unified locus of sentient states, experiences these as if in the environment; thus emotions and feelings are felt to be bearing down upon the embryonic self, rather than belonging to it. If, for example, the supply of milk is satisfying, the infant's apprehension is that the breast itself is benevolent; if it is not, the infant feels a murderous hatred, but experiences this as if the breast itself were malevolent and persecutory. The feeling and knowledge about the good and the bad breast are, at first, 'split' (or at least, not integrated); why, when the experiences associated with them are so different, should they be recognized as the same object? In Klein's own work the breast seems often to be taken literally; but we may take it more broadly as a metaphor for the quality of nurture that the infant receives; whether, or not, in these early months of absolute dependency, needs are met with skill and empathy; and so, whether or not the infant is generally given a supply of good feelings. At all events, everyone must pass through this stage of fragmented and sometimes deeply contradictory experience (which Klein termed the paranoid-schizoid position), with its complement of persecutory fear. When development proceeds with sufficient care, and with a preponderance of benign experience, the good breast and the bad are integrated, and the paranoid-schizoid position is transcended. A less dramatic psychology might simply say that here the very first stages of the separation-individuation process are not too problematic.[10]

It is in this context, during the first few months of life, that the infant receives a diversity of intimations of being, or having, a self. Winnicott hypothesized that these first arise as a result of 'raw' experiences; when stimulation, or pleasure, or frustration, or pain, are far beyond the ordinary.[11] It is when the status quo of general, if modest, satisfaction is disrupted that the infant is precipitated into a rudimentary awareness of 'I am'. To be an 'I' is tremendously exciting, since it is an awakening to life and relating; but it is also fraught with terror, because at that point the infant knows that he or she is excessively vulnerable, infinitely exposed. At first the immensely fragile 'I' is in the gravest danger of annihilation. So, Winnicott suggests, for the 'I am' experience to be tolerable, for the first sense of separate being to be endured, the infant needs empathic support of very high quality. Well supported, the infant can relax, and slowly come to feel 'at home' in the world. All this, incidentally, has very little to do with the parents' or care-giver's intellectual attainments. As Schaffer (1971) and others have shown, through very detailed study of adult–infant interaction, it is largely a matter of how sensitive the care-giver is to the moods, phases, and messages of the infant – whether there is empathy and a kind of 'resonance'. Care-givers who are preoccupied or depressed are not good at providing a satisfactory 'holding environment'. Those who are relatively free of care, and have good feelings about themselves, are more likely to do it well; it is they who may be able to follow, in relation to the infant, the precept, 'Feel the consciousness of each person as your own consciousness. So, leaving aside concern for self, *become each being*' (page 25). At this crucial point their theoretical morality is irrelevant.

So self-hood arises, in a sense, as a negation, a parting. Under conditions where the care-giving is 'good enough' (to use Winnicott's phrase), however, it is not a terrifying journey into a void, but a movement from symbiosis into a relationship that brings its own new excitements and satisfactions. Thus the self is relational, and in a sense, moral, in its very essence; and we may well suppose that the strength of the self – the person's 'onto-logical security' – depends on the extent to which that relationship embodies empathy, respect, concern, and reliable provision: qualities that are usually taken to be of the essence of morality. The infant comes to an awareness of self as one-who-trusts.

Every person, so some psychoanalysts claim, carries a buried memory of the time before this primary separation occurred; when, as in the legend of the garden of Eden, the human being had a magical potency, and every need was supplied without effort.[12] In the process of becoming a person, however, the infant suffers a severe 'narcissistic wound', having to face for the first time the fact of weakness, dependence, and existential separateness. In those for whom the passage has been too fraught with pain and disillusionment, it is suggested, the memory of the primal state becomes transformed into an ideal, for ever unattainable. This can manifest itself in adults as a 'malady of the ideal', where people try to create for themselves a heaven on earth: through being in love, through membership of a group that takes the place of a powerful and enveloping mother, or through Utopian projects to create a perfect society, and other forms of 'impractical morality'. The truth, which we all know but may perhaps resist at some 'deeper' level, is that human life always involves frustration, disappoint-ment, and failure. A mature moral outlook is not naïvely idealistic but takes these facts into account.

The 'I am' experience is probably fragmentary at first. Gradually, however, if sufficient support and care are provided, the infant becomes endowed with a secure and continuing self, and finds a variety of ways of expressing desires and feelings, in a purely bodily way. With this also there is a growing sense of agency, of being able to make an impact. One child psychologist puts it in this way:

> Through the prompt action of his caretakers the child learns that specific activities have 'signal value': he cries, and his mother appears: he coos and gurgles, and the adults around him respond with delight. He thus finds out that crying and cooing each produce a particular effect, and that he can employ one or the other to manipulate his environment in particular ways. But possibly this is only part of the lesson he learns; much more importantly, he may develop a general expectation that he can indeed affect his environment. A baby therefore develops an 'effectance motive' . . . to develop such a motive a child's actions must be consistently and promptly reinforced.

> (Schaffer 1977: 62)

Psychoanalysts tend to make the same point, but with a rather different emphasis, suggesting that the infant acquires an 'internal environment', which includes the sense of being a centre of original action. With the inevitable decline in the feeling of omnipotence, founded as it is on total fantasy, it is crucial that there is a realistic sense of being able to bring about effects upon others and the world. The infant comes to an awareness of self as one-who-acts.

The idea of acting can be contrasted with that of reacting. Suppose that the care-giver is unable to allow the infant's growing sense of personal being to have sufficient scope; perhaps because of being too tired, or harassed, or preoccupied with personal need. Under these circumstances the spontaneity and agency of the infant are stifled, and he or she is put into the position of a reactor – rather as the person is conceived to be in the more naïve forms of behaviourism. Winnicott, on the basis of his many observations, suggests that the infant will resist this strenuously, and will only capitulate after enormous struggle. Immorality, for the infant, is 'to comply at the expense of a personal way of life'. If the infant is forced into compliance, depth psychology suggests that the way is set for all manner of falsehood and inauthenticity in later life.

Perhaps we can see here the origins of what Transactional Analysis calls the ego-state of the 'adapted child', where the person has lost touch with, or confidence in, his or her own desires and spontaneity, and is excessively attentive to what are perceived as the needs or demands of others.[13] If the failure to validate the infant's subjectivity and agency is extreme, the way may be set for the development of the schizoid disturbance, and for a basic failure in trust and engagement (cf. page 84). When a person becomes so preoccupied with psychological survival under conditions of severe and continuing threat, it may prove impossible to develop a concern for others. There are clear links here with the psychopathic and affectionless personalities manifested in later life, which seem to be associated with early privation.[14]

A SELFISH CONCERN

Some, at least, of the first manifestations of concern for others seem to be relatively spontaneous and straightforward, the 'natural' movements of a highly social being. These occur just as the infant is moving on from the first and (as adults would say) unrealistic apprehension of the world, where nothing is permanent and there is only the most rudimentary awareness of persons. The knowledge of persons grows through specific attachments; not generally towards one, as many early researchers such as Bowlby had supposed, but (even in western societies) more typically around three to five, including fathers, grandparents, and older brothers or sisters.[15] The infant's milieu is changing from one of extreme dependence and symbiosis to one of interdependence, dependence-in-relationship.

The care given to infants and young children is never perfect. If it were, it would be a very misleading preparation for life in a far from perfect world. It is clear from simple observation that infants can have, at times, highly ambivalent feelings towards their main care-giver(s). Precisely what they experience can only be imagined. It seems likely that they feel something similar to what adults would term love, warmth, and attraction when their needs are met and generally their being is affirmed. It is perfectly plausible to suppose that they feel intense anger and hatred when deprived or radically misunderstood. The work of Klein and others who have used play analysis and play therapy certainly indicates that young children may have to deal with very intense negative emotion, almost too great for the psyche to manage; at times they have been known to rip off the head or arms of dolls, or to cut into them violently with scissors, as if 'acting out' some powerful desire for vengeance. Perhaps the very first 'ought' that a child truly understands is linked not to a sense of duty but of outrage: 'This ought not to be done to *me*.' It is not necessary to be a psycho-analyst to realize that it may be very hard for a young child to reconcile feelings of love and hatred, when they are directed against the same person. Many adults have difficulty with precisely the same problem.

Depth psychology, based both on work with 'normal' and 'disturbed' children, suggests that this ambivalence, which may at times be intense and frightening, contributes something very significant to a person's moral outlook. This is where the controversial work of the Kleinian school has the most to say.[16] The suggestion is that a young child who is overwhelmed by his or her own destructive feelings fears that the care-giver may actually be destroyed; the sense of power is quite unrealistic, although it is clear that some care-givers are really disturbed by their children's rage. Dreading the annihilation of a person who is loved, and on whom life itself depends, the young child feels a deep concern, a sense of guilt, a desire to make reparation. Some actually seem to go through a period of depression, as they deal both with their own feelings and their growing awareness of their need. The motive for their concern here is partially selfish, but the feeling is real and profound. It is grounded in a double negative, not a simple positive: a desire that the other person should not be destroyed. For a young child to work through the 'depressive position', as Klein termed it, two conditions seem to be necessary. First, there should not be too great a measure of privation and frustration in relation to what brings satisfaction and joy. Second, the care-giver should be present, as a real physical being who holds, reassures, and comforts, and so is able to 'contain', to help to make manageable, emotions such as rage and fear. Perhaps most crucially, this real presence provides a reassurance that the one who is destroyed in fantasy is not destroyed in reality. Under these conditions it is suggested that the child can come to accept and integrate his or her ambivalent emotions, learning that a truly personal relationship is robust enough to withstand it all. At a deep level, he or she is validated as a sentient being.

What, however, if these two conditions do not obtain? What if there is too much 'bad' experience for the child to deal with; if he or she is left alone unsupported, or left alone with feelings of destructive rage? (This is, in a sense, to say that the conditions are immoral.) Now it may be much harder to integrate the ambivalent emotions; or, in Kleinian terms, they remain 'split'. Generally, so the psychoanalytic account goes, the positive feelings are acknowledged, and taken into consciousness; the child might, indeed, idealize a clearly inadequate mother or father. The negative feelings, however, are 'introjected', and become bad feelings about the self. All this occurs, of course, without the intervention of propositional, logical thinking, but it can be expressed it in the form of a syllogism that is based on false premises:

My mother (or father, or whoever) behaves unkindly, insensitively, critically towards me.
My mother is powerful, wise, and good.
Therefore I must be unworthy, stupid, or evil.

Putting it in this way, the force of the argument lies in the second line. It is necessary for the child to hold to this assumption, or his or her moral world would collapse in ruins. But the price that is paid is a high one. In the psychotherapy of depressed people in later life, it is often found that they have an extremely strong resistance to admitting deficiencies in their nurture, and to experiencing the accompanying feelings of hatred or rage.

This is the form of the story that emerges, when child psychology and depth psychology are brought together in attempting to understand the early origins of concern for others. Many details remain to be filled in; perhaps they never will be, because there are insuperable difficulties in building up a theory that deals with an infant's subjectivity. The formation of a person is an extremely delicate relational process, and one which can go disastrously wrong if 'good-enough' care-giving is absent. There seems to be a natural propensity to develop concern for others, if a young child is given an environment which is sufficiently stimulating, and yet free from anxiety. But depth psychology seems to point also to more convoluted processes, because being human involves so much imperfection, and because the concern showed to the child can never be all that he or she might desire. So, in the theory of Klein, and various other schemes based on the idea of 'object relations', there are two 'positions' to transcend: the paranoid-schizoid and the depressive, each with its particular type of anxiety. Here there is much that is controversial, such as the age at which a child is able to feel guilt and the desire to make reparation. There seems to be broad agreement, however, that a form of care-giving is required that takes the infant really seriously, that accords to him or her the status of a person; in other words, one that embodies a thoroughgoing and well-rounded practical morality. It is from an 'inner' abundance that an infant can develop a rich subjectivity, a sense of agency, and the beginnings of a genuine concern for others. Scarcity of nurture, a failure of 'resonance' and empathy, however, is liable to make a child insecure and unrealistic, a mere responder to stimuli, having no space to take others into account, and constantly living on the borderland of relapse into solipsism and negativity.

GENDER AND EARLY MORAL CONCERN

During the last fifteen years or so, depth psychology has produced some highly speculative ideas in the search for a fundamental explanation of the (allegedly) differing emotional and relational capacities of men and women. Chodorow (1976), for example, attempts to re-work clinical material from classical psychoanalytic sources, but with a perspective that takes gender into account, and which recognizes that 'mothering' is a social construct. Dinnerstein (1976), without direct use of evidence, draws on the work of Klein and the 'object-relations' psychoanalysts to give a sketch of the way existing gender arrangements tend to create both men and women who are not, in a sense, fully human. Some of the best evidence comes from psychotherapy itself, although here much more has emerged about the psyche of women than men. The work of Orbach and Eichenbaum (1986), for example, gives clear and direct evidence about the way certain needs of women tend not to be fulfilled under existing gender arrangements. As with the work we have examined thus far, depth psychology leads to the telling of a story, which is consistent with, but goes some way beyond, the available evidence.

Every infant has to go through the fraught process of psychic parturition in order to become a person. On the successful accomplishment of this, without excessive fear, the later security of the self will depend. There may be some differences even here in the way in which male and female infants are treated; probably these are not important in relation to our topic. But from the age of about one year, there is a crucial difference. The boy child, in order to acquire his gender identity, typically has to undergo a further separation. Under conditions where the main care-giver is a woman, he has to define and experience himself as different from, apart from, her. To the extent that there is not an equivalent care-giver of his own sex to provide another source of closeness and security, his personal identity will be founded upon a sense of being separate. This may well carry with it a residue of unresolved anxiety and pain, and a hidden resentment against the woman who, so to speak, cast him out. Thus a boy child may long for an intimacy that he has been denied in taking on his masculine identity; but at the same time fear it deeply, because it would threaten the very basis on which that identity is founded. So, typically, boys from the age of about three upwards frequently show a resistance to tenderness, and begin to put on the 'hard' exterior that is taken to be typical of their sex.

There is, clearly, a wide variation in masculine experience; depending, for example, on whether or not a father-figure is available and emotionally aware. The most damaging combination seems to be that of inadequate mothering and a remote or absent father.[17] Men who have experienced this are apt, as adults, to relate to any woman to whom they become close with the deeply ambivalent feelings typical of an anxious two-year-old. Here, perhaps, is the early formation of the 'soft male', who has abundant nurturing qualities but is deeply unhappy, always yearning for intimacy with a woman but unable to attain it; also of the male who batters women, in whom intense unresolved anger is aroused under even minor conditions of frustration.

In comparison to the boy child the girl is not 'cast out' into separateness. She is like-mother, and can remain so. Her sense of self thus tends to be more diffuse, more relational, less tightly contained, than that of a boy, and from an early age in childhood she begins to imitate the nurturant role that society accords to women. The world of persons becomes and remains that which she takes as 'natural', and there are plenty of opportunities for her relational capacities to develop. Later, during adolescence and early adulthood, it may be difficult for her to become sufficiently separate, to define herself and her life-direction autonomously. Being self-assertive may even cause a considerable sense of anxiety and guilt.[18] It is claimed, then, that the differentiation of gender, as we know it in the modern industrial societies of the west, thus tends to bring about a greater degree of emotional and relational maturity in female children and young adolescents. However, we live with the legacy of centuries in which women and the roles to which they have been allocated have been devalued; for many girls the process of becoming a woman is also that of 'internalizing' an inferior status. Furthermore, the mother and other females with whom a girl identifies generally belong to the category of those-who-supply-the-needs-of-others, their own needs for nurturance and validation often deeply unmet. In due course she too may well join the ranks of the 'un-nurtured nurturers', and take her part in the reproduction of the gender inequalities, whether as a mother or in some other socially given role. So there is a tendency for females, too, although in a rather different manner from males, to lose touch with their own lives as sentient beings. Their unmet needs may remain deeply buried. A tragic tale that emerges frequently during psychotherapy is of these needs being awakened during adult experiences of love and sexual intimacy; but then being totally frustrated because the partner does not have the resources to meet them.

A story such as this is very close to stereotype, although many people seem, intuitively, to find it convincing. At best it can only point to certain prevalent patterns around which individual variation occurs. There are numerous exceptions, and of several main kinds. For example, many children are forced into a second separation from the main care-giver not because of their sex, but because of the arrival of a new baby; also, in families where there are several children it is not only girls who are cast into the role of subsidiary parent. For this kind of reason many people who work in counselling and psychotherapy are wary of broad gender analyses, believing that it is far more important to attend to the uniqueness of each person's personality and life-history. Psychoanalysis, at least, is better at providing 'thick histories' of particular individuals, than the foundations for wide-ranging social theory.[19]

If, nevertheless, the story does have some substance, it suggests that in some societies there might be important differences between the sexes, both in the way they hold their earliest moral knowledge, and in the content of that knowledge. This would appear, although transformed, in their adult moral outlooks. Men might have a deep tendency to view the moral predicament as that of relatively isolated individuals, complete in themselves, and negotiating their interests, so to speak, from a distance. More psychodynamically, it may be the case that it is harder for some male children to work through the ambivalences of relating to the main care-giver, and they may have a greater tendency than females to retain the split between positive and negative feelings. Also, perhaps, the narcissistic wound associated with the fact of separation is greater for them; maybe they find a need to compensate by developing grandiose self-images, and more frequently become victims of the 'malady of the ideal' – especially those forms of it that are associated with power and control. But there may also be a positive side to their greater sense of separateness. When they do take on the role of care-giving, perhaps as parents or as husbands looking after their wives in old age, they may be better than some women at seeing clearly the one they are caring for, without the projection on to that person of their own unacknowledged needs. This is a period when many men are discovering, to their great surprise, their hidden abilities as care-givers.[20]

Women, in contrast, may well develop their earliest moral feeling and understanding primarily on the basis of a sense of connectedness, relatedness, and closeness to others. Their typical view of the person is, perhaps, far less that of the separate individual. This certainly seems to have been found in the research of Carol Gilligan, to be discussed in Chapter 5. Women may, however, have considerable problems over boundaries, finding it difficult at times to distinguish clearly between their own needs and desires, and those of others with whom they are involved. The intense, and sometimes malignant, psychic entanglement of mothers with their daughters is well documented.[21] Also, in societies where the male sex is strongly dominant, some women carry not only the psychological burden of their low social evaluations, but also, perhaps, a poor sense of self-worth derived from inadequacies in primary care. Where this is the case, there may be great difficulties in feeling valid and effective. Perhaps, in moral terms, the most pathological script is that of the *mater dolorosa*: one who is continually, even compulsively, attempting to carry the burdens of others, while being totally out of touch with the extent of her own deprivation. Her caring is a form of clinging.

PRE-CONSCIOUS MORAL KNOWLEDGE

There are grounds, then, for believing that the moral life of an individual begins with self-hood itself. It is not a question, as many moralists have supposed, of there being first an individual who is essentially egocentric, impulsive, and pleasure-seeking, who must later be tamed into social conformity and morality. A psychology that enquires carefully into infancy and early childhood seems to confirm what several philosophers have arrived at by a very different route: that personhood is an ineluctably moral concept.

Consistent with the view examined in Chapter 3, it would seem to follow that a young child of around, say, three years old does already have, in some sense, a good deal of moral knowledge. Part of it, as we have seen, can even be detected by the fairly crude methods of verbal enquiry, with all the attendant problems of making sense of what children are saying, while their thought is, in Piaget's terms, pre-operational. Most of that knowledge would be held as a kind of feeling-knowing, only from time to time expressed accurately in words. This later recedes into the background as the child develops operational thinking. What children can articulate clearly never matches their experience exactly, but comes largely from the available discourse. In a culture that both emphasizes the individual and is also moralistic, they may well learn first the cruder languages of egoism and convention, and be unable to say much about the heart of their 'true morality'.

If the account given in this chapter has substance, it suggests that one crucial condition for a child's earliest sense of concern for others to develop into a mature and effective practical morality is a set of 'good feelings', both about the self and others. If these feelings were translated into propositions, they might consist of items such as the following:

1 I have a life of my own, that is valid in its own right. I am a *person*.

2 I am loved and cared for by others. It was they who, generously and tolerantly, gave me my being as a person.

3 Some relationships can be absolutely relied upon, even though those concerned have their weaknesses and foibles.

4 There is enough love and care to go round. I can both dare to make demands, and afford to be generous.

5 My own emotions and feelings, including my fear, anger, hatred, and grief, are valid. They will not engulf me or destroy others.

* 6 The life and being of other people is as valid as my own.

● 7 Living and relating is not always easy. But it is exciting and worthwhile, and I can do it.

All this may seem over-speculative to psychologists who insist on all statements being rigorously grounded on empirical data, although it follows Galileo's method of the 'thought experiment'.

Also, some at least of these items could be operationalized, and tested by purely behavioural means. Indeed, something of this kind has already been attempted in the many studies of the morality of very young children. It is easy enough even at an informal level to discern the differences between, say, those three-year-olds who show little emotional inhibition, those who readily attend to others, those who move adventurously into new situations, and those who do not. In all of this we can at least catch a glimpse of their tacit knowledge.

Let us return, for a moment, to the moral theory of Nagel, to which reference was made on page 53. Nagel develops a philosophical thesis: that morality is grounded in a metaphysical standpoint where a person sees himself or herself as 'one among others'. He leaves us, however, with a psychological question: under what conditions is it possible to take that standpoint? Perhaps here we have part of the answer. It is that in the unconscious and pre-conscious psychic life there should be a continuity of good feelings, a sense of inner abundance, and that these should be continually nourished. If good feelings dwindle, or if they fail altogether and 'inner' life is reduced, as Kleinians might say, to 'chaos and ruin', an individual will, in certain senses, lose his or her personhood and come perilously close to solipsism. Putting it another way, there will be an id where there is, or was potentially, a moral being.

MORAL LEARNING AT A CONSCIOUS LEVEL

The roots of 'true morality' lie far deeper than the child's encounter with the mores that belong to society at large, and do not involve the various attempts of adults and others to convey moral knowledge through the medium of language. However, there is an overlap between processes such as those we have been considering and those involving language, since these are well in hand during the second and third years of life. By the age of six or so the child, in Freudian terms, has already consolidated a superego; and around this age, or soon after, he or she is likely to be in the stage which Piaget called that of moral realism, when views about rules and punishments are harsh and literalistic, taking no account of intention. Here we have rival terminologies to describe what may be virtually the same phenomena. Freud's rather strange account focused on the alleged sexual rivalry between sons and fathers in the Oedipal situation (which left him with difficulties in dealing with the superego of girls); Piaget talked about a situation of unilateral respect, where the child is subject to authority. It is questionable whether either of them was dealing here with what might be regarded as the authentic part of moral development, as opposed to forms of moral pathology; and it is typical of the period in which they were writing – one still strongly influenced by nineteenth-century moralism – that the two were often totally confused.

Depth psychology, as characterized both here and in Chapter 3, puts matters in a very different light. Perhaps we can detect two highly contrasting movements into conscious and verbally communicable moral knowledge, according to the type of feelings which a child is developing about the self and others. Suppose, on the one hand, that propositions such as those listed on pages 118–19 are known as experiential truth. With a life as a sentient being that is already well integrated, the child is likely to engage with moral teaching primarily in a constructive way. That is, he or she will do something actively with it, maybe trying it out in practice, rejecting, rebelling, compromising, and innovating – in short, *assimilating it at an experiential level.* The form and content of the moral instruction is perhaps less relevant than the quality of subjective life that the child brings to it; above all, whether he or she is able to engage with it while still maintaining a truly personal way of being. A child who already had plenty of good feelings might, for example, be able to deal with a highly punitive school environment without the slightest psychological damage.

On the other hand, we may envisage a situation in which the child does not have a core of good feelings about the self, and where a fundamental compliance has already taken place. Such a child, in terms of the propositions on pages 118–19, does not feel valid as a person, is doubtful about the love and reliability of others, and is afraid of his or her emotions and feelings because they contain too great an element of negativity. Here it is more likely that the mores and moral instruction will not be assimilated but *introjected*: that is, metaphorically, swallowed without digestion. To outward appearances the child may be a model of goodness and obedience. Psychologically, however, he or she has acquired an alien voice; one which does not belong authentically but which, so to speak, occupies the space which subjectivity should rightfully occupy. This voice is the superego of which Freud spoke. Freud pointed out that the superego is often harsh and vindictive, sometimes crushing a person with a sense of worthlessness and guilt. He linked its power to the instinctive drives of sexuality and aggression. In terms of our account, however, its strength relates to the conditions of personhood itself: the terror of annihilation, the fear of persecutory 'bad objects', and deep anxieties about destructive feelings towards care-givers. It is a tragic irony that the very parents who are highly moralistic in their dealings with children are likely to be those who also failed them earlier as infants, engendering the deepest archaic ambivalences; and so setting the scene for profound irrational guilt and moral anxiety.

The problem of moral alienation is now traced back to its early origins. The child is an embodied, feeling being, whose experience in a total sense does not completely match what he or she is learning through the medium of language. Thus, on the one hand, there is a great deal of genuine experience which is not represented to consciousness; and on the other, there is much that has been learned at a purely verbal level, but is not grounded on what the child knows experientially. Some degree of alienation is present in all persons, and is not particularly damaging. But when the alienation is severe, it seems to be associated with the most dire pathologies; the mass murderer who as a child was, apparently, meek, mild, pious, and good-mannered, is a case in point.

MORAL CHARACTER

Perhaps it is in the dialectical interplay between lived experience and the attempts by parents and others to 'moralize' a child that we can see the beginning of the formation of what an older generation of psychologists called 'character'. This is a topic that we shall examine more closely in Chapter 7. Here, however, it is worth looking at one very detailed and intensive study, since it has a close relationship to what has been discussed in this chapter. Peck and Havighurst (1960) followed the development of seventeen boys and seventeen girls from the ages of approximately ten to seventeen. Their research method was eclectic, involving observation, interviews, essays, and psychometric and projective tests; also, since the researchers came to know their subjects very well indeed, the enquiry had something of the detail of clinical work. Drawing on the ideas of Freud and Fromm,[22] Peck and Havighurst postulated five main characters: amoral, expedient, conforming, irrational-conscientious, and rational-altruistic. Each is an 'ideal type', to which any real person might only partially correspond. The amoral character is grossly egocentric, pursuing immediate gratification; internally disorganized; and lacking any set of values. The expedient character is also largely preoccupied with self-gratification, but is more socially skilled than the amoral. The conformist is supremely other-directed, concerned above all else to abide by the prevailing mores; afraid of taking responsibility, always in 'bad faith'. The irrational-conscientious character is similar, but has 'internalized' the social norms to such a degree that they largely constitute his or her identity. The rational-altruist is one who is capable of a genuine concern for others, who can assess situations accurately, whose psyche is well integrated, and who lives by a set of values. Roughly speaking, the five character types were viewed as forming a developmental sequence; many individuals, however, were assumed to become fixated at some stage below that of rational-altruism.

Among the thirty-four subjects, twenty-four seemed to approximate to one of the types, while five were partially expedient, and five had a considerable component of rational-altruism. Six personality correlates of moral character were also measured; re-working the data a little, the approximate means for each group, on a scale of 1 to 6, are shown in Table 4.1.

Table 4.1

Character type	Number of subjects	Moral stability	Ego strength	Superego strength	Spont- aneity	Friend- liness	Hostility- guilt
Amoral	5	0	1	1	4	1	5
Expedient	4	1	2	2	2	2	3
Conformist	8	4	2	3	1	4	3
Irrational- conscientious	3	5	3	6	1	1	3
Rational- altruistic	4	5	6	5	5	5	1

In simple Freudian terms, the amoral character is weak both in ego and superego (presumably being largely id); the irrational-conscientious character is weak in ego, strong in superego; and the rational-altruistic character is strong in both. This, however, may be an inadequate way of framing the research findings. Perhaps in the amoral character we can catch a glimpse of one whose basic ontological security is not well established, and who is having to deal with many bad feelings about the self and others; the same may be true, to some extent, of the expedient and conformist characters – but perhaps there has been a different history of social learning. The irrational-conscientious character looks distinctly like the person who, in our terms here, has been psychologically blackmailed into compliance; the 'morality' is stable, but there is little spontaneity and a good deal of hostility. On the other hand, the rational-altruist seems to be a person who has managed a remarkable experiential assimilation; who is able to be both friendly and spontaneous, and yet also to maintain a moral position. Developmentally, the research showed a definite persistence of character type through the maturational changes, both physical and intellectual, of adolescence; in other words, the character structure formed by late childhood corresponded closely with that of young adulthood. Also (and this seems to bear out the rather general comments made earlier in this chapter), there was some correlation between character and type of family. The amoral subjects came from homes where parents appeared to be inconsistent, distrustful, and disapproving; conformists, from those where there was severe and consistent discipline, but little love and respect; rational-altruists from homes where the regime was consistent, democratic, and trusting.

This is but one study of moral character, although it is one of the most detailed that has ever been carried out. Peck and Havighurst had an essentially Freudian theoretical frame, and tended towards the view that a very young child was to be seen not as a proto-person, but as id. Their findings, however, can perhaps be better interpreted along the lines of this chapter, in which the child's relational experience, right from the beginning of life, is the crucially important thing. The more general inference would seem to be that it is a person's character, grounded in the quality of relational experience, that is most constitutive of his or her life as a moral being. Character undergoes many vicissitudes, as Horney's analogy of the traveller so powerfully suggests (see page 89). But its origins are indeed to be found in infancy, and derive from a few primary relationships. However, human life is subject to no overriding determinism. For some persons who made a difficult start it may be possible to undergo a process of moral restoration; and many who have had a sound foundation of care and validation in childhood may well, in later life, be seriously corrupted.

Chapter Five

THE STUDY OF MORAL JUDGEMENT

Even very young children, down to the age of about three years old, and possibly even earlier, are capable of showing concern for others. On this psychologists of morality are now agreed. If the claims of depth psychology are true, moreover, that concern has even more archaic origins, in the actual emergence of self-hood. When, however, young children are asked to articulate their concern, or to make judgements of rightness or wrongness on their own or others' actions, they are often lost for words. Sometimes they use the language of desire ('I wanted . . .', 'I didn't like that . . .'), and they show intense emotional reactions to what adults might regard as moral violations.[1] But they have no clear intellectualized conception of the person as a moral agent, and they are incapable of drawing general inferences: they do not yet have a 'theoretical morality', one that uses fixed categories. The capacity for making judgements, which is the essential feature here, is acquired at a rather later age, and through a succession of stages. Moral judgement is generally considered by western thinkers to be relatively detached from emotion, and it is clearly grounded in conscious, rational thought (see Figure 3.1, page 82). How judgements relate to feelings is complex, as we shall see, and the connection between moral judgement and moral action is extremely problematic. For theorists who accept the western tradition of moralism as definitive, moral judgement is the central focus of the whole problem area. If, however, the account of the person developed in Chapter 3 has substance, it is only a small part of the whole story, and does not even exhaust the topic of moral knowledge.

125

PIAGET'S STUDIES OF MORAL JUDGEMENT

It was Piaget, of course, who laid the foundations of the cognitive-developmental approach; his project, in his own terms, was to create a 'genetic epistemology', in which the knowing-capacities of human beings would be traced back to their origins, both in the species and in the individual.[2] Piaget came to this with a background in zoology and natural history, having already carried out distinguished work in those fields. A biological interest pervades his work, and in one of his later books he explicitly took up the theme of biology and knowledge.[3]

From biology Piaget brought two main ideas into epistemology. The first is that of interaction. Each living creature is involved in a continuous interchange of matter and energy with the environment, and achieves some kind of dynamic equilibrium with it. This interchange begins in the earliest phases of development, and continues until the organism dies. An ecological system, too, is one in which a number of species coexist in continual interaction. So, psychologically, Piaget was concerned with the way in which human beings acquire modes of knowing by interacting with their world, thus gaining a kind of equilibrium with it. The second idea which he took from biology was that of form. One of the core assumptions here is that all the members of a particular species show a distinct set of relations between their parts, even though the shape and size of the parts may vary. The medical student, in dissecting one arm, in a sense comes to know all arms; or (close to Piaget's own concerns) the basic form of a species of freshwater snail remains the same, across many minor variations. It was Piaget's belief that human knowing has similar properties: that there are forms of knowledge which remain as constants, indeed as universals, even though the content may vary. As a person develops, he or she acquires fresh knowing-capacities, thus gaining a new and more satisfactory equilibrium with the environment; change occurs when the equilibrium is disturbed.

Through a vast body of observational and experimental work Piaget and his colleagues claimed to have found the succession of stages through which human beings develop in their knowing-capacities, culminating in the sophisticated abstract thinking that underlies modern science. There seemed to be a continuing progression from the reflexes and spontaneous movements typical of the infant to the acquisition of complex action-schemes such as reaching, holding, and walking, so that by the age of about two a child had an elaborate and sophisticated practical knowledge of the world. Out of this there emerged a more reflective understanding involving the use of language and number, where knowledge was stabilized by logic of progressively greater sophistication. Piaget explained these changes through the related concepts of assimilation and accommodation. A person generally takes in information from the environment in such a way that it fits the schemes of action or intellect that are already present – acquiring new knowledge with existing knowing- capacities; this is assimilation. However, there are times when seemingly important information cannot be assimilated, and a disequilibrium ensues. This may provoke the person into acquiring new and more elaborate knowing-capacities; in other words, to undergo the process of accommodation. Thus, as children mature, their cognitive structures become increasingly sophisticated, and cognitive challenges are more easy to handle. Cognitive development is assumed to take place below the level of conscious control. The conflicts set up by new situations or problems lead to an unconscious revision of cognitive structure, and hence in due course to a resumption of equilibrium. Piaget's unconscious is not like that of Freud, since it is free from serious conflict; and if it 'contains' a motive, it is the single one of curiosity.

According to the Piagetian school, cognitive development occurs through four distinct stages.[4] In each one knowledge is actively constructed through interaction with the environment; each stage has its own inner logic, and the sequence is invariant. The first, the sensori-motor stage, covers approximately the first two years of life. Here the infant is learning to differentiate objects and to appreciate their permanence through direct bodily actions; reality comes to be structured in terms of space, time, and causality. The second stage is that of pre-operational thought, where much that has been learned in a physical way now comes to be known theoretically. Children at this stage have the use of language, but the meanings they hold are often highly idio-syncratic. They can do simple operations with numbers, but are unable to comprehend the logic that underpins their use. Only to a very limited extent can they rationally appreciate another's point of view. They have no more than a fleeting and transitory grasp of the categories of adult cognition. Around the age of seven most children who go through a western style of education begin develop the capacity for concrete-operational thought. Now they can understand some of the rudiments of logic; they can grasp rules and apply them strictly; for example, in basic mathematics and physics, in grammar, and in games. Children at this stage are often more evidently socialized, and able to conform to others' expectations. The final stage, which is attained by some 20 to 40 per cent of children over eleven years old in the industrialized societies[5], is that of formal operations. Thinking here is more flexible and abstract. A person can link concepts, can stand back from concrete operations and reflect upon them; can envisage situations that do not in fact exist, structured by novel rules. Formal-operational thought is, pre-eminently, the mode of the modern scientist, whose creativity lies in formulating bold hypotheses that can be subjected to rigorous empirical testing.

Although Piaget's main work was in the development of thought related to logic, mathematics and science, he did make a major foray into the study of morality, which was published in English in 1932 as *The Moral Judgment of the Child*. His developmental work in this field was not the first by any means, as he freely acknowledged, but it has proved in many respects to be foundational; a large part of the psychology of morality, as presently structured, is an elaboration of his basic ideas. Consistent with his whole approach, Piaget saw the human being as one who actively constructs moral knowledge through interaction with the environment. Here, however, it is primarily the environment of persons; and the developmental scheme that emerges is far less neat and tidy than that which applies to knowledge of the physical world.

Piaget's empirical research, with children up to the age of about twelve, was in three main parts. In the first, he looked closely, as a participant observer, at the game of marbles, and asked his subjects to discuss the rules and their beliefs about them. In the second, he elicited children's moral judgements on descriptions of behaviour; his interest was not simply in the content of the judgements, but in the rationale that lay behind them. In the third part, he explored children's ideas about punishment and justice. From all this Piaget believed he could discern certain developmental patterns. The core of his theory was that there seemed to be two distinct moralities: one of unilateral respect, based on deference to authority; and one of mutual respect, based on co-operation. Developmental change was in the direction of the latter. It was a consequence, on the one hand, of the child's increasing cognitive sophistication, particularly becoming able to transcend an egocentric standpoint; and on the other, of changing social experience. He believed, moreover, that what he found in the development of individuals was, in some sense, a recapitulation of changes that had occurred in the moral standpoint of societies, as they moved from older authoritarian forms to those of modern democracy.

In relation to the rules of the game of marbles, Piaget believed that the youngest children were, essentially, playing by themselves according to their own whims, even when they were with others in a group. It is possible, however, that he was very insensitive to the communications of young children, sometimes quite ineptly interpreting their discourse as 'collective monologue'.[6] Slightly older children saw the rules as fixed and eternal; paradoxically, the rules were honoured in the breach as well as in the keeping. Those who were approaching formal operations, however, while more scrupulous in following the rules, recognized that these were human inventions, and therefore changeable. It is only a short step from there to the assertion that in fact it is only fair to change the rules if all players agree to do so; a set of rules agreed upon by all is an essential condition for the game to proceed.

There was some parallel to this in the children's moral judgements, which Piaget elicited by presenting them, in story form, with a variety of hypothetical dilemmas involving clumsiness, stealing, and lying. Younger children simply judged the wrongness of an action by its objective effects (a feature Piaget termed 'moral realism'): breaking fifteen teacups accidentally is far worse than breaking one deliberately, and so on. Similarly, lying was not considered to be wrong unless the lie was discovered by an adult. These children, then, had certain rudimentary ideas of right and wrong, but the criteria were determined by adult authority; their verbally expressed morality was heteronomous. A more sophisticated understanding was present in older children, who were able to take account of such factors as intention, and were able to give a rationale for the wrongness of such actions as stealing and lying; essentially, it is because they destroy the basis for trust and co-operation in social life.

In relation to conceptions of punishment and justice, Piaget again found a marked age difference. Younger children, reflecting the constraint under which their morality is often formed, seemed to believe that the extent of the punishment should be related to the gravity of the misdeed. Punishment is essentially a form of retribution. Associated with this was the superstitious belief that if a misfortune occurs to a person who has committed a misdeed, this is a form of punishment – as if there were some force of immanent justice at work in the world. Punishment was viewed in a different way by some of the older children. Its purpose is to help the offender to be aware that the misdeed has brought about a breach in his or her bond with others, and to deter from future offences. This idea of punishment can only arise as an emphasis on co-operation and on rules of equality gains ground. The important change is that moral rules are not felt as constraints from outside, but rather experienced as a necessary part of a relationship between persons in which mutual respect predominates.

That, briefly, is an indication of Piaget's line of empirical enquiry. His work has been amplified in many ways, for example, by extending the age range, and by looking at the effect of social class and other variables.[7] The main points that emerge from later studies are a general empirical validation of the conception of two types of morality, and a serious questioning of Piaget's findings about the time when a transition between the two occurs. It now appears that the transition usually takes place at a considerably later age; and this tends to be confirmed by the work of Kohlberg and his associates, which we shall examine in due course. There is also ground for believing that in some persons the transition never occurs at all.

Let us look more closely now at the two moralities. The first is one in which the rule is pre-eminent, and the moral motive is very largely a self-interested submission to powerful authority; the attitude to authority has a large ingredient of fear, even if also there is love. 'What constraint imposes is an already organized system of rules and opinions; you can take the system or leave it, but any form of argument or personal interpretation is irreconcilable with conformity' (Piaget 1932; Penguin edition 1977: 333). The second morality is one that is based on a respect and concern for persons rather than rules, a recognition that each human being is autonomous and unique. No one imposes a solution upon others. The common ground, as Piaget put it, is a method, one in which each person is free to express a view and to attempt to persuade others, and where each is attended to with respect. The only rule, then, is that of reciprocity, aimed at bringing about the equilibrium that consists of mutual understanding. 'What we seek in the other person is the very thing that enables the other person to come out of himself while yet remaining most profoundly himself' (ibid.: 339).

Both moralities are present, in embryo, from a very early age; yet it seemed to Piaget that in younger children the morality of constraint generally tended to predominate. How, then, does the transition occur from one type of morality to the other? Piaget believed that it came about in part as a consequence of the intellectual maturation of the child; the acquisition of concrete operations makes it possible to understand moral rules, even if somewhat rigidly; formal operations enable a person to understand at a meta-level that rules are no more than social constructions, and therefore changeable. But Piaget placed his greatest emphasis on the causal efficacy of changing social experience. A young child is confronted by the powerful presence of adults and older children, and is strongly inclined to defer to them, conforming to the rules they lay down. As he or she grows, however, the gap is diminished, parental authority declines, and there is usually a greater interaction with peers. Under these conditions, which are objectively more egalitarian, relations of reciprocity are more likely to emerge, and hence the morality of mutual respect. Piaget did not envisage a stage change comparable to those in his cognitive theory. Rather, the two types of morality were, to some extent, already in coexistence; but as the child grew the first morality became, so to speak, outmoded, while the second was increasingly consolidated, since it corresponded to the reality of social experience. Piaget was aware, of course, that he was portraying ideal types, and that in fact the two moralities are usually mixed together. Also, there was no simple equation between constraint and the child's relations with adults, and co-operation and relations with peers. The most authoritarian morality of all might be that imposed by other children, and it is often with parents that the foundations of co-operation are laid.

What he missed here, however, was any sense of the respect towards and co-operation with infants which seems to be essential to 'good' parenting, and to which both depth psychology and child psychology bear witness.

The title of Piaget's monograph is, in a sense, misleading, because he was concerned with much more than the moral judgement of children. In this piece of research, which is the most truly social-psychological of all his works, he was attempting to discover the social – or rather, interpersonal – origins of the most basic sense of concern for others, later to be articulated as morality. Also, although only a small part of his empirical enquiry focused on action, his fundamental concern was with practical morality. How, then, did Piaget attempt to specify the relationship between theory and practice? The key to this, as Wright (1983) has pointed out, is the term '*prise de conscience*', for which the accepted translation is 'conscious realization'. In French usage this denotes both a process and a new situation; after a *prise de conscience*, some part of the world appears in a new light, and nothing can be quite the same again. In Piaget's work the term is not used precisely or consistently, but its meaning as applied to morality is roughly as follows. A person at some particular point in time already has a certain practical morality: a way of treating others, a set of action-schemes, acquired largely without conscious awareness, simply as a result of being thrust into situations where interaction must occur. As daily life continues, from time to time the problem of how to treat others is forced into the foreground of thought, perhaps as some new type of situation arises for which there is no ready-made solution, or as a result of reflection on what has clearly been a failure. Thus, gradually, a person acquires a conscious grasp of the morality that he or she has been living by, and a stronger sense of the self as a moral agent. All this, perhaps, leads to a greater moral consistency and resourcefulness. If the conscious realization had a perfect simplicity, a person's theoretical morality would be isomorphous with his or her practices, or at least those which are best. In fact, however, as Wright (1983) points out, theoretical morality is very liable to distortion, and to intrusion by elements that do not really belong to the experience of the one who holds it. This is one of the prime arenas of self-deception, as we have already seen.

In all of this Piaget comes quite close to a view of the person such as is held in certain forms of depth psychology; in the idea of the *prise de conscience* his theory is totally compatible with the image presented in Chapter 3. The moral agent is, however, conceived as a rather harmonious and reasonable being, for whom justice is the most rational of all moral notions. There is scarcely a hint of awareness of the personal distress, inner division, hidden rage, unwitting blindness, and capacity for violence to which psychotherapy bears witness. Piaget often nodded his head in the direction of the feelings and emotions, but granted his method he could not integrate them adequately into his theory. Also, he had only a very poorly articulated view of intersubjectivity; he was always happier in dealing with a person's relationship with objects. In the field of moral development he simply concluded that although the affective aspect of co-operation and reciprocity is absolutely essential, it 'unfortunately defies interrogation'. Thus, we might conclude, Piaget approached the problematic of thought and action in a most fruitful way, but he worked with too simple a conception of the person. In this he was true to the tradition of the Enlightenment, and its extreme faith in the intellect and science.

Despite these limitations, one of the most powerful features of Piaget's work is that he never takes the person merely as an isolated individual. Just as the biologist looks at organism-and-environment, so Piaget took person-and-social-milieu as his unit of analysis in the study of morality. Practical morality is constructed dialectically, in engagement with others. This view led Piaget to some broader sociological reflections. In the general field of knowledge he envisaged stages similar to those he had found in individuals, culminating in the sophisticated scientific knowledge of the modern western societies. In the field of morality he saw a parallel between the change from constraint to co-operation that occurs in the individual as corresponding to the social change marked out by Durkheim, from the 'mechanical solidarity' of the traditional societies to the 'organic solidarity' of those of the modern age.

To relate morality to the broader social context, and to make a moral critique of that context, is of central psychological importance. Piaget, however, seems to have had rather simplistic views about society. In his work on morality he shows only a very meagre anthropological knowledge. His notion of 'primitive societies' is extremely undifferentiated; they are all conceived as theocratic and authoritarian, and there is no awareness of those earliest forms of social organization in which practical morality came very close to his own ideas about co-operation. Also, although he clearly understood some of the deficiencies of modern societies, he may have grossly overestimated their potential for fostering autonomy in the individual, and the kind of mutual respect which he so admired. In the individual Piaget saw the morality of constraint as inherently unstable, tending almost effortlessly towards that of co-operation. He envisaged something similar at the societal level, through an easy path of evolution. Now, in the era that has been described as postmodern, we may perhaps be less naïvely optimistic. We need a much more incisive understanding of the conditions which the advanced industrial societies provide both for individual development and for interpersonal relations.

THE WORK OF LAWRENCE KOHLBERG

By far the most influential research in the tradition of moral psychology inaugurated by Piaget is that of Kohlberg, although the similarity between their two approaches can be overemphasized.[8] Like Piaget, Kohlberg was concerned to discover the way in which people's moral outlooks developed. Here he dealt primarily with theoretical morality; he posed the question of how moral judgement relates to action almost as an addendum, and it caused him many problems. Piaget's central focus, however, was on the dialectical construction of practical morality, and its subsequent conceptual articulation.

In his original study[9] Kohlberg examined the moral reasoning of seventy-five boys aged ten to sixteen years. This was done by presenting them with a series of stories which posed a dilemma between the following of authority-based laws, rules or conventions, and considerations of human need or benefit. The best-known is the Heinz dilemma, in which a man whose wife is dying wonders whether he should steal a drug for her which he cannot afford. The judgements of the boys were sought, followed by various probing questions designed to take them to the limits of their competence in moral judgement. From the interview material, various aspects of moral judgement were isolated (for example, the motive expressed for obedience to a rule, or the nature of arguments concerning the value of a human life). Out of this Kohlberg attempted to reconstruct his subjects' moral outlook. He claimed, at first, to have found six stages of moral reasoning, which formed a genuine developmental sequence. Broadly speaking, this seemed to be confirmed by the continuing longitudinal study of his first subjects, over the subsequent twenty years.[10] The six stages could be regarded as three levels, which relate to some extent to the findings of Piaget. Level I was seen as pre-conventional, where the orientations are towards obedience and punishment (stage 1), and to the satisfying of self with occasional consideration of others (stage 2). Level II was that of conventional morality, characterized by the desire to gain approval, to please and help others (stage 3), and to maintain the social order (stage 4). Level III was that of principled morality, which Kohlberg originally divided into an outlook characterized by a concern for equality and mutual obligation (stage 5) and finally one governed by personally accepted principles (stage 6). As development takes place, so Kohlberg claimed, a person's moral outlook approximates more closely to one that can be justified in philosophical terms. Clearly, a person would need to be capable of advanced formal-operational thought in order to attain the third level.

Some time later Kohlberg re-formulated the stages, making them less dependent on a variety of aspects of moral understanding, and giving them a more social perspective; that is, focusing on the way in which a person views the self, relations to others and to society.[11] Stage 1 is one of undifferentiated egoism, and stage 2 involves two actors who are aware of each other, able to co-ordinate their actions reciprocally, although in an instrumental way. In stage 3 a person is able to understand another's point of view, in the context of shared agreements and expectations: in stage 4 relations are considered in the context of a less personalized set of norms and roles, as the person comes to appreciate the significance of the social system. The principled morality of stage 5 involves an awareness of values and rights that are held as being prior to society, and a moral point of view that is logically justifiable in some fundamental way, granted certain assumptions. With this re-formulation it became somewhat clearer how Kohlberg's scheme relates to that of Piaget. Morality, in Kohlberg's terms, grows from egoism through social constraint, to a condition of autonomy in which all persons are recognized as ends in themselves. One puzzling disjuncture concerns age; moral autonomy, in a full sense, arrives in Kohlberg's subjects some ten years later than in Piaget's, and in a much smaller proportion. Here Kohlberg seems to be on much stronger empirical ground.

In his early studies Kohlberg used a method that was primarily interpretive; he attempted to 'get inside' his subjects' moral outlooks, and he inferred the structures characteristic of each stage as ideal types. This method was strongly criticized as lacking in rigour, notably by Kurtines and Greif (1974). Accompanying the general re-formulation a new method of scoring the interview material was developed, much closer to standard psychometrics. The analysis now made a much sharper division between the content of moral judgements and the nature of the arguments by which they were supported, and also looked at the kind of value content appealed to in these arguments (Colby *et al.* 1983). The new scoring method was claimed to combine the virtues of hermeneutics and sound objective methodology. With it, some earlier anomalies were resolved, such as the apparent regression of some persons to stage 2 before advancing to stage 5; also, claims for stage 6 were considerably modified, with all the principled moral reasoning now being re-classified as belonging to stage 5, an amalgam of the previous stages 5 and 6. A 'true' stage 6 remains as a necessary requirement of the whole theory, as that towards which moral reasoning ideally tends; 'but we cannot say that we have empirically evidenced it' (Kohlberg, Levine, and Hewer 1983: 17). Granted these modifications, it is now claimed that the stages of moral reasoning determined by the Kohlberg method form a true sequence, meeting the criteria of genuine, or 'hard', cognitive-developmental stages: each stage has a definite structure, the developmental succession is invariant, and a higher stage integrates and incorporates all that was present in a lower, while bringing more considerations to bear (ibid.: 31).

In common with almost all workers in this field, Kohlberg had a serious methodological problem, in that he both wished to undertake an objective empirical enquiry, and that he held a distinct normative position in moral philosophy. Thus he used his philosophical views both to define the domain of his empirical investigation, and (to some degree at least) to point to the direction in which he might perceive development. He explicitly identified his stance in moral philosophy with that of Rawls (see page 32). So justice is the key element in his understanding of morality. And, like Rawls, his work is based on a prior-to-society perspective: that is, a society is viewed, for theoretical purposes, as being formed through some sort of agreement between pre-existing individuals, devoid of commitments or organic ties. The role of justice in the moral sphere is seen as parallel to that of science in our engagement with nature, in that it supposedly offers a way of balancing and equilibrating all social interests and relations.

As in the case of Piaget's theory, moral development according to Kohlberg requires much more than an increase in cognitive competence, although that of course is a necessary condition. Factors relating to social experience and stimulation must always be present, and in particular the opportunity for 'role-taking', or standing in the shoes of another person. There are clear parallels throughout with the scheme for the development of role-taking ability put forward by Selman (1980). In general, Kohlberg's approach has given relatively little attention to the emotions and feelings in role-taking, where empathy might be regarded as a key element. Rather as in the theory of George Herbert Mead, it has focused on the cognitive aspects. Role performance is seen as the organized structural relation between self and others, and there is an emphasis on the relevance of all social interactions and communications, not merely those which arouse empathic feelings. Here, then, is the bridge between the cognitive and the moral; its essence might be termed 'social cognition'. Something of Piaget's sense of the delicate interplay of action, thought, relationship, and affectivity is lost, in a relatively crude emphasis on the role rather than the person.

Also in contrast to Piaget's work in this field, here we are dealing almost exclusively with theoretical morality, and moving closer to pure cognitive-developmentalism. In the attempt to refine the scoring procedure, and in particular to separate form from content, a division was made within each stage, reflecting a 'moral orientation'. The A sub-stage corresponded roughly to Piaget's heteronomy, and the B sub-stage to autonomy. Further, the justifications made in the B category were more Kantian, involving appeals to concepts of fairness and justice. At a later point, roughly from 1985, this tactic was changed into an attempt to distinguish between moral types, regardless of their stage. Persons of type B would be marked by autonomy, by mutual respect, by reversibility in their judgements; those of type A would have a heteronomous morality. In both the sub-stage version of the theory and that of moral types, it was supposed that autonomy would be associated with a closer correspondence between moral judgement and action. At the start of his work Kohlberg had rejected approaches that attempted to deal with moral character; but towards the end, in this oblique way, character was reinstated.

Although Kohlberg's approach is thoroughly (and some would say narrowly) cognitive, there has been a generous recognition of the relevance of other developmental schemes that are, in some way, pertinent to the whole topic of morality. Some of these are said to involve 'soft' stages, as compared to the 'hard' stages of moral cognition. Most significantly, it is clear that many kinds of personal change take place during adulthood; and these may have little counterpart in the level of moral cognition as assessed by fairly simple testing. One problem for the Kohlberg school, then, is whether a genuine synthesis can be brought about between 'hard' and 'soft' stage schemes. In principle it is possible; but only, of course, by coming fully to terms with the topic of personality, and its moral subset of character.

These points illustrate a highly paradoxical feature of the whole approach. On the one hand, it has a firm grounding in a specific way of testing moral judgement, and clearly it has something very important to say on this topic. On the other hand, through numerous accretions and *ad hoc* modifications, it has endeavoured to encompass the whole field of morality – and here it has been far less successful. When expansive, then, the Kohlberg school attempts to be all-embracing; but when pressed hard, it simply defines its project as the elucidation of stages in a particular way of reasoning about justice, through empirical enquiry and rational reconstruction; and in this there can be no complaint.

The most assured conclusion from the whole body of research using Kohlberg's moral judgement interview is that, in western societies at least, the postulated set of stages is well substantiated, and that it goes a long way towards meeting rigorous criteria for a truly cognitive-developmental sequence, at least as far as stage 4; stage 5 is more controversial.[12] From Kohlberg's own longitudinal study, as well as numerous others in the literature, the picture that emerges is approximately as shown in Table 5.1:

Table 5.1

Stage	Percentage at each stage for a particular age in years				
	10	15	20	25	30
1	30				
2	60	35	15	5	
3	10	55	60	40	40
4		10	25	45	50
5				10	10

These figures are only approximate, and in any case it must be borne in mind that only about 50 per cent of a person's moral reasoning belongs unequivocally to a particular stage. But three points are especially noteworthy. First, by far the majority of persons in adolescence and early adulthood are conventional theoretical moralists. Second, very few persons – perhaps of the order of 10 per cent – ever attain to principled moral reasoning as Kohlberg defines it. Third, there is relatively little stage change after the age of about twenty-five; in detail it is found that 'progress' largely consists of bringing more judgements up to the highest level that has already been attained, rather than breaking into a new one. Whatever changes do occur in adulthood, they do not seem to be registered by the Kohlberg methodology.

The theory has been subjected to considerable testing in non-western societies, with the stories being modified so as to be relevant to the culture concerned, while preserving the main features of each dilemma. Studies have been carried out, for example, in China, India, Israel, Mexico, Taiwan, and Turkey.[13] The clearest finding is that conventional morality predominates to an even greater extent than in western industrial societies, although some principled reasoning has been found among persons in Israel, India, and Turkey who are either urban or who have had some higher education – or both. In small village societies it is exceedingly rare for reasoning about justice to rise above stage 3. One interpretation of these findings is that, while the sequence represents a genuine cross-cultural universal, in some cultures the social experience is not such as to elicit the higher levels of reasoning. There is, however, an alternative view, which is presented in several of the sharpest critiques of the whole approach. It is that the scheme is far more oriented to western concerns than its proponents care to admit, and reflects a bourgeois-liberal ideology. As such, it is thoroughly unsuited to a cross-cultural study of morality. An approach that is adequate to the task would need to be much more sensitive to the meanings held within each culture, and their relation to the material and social conditions of each one.[14]

The whole approach has been criticized on many grounds; some of these are discussed, together with attempted rebuttals, in Kohlberg, Levine, and Hewer (1983). The most dubious claim of the Kohlberg school – and, as we have seen, it is one from which its adherents retreat when under pressure – is that a cognitive-developmental scheme focusing on a particular idealized view of justice can be a basis for a general understanding of the psychology of concern for others, and of practical morality in everyday life. In the moral judgement interview the dilemmas are presented with extraordinarily little contextual material, and even here none of them deals with what might be regarded as the focal issue of western moralism – the relation of duty to desire. Of the interview content only prescriptive material (that which is clearly related to the category of 'ought') is scorable; and this might be as little as half-a-dozen sentences in an interview which typically lasts about one hour. As a result, a vast amount of information which relates a person's moral experience and action to the real social context is passed by. Moreover, the training for those who would use the moral judgement interview is wholly oriented to content, with the aim of eliciting scorable material; there is no sensitization to the subtleties of process in interaction to which all counselling and therapeutic work bears witness.[15] Thus the method is intellectual in an extraordinarily narrow sense, and gives very little respect to the subject as a social, political, and sentient being. Wright (1983) suggests, optimistically, that Kohlberg's approach might elicit the successive conscious realizations of a person's lived morality; perhaps, in some cases, it does. But it might also be argued that the approach dissociates the subject from lived experience and forces him or her into a particularly artificial role: that of the speculative casuist. As such it is totally inept at dealing with what, in Chapter 3, we termed the problem of moral alienation. Educational programmes based on arguments around Kohlberg's scheme, while providing no new lived moral experience, might actually make that alienation the more intense; flattering the intellect but contributing little towards a person's integration.

GENDER AND MORAL JUDGEMENT

For a long time a stereotypical view has been held in western culture, suggesting that women are, in some way, morally inferior to men. Although they may be sympathetic and kind-hearted, so it is alleged, they have a less clear and incisive moral understanding, and tend to be weak and vacillating in their judgements. This view is reflected also in some areas of moral psychology. Freud, for example, with his typical tendency to confuse the natural and the cultural, asserted that the superegos of women were often poorly developed, and that their sense of justice was deficient. Piaget, in the studies we have examined, noted that girls were less concerned than boys about the nature of the rules, and suggested that this implied a lag or deficit in their moral development.

This evaluation of female capability (even were it empirically valid) is, of course, entirely dependent on the way moral excellence is defined. If the essence of morality is to be rational and objective, and to make judgements in which feeling, emotion, and intuition have no part, then it may well appear that men are morally superior. The construction of concern for others in the categories of western moralism is paralleled by the social construction of masculinity. If, however, those twin constructions are dismantled, matters appear in a very different light.

This, essentially, is the challenge presented by Carol Gilligan (1982), whose work was developed at first as a reaction to a sense of gender bias in Kohlberg's scheme. The study which provided the foundation for all his later work was with boys; the principal moral agents in the hypothetical dilemmas were males; and the scoring method was, allegedly, grounded in a masculine orientation, in which there is little sense of human connectedness and relatedness. One particularly striking point, which came directly from Gilligan's own work with the Kohlberg group, was that among women a relatively high proportion were found to be at stage 3; and it seemed implausible that those who showed, in other ways, many signs of experience and maturity should 'really' be morally inferior. Also Gilligan had worked on the problem of apparent regression in the stage of moral judgement, shown by some persons in late adolescence and early adulthood.[16] What appeared to be regression in terms of Kohlberg's idea of a 'pure', detached reasoning about justice was clearly an advance within the framework that had been produced by Perry (1968); here moral development was seen as a movement from identification with group values, to relativism and scepticism, and finally to the co-construction of values with others. Perry's scheme, then, was far more oriented to real-life relationship and commitment than that of Kohlberg, and pointed towards a different view of morality, one that seemed to be far more relevant to the life of women.

Out of these doubts about the universal validity of Kohlberg's scheme, and then her own empirical work with women, Gilligan produced an account of another dimension of morality. Its core components are care, responsibility, compassion, and relationship, as compared to fairness, rights, and autonomy in Kohlberg's scheme. Very much along the lines suggested by the depth psychology of Chodorow and others (cf. page 114), Gilligan grounded her work in the idea that men and women tend to have a very different sense of their being in the world; men founding their identity on separateness from, and women on closeness to, others. Within the ethic of care Gilligan postulated three developmental levels. The first is one where the individual is mainly concerned with survival, and transition occurs with the emergence of a sense of responsibility for others. The second level comes close to the stereotypical view of women as care-givers, where goodness is linked closely with self-sacrifice and gaining approval from others. Transition comes about as a person begins to include the self within the domain of care; seeking to be 'good', but also to be 'honest' and 'real'. The third level involves a commitment to an ethic of non-violence; care has become a universal obligation, accepted not out of compulsion, but out of a sense of connectedness with other sentient beings. The sequence is not claimed to be strictly cognitive-developmental, based on so-called 'hard stages'. In a sense it might be regarded as a detailed developmental articulation of what Kohlberg identified as a stage 3 moral outlook, but more oriented to real life, and revealing complexities to which his theory is largely opaque.

Gilligan's original research was with twenty-nine women, all of whom were facing the real-life dilemma of whether or not to have an abortion; this raised, in a very crucial way, issues relating to care and harm. She then extended her work in other studies, again focusing on her subjects' lived experience, and involving both men and women. In one of these she found that 75 per cent of the women used predominantly an orientation of care and 25 per cent that of justice. Among men the balance was reversed; 79 per cent were oriented predominantly towards justice, 14 per cent towards care, and 7 per cent about equally towards both. Her sample was small, but the figures are suggestive. Virtually all Gilligan's research in the moral field is small-scale, qualitative, and interpretive, and so is open to the kind of criticism that was raised against Kohlberg's early work: doubts have been voiced, for example, about the representativeness of her quotations and the validity of her generalizations. It must be pointed out, however, that Gilligan has made no broad claims implying universality or inherent necessity in her scheme. Also, she does not assert that a caring orientation is unique to women, nor that it is determined biologically; its prevalence probably varies within the different groupings in any one society, as well as between different cultures. Her view seems to be that both an ethic of justice and of care are desirable; a person might hold both, in creative tension.

Gilligan's first departures from the Kohlberg scheme drew strongly on the work of Perry, for whom a discourse among peers (who had, so to speak, discovered one another in their alienation) was the prime factor in developing a mature moral orientation. Her later work, however, has been criticized by Philibert (1987), for neglecting to follow this through into the understanding of an ethic of care. Her writings carry a pervasive rhetoric of connection and community, but give no clear indication about the way in which a person might grow morally through relationship and exchange with others. In this sense, then, Philibert argues that her work has a methodological weakness similar to that of Kohlberg, which she criticized for its masculine bias. 'If, with Kohlberg, we have a morality of rights without effective cooperation, with Gilligan we have a morality of caring without effective co-construction' (p. 187). The theory of caring is still very incomplete; and, as will be argued in Chapter 7, needs to be carried through with a depth-psychological emphasis.

Whether there are gender-based differences in moral judgement is now open to considerable doubt. The empirical study of a caring orientation along the lines explicated by Gilligan is only in its early stages, and as yet there is little good evidence for comparing men and women. Also, in relation to Kohlberg's scheme, there is now a vast body of empirical data that calls into question the early findings which suggested that females scored lower in their reasoning about justice. Walker (1984), for example, has reviewed no less than seventy-nine studies using the Moral Judgement Interview, the majority of which showed no significant differences. These studies implied higher levels among males in late adolescence and early adulthood. The differences found in the latter, however, do not control adequately for either educational attainment or occupation, and Walker concludes that such differences as do appear may be largely artefacts of method. Similarly, Rest (1979) reviewed twenty-two studies using the Defining Issues Test, the psychometric instrument he devised from Kohlberg's scheme. Only two studies showed differences, both giving higher scores to females. His conclusion is that gender seems to be a relatively unimportant factor. The findings of Walker, Rest, and others are confirmed in a more recent review by Brabeck (1986); her opinion is that few if any significant gender differences have been shown in moral judgement, whatever other differences there may be. The matter is, however, by no means closed. Recently, for example, Watson (1988) has found highly significant differences between fifty-five male and thirty-five female British teachers of similar social class, experience, and educational attainment, the males scoring higher. Moreover, only eleven males and three females clearly reached stage 4 or above. If any conclusion can be drawn at present, it is that many women may be more resourceful than men in western society, having a readier access to different types of moral orientation; also that a person's level of moral judgement may be more variable than was hopefully supposed.

The work of Gilligan has been a notable contribution in a number of ways, as Kohlberg and his colleagues have themselves acknowledged, if a shade reluctantly. Perhaps the most significant point is that she has promoted a shift away from the rather obsessive concern with reasoning about justice that has been prevalent in the field of moral psychology ever since Kohlberg's work became well known. We saw in Chapter 1 how, in the western tradition, there was a growing division between theorizing about interpersonal and societal morality, corresponding to the rise of mercantilism and then industrialism. This is reflected explicitly in the work of some contemporary philosophers, who have pointed to the coexistence of two moralities, oriented respectively towards care and justice.[17] Gilligan has brought this matter right into the heart of psychological enquiry; and this may, in the long run, be more important than her findings related to gender.

Through the way in which she has drawn attention to the ethic of care, and shown that people may indeed be deeply concerned with moral issues without making any reference to broader notions of justice, Gilligan has made the study of moral judgement much less of a detached academic exercise, and brought it closer to lived experience. Moreover, whereas the study of reasoning about justice has very largely excluded the feelings and emotions, these are much more integrated in Gilligan's scheme. In other words, she has gone some way towards dealing with the problem of alienation that is so salient in Kohlberg's work. It may, of course, be claimed that the cost of this is that her work is imprecise, and that no 'hard' stages of cognitive development have been shown up within the orientation of care. This must be conceded, but it is not necessarily a disadvantage, except for the purpose of tidiness. For the development of concern for others, as an expression of a person's mode of being, is not primarily cognitive; it is as complex and convoluted as life itself. This is a point to which we shall return.

MORAL JUDGEMENT AND MORAL ACTION

The strong emphasis that psychology has lately placed on moral judgement, especially as a result of Kohlberg's work, highlights an issue that has been seen as supremely important in western moral discourse at least since the time of Socrates. What is the relationship between what a person judges to be right, and what he or she actually does? It seems to be self-evident that people often fail to live up to their beliefs about what they ought to do. One solution – and it is a very extreme one – is to 'save the appearances' through definition. 'To know the good', we might say, 'is to do it.' Thus, if a person did not do the good, it follows that he or she did not know the good, according to a proper definition of knowledge. This, effectively, was the position taken by the moral philosophe r Hare, in his famous work *The Language of Morals* (1952). It is logically consistent; but it would only be psychologically plausible if we could believe that each human being was a unitary subject, whose total range of actions came within the scope of a single rationality.

It is far more common, however, to deal with the apparent gap between moral judgement and action in terms of weakness of will, or *akrasia*: that is, to hold that it is indeed possible to know what is right or good, and yet to fail to do it. In conventional psychology weakness of will is re-formulated in terms of such concepts as lack of ego strength, or failure of attention. Depth psychology, as we have seen, offers a more radical solution. For it suggests that the person is very far from being a unitary subject, and that only a part of experience is well integrated into the consciously held schemata of rationality. The problem of *akrasia* is, in terms of Chapter 3, related to that of moral alienation.

Kohlberg and his co-workers have returned to this question again and again.[18] Several fairly early studies did suggest, *prima facie*, a degree of correspondence between a person's stage of moral reasoning and the likelihood of engaging in actions that would commonly be judged as morally praiseworthy. For example, Haan, Smith, and Block (1968) studied students' self-ratings on political activism; also whether they had been arrested in demonstrations concerning free speech. Few of the activists were conventional in their moral judgements; the majority were at stage 5 or 6, while some were, apparently, at stage 2. (This latter anomaly was one of the main incentives for re-working the scoring system on the Moral Judgement Interview.) Even more convincing was an experimental study by McNamee (1978). Here a collaborator, feigning to be suffering from the effect of drugs, interrupted the experimental situation, evidently needing help which the experimenter professed to be unable to supply. The participants were thus faced with the dilemma of whether or not to help. Later their moral judgement level was measured. The results, for eighty-six persons, are shown in Table 5.2.

The evidence seemed to be impressive that moral judgement and moral action converged at the higher levels.

Table 5.2

Stage	% at each stage	% of those at any one stage who gave help
2	13	9
3	33	28
4	20	38
5	28	68
6	6	100

Matters turned out, however, to be much more complex. Blasi (1980) reviewed seventy-two studies in which moral judgement levels were related, respectively, to delinquency; specific behaviours or traits (such as leadership, gregariousness); honesty; altruism; and conformity (both to others' opinions and actions). His overall conclusion was that there was indeed ground for believing that moral judgement and certain behaviours were related. The strongest evidence was that 'delinquents' scored low on moral judgement, and that those who scored high were generally able to resist pressure to conform to others' opinions. There was some evidence, but less robust, that sophistication in moral judgement was positively correlated with honesty and altruism; and only weak evidence that it might be related to resistance to social pressure at the level of action. Blasi pointed out that research such as he had reviewed shed very little light on the problem of how moral judgement and moral action were related 'within' any one person. The 'behaviours' studied generally made no reference to the actors' own definitions of what they were doing. Straughan (1983) has also pointed out that in the greater part of this kind of work there is a confusion between the problem of 'consistent action' (whether a person conforms to his or her own judgement) and that of 'virtuous action' (whether a person conforms to ideas held by certain others, or 'people in general', about what is right or good). Most of the work reviewed by Blasi addresses the latter problem. And it does so in a weak way, because it is a compromise between the behavioural and hermeneutic approaches; between mere correlation, and trying to understand from the viewpoint of the moral agent.

The critique made by Blasi and others led Kohlberg and his associates to examine much more closely the relationship between moral judgement and moral action. They hypothesized that there might be three intermediate stages. First, a person makes a fairly detached judgement of what is right or just in the given situation (a 'deontic choice'); second, makes a judgement about whether or not the self has an obligation to carry out the judgement; and third, brings the action into effect. Thus there would be two areas in which *akrasia* might operate: between deontic choice and judgement of responsibility, and between acceptance of responsibility and action itself. More recently Rest (1983) has extended these ideas in attempting to create a comprehensive framework for the understanding of moral action. He takes the three components above, and elaborates them considerably. He also adds a fourth, which is in a sense prior to the deontic choice; this is interpreting a situation and identifying the moral issue that lies within it. There might, then, be a third area of *akrasia*: a person whose judgements were sound might be inept in appraising a moral situation, perhaps through lack of empathy or awareness.

Some of these ideas are well supported by evidence. For example, it does now seem to be established that judgements of responsibility become more consistent with deontic choice at the higher stages in Kohlberg's scheme; and for those of a B-type (autonomous) moral orientation.[19] Conversely, a heteronomous moral thinker typically at stage 3 might believe that it was right to take a certain course of action, yet not feel responsible for carrying the action out. Evidence that action itself becomes more consistent with judgement at the higher stages is considerably less strong; and as Blasi pointed out, is weakest in the crucial case of actions which are out of conformity with those of others.

One of the most serious difficulties in this whole approach is that it is highly rationalistic, assuming that the flow of movement is primarily from thought to action. Piaget, as we have seen, did not hold this view, but believed that genuine moral understanding arose after action, through a *prise de conscience*. Some concession in this direction is indeed made by the Kohlberg school; for example, in recognizing the validity of Gilligan's work, and her finding that development in practical morality does not necessarily follow development in moral judgement as measured by the standard interview. There may indeed be truth in the 'rational decision-making' approach adopted by Kohlberg, Rest, and many others, when we are dealing with those crucial dilemmas that do occur from time to time, and where there is an opportunity for careful reflection; whether to end an intimate relationship, perhaps, or whether to put a confused and ageing relative into a residential care. Even here, however, it is unlikely that people generally try to resolve such dilemmas in isolation; this has certainly never been demonstrated by careful research.

The major moral dilemma is not, however, the quintessential feature of the moral life, nor is its wise resolution the prime evidence of concern for others.[20] Much more important, surely, are our countless small and unreflective actions towards each other, and the patterns of living and relating which each human being gradually creates. It is here that we are systematically respected or discounted, accepted or rejected, enhanced or diminished in our personal being. Once this is acknowledged, the arena must be recognized not primarily as one of rational decision-making, but of skilled practice. Here, as suggested in Chapter 3, a very different process may be called into play, one towards which social learning theory points. Perhaps it is that each person acquires a repertoire of actions, through observation, imitation, practice, and so on, and has these available for the contingencies of everyday life. A situation arises, and it is defined in some way, both consciously and pre-consciously; then action is produced, virtually ready-made, from the repertoire. A skilled moral agent would, from this point of view, be one who not only was sensitive to the moral content of situations, as Rest suggests, but who also had a wide range of appropriate actions. The parody of Kohlberg's approach would be found in a superlative moral philosopher who was incapable of staying gently and quietly with a person in bereavement, cleaning a kitchen, or wiping a small child's running nose.

Perhaps it is in the direction of the understanding of skill, then, that we might look for some of the keys to practical morality. Conversely, the further elaboration of a rational decision-making model may not get us very far. This point has been strikingly brought out in the research by Haan et al. (1985) on moral interaction. Their study involved a number of role-plays that centred on moral issues (for example, a simulation of ghetto life, where individual gain and the common interest came into conflict). Some of the games were apparently quite stressful, and engaged the participants' emotions deeply. One of the crucial findings was that skill in moral interaction was not strongly associated with sophisticated moral reasoning on hypothetical dilemmas. Moreover, in some cases those with high cognitive scores were also liable to engage in ego-defensive tactics such as isolation and rationalization. In other words, to be a clever and individualistic moral judge can at times be a defensive manoeuvre, enabling a person to avoid the threat of moral encounter, and the conflict which it often entails.

TOWARDS A BROADER CONCEPTION OF MORAL DEVELOPMENT

Beyond all the detailed criticisms that might be made of Kohlberg's approach to moral development, there are two much larger problems; both have surfaced already within this chapter. The first is that the 'pure' study of moral judgement necessarily involves abstracting from the real person to what Kohlberg (following Piaget) calls an 'epistemic self': in effect, a head without a body, an intellect without emotion. This has, of course, been the tactic of Platonism all along, and it seems to bear some relation to the schizoid disturbance (see page 84). The other problem is that the focus is very much on the first third of life; those who work strictly within Kohlberg's frame tend to lose interest in the person after the age of about twenty-five years, when development in reasoning about justice seems largely to come to an end.

It is clear, however, that there is much more to a person than an 'epistemic self', and much more to being a moral agent than having the capacity to reason clearly about difficult dilemmas. These points were explicated in some detail in Chapter 3. It is clear also that a great deal of development occurs during adult life, and indeed into advanced old age: all this is highly relevant to the way a person functions as a moral agent. If simple cognitive advance, oriented strongly as it is in the west to the educational system, tends to reach a plateau fairly early, for many people it is during adult life that their existential development really begins: when they have, to some degree, got their bearings in the world. During adulthood almost all people have to deal with responsibility, commitment, success, failure, suffering, betrayal, contradiction, the fulfilment, and the abandonment of hopes; and gradually to come to terms with the meaning of a human life, together with the prospect of approaching death. In this process a person may come to acquire values, although not necessarily so;[21] and perhaps to find a coherent and enduring way of living out of a felt concern for others. Here, perhaps, the key moral concept is integrity. None of these things can be encompassed by a purely cognitive approach whose topic is reasoning about justice. There is indeed some evidence that as people move into adult life the sort of considerations with which Kohlberg's theory deals may become irrelevant, although development as measured in other terms is apparently continuing. Some aspects of this are brought out in Perry's scheme.

The psychological literature does, of course, contain several developmental frameworks that apply explicitly, or at least potentially, to the whole of life, such as those of Erikson or Loevinger. Their existence, and their relevance to moral development, is certainly acknowledged by the Kohlberg school.[22] Its general tactic in engaging with them, however, has been to maintain the centrality of its own approach, and then to append insights from elsewhere in an *ad hoc* fashion. As a result, the larger theory of moral development which is gradually being assembled has something of a baroque character: a mass of embellishments without a coherent structure. If the argument of this book is valid, it is a serious mistake to place reasoning about justice at the core of a general theory of morality. Piaget's own work in this field provides an important lesson, for he saw relationship and action as prior to cognition. Piaget, it might be argued, made his own mistakes; he may have been naïvely optimistic both about individuals and about society, and he was somewhat inept at dealing with the emotions and feelings. Nevertheless, there lay within his work the potential for a broad and profound under- standing of the psychology of concern for others. In particular, Piaget implied that it is to the form of social life that we must first look with psychological intelligence in order to create a sound theory of moral development. However, if we are to do justice to the 'therapeutic' facts, it is clear that a richer conception of the person than he employed even in his most humanistic work must inform our understanding.

Chapter Six

ON ORGANIZATIONS:
THEIR IMPERATIVES AND
CONSTRAINTS

When dealing with the effect of 'socio-moral atmosphere' on people's judgements and behaviour, Higgins, Power, and Kohlberg write:

> In the massacre at My Lai during the Vietnam War, individual American soldiers murdered non-combatant women and children. They did so, not primarily because their moral judgment that such action was morally right was immature, or because, as individuals, they were 'sick' in some sense, but because they participated in what was essentially a group action taken on the basis of group norms. The moral choice made by each individual soldier who pulled the trigger was embedded in the larger institutional context of the army and its decision-making procedures. The decisions were dependent in large part on a collectively shared definition of the situation and of what should be done about it. In short, the My Lai massacre was more a function of the group 'moral atmosphere' that prevailed in that place at that time than of the stage of moral development of the individuals present.

(Higgins, Power, and Kohlberg 1984: 75)

This passage raises some fundamental, yet curiously neglected, moral issues. For we are social beings, and the greater part of most people's lives takes place in relation to collectives of some kind. Thus it is relatively rare for people to act purely as separate individuals, and the psychology of morality would make a great mistake if it failed to take the special dynamics of collectives into account. The behaviour of organizations, their internal social relations, the psychological effects they have on their members,

152

and the part they play both in the nation state and the world system, all are valid subjects for consideration. The My Lai example points to one crucial aspect: that some of the greatest atrocities are committed under the imperatives of the collective. But possibly of greater significance, and nearer home, is the fact that many organizations, *qua* organizations, are blind to moral issues, and quietly and persistently commit acts of violence both on their own members and outside. A sea is devastated by pollution; a rain forest is decimated in order to grow pineapples for the affluent; a Third World city is massacred through a chemical disaster; a settled community is wiped out because production is found to be more 'economic' in another part of the globe; confused and helpless people are subjected to cruel or even violent treatment in institutions. Perhaps such events take place, not because those involved are especially wicked, but because in some way the organization has incapacitated them as moral beings. It is necessary, then, to look carefully at the way in which collectives operate. One of the most searching questions for humankind, at this point in history, is this: are there ways of carrying out large-scale tasks 'efficiently', but under a social-psychological dynamic that is healthy and creative, as judged in moral terms?

In social science there has been a tendency to look at behaviour in collectives using some form of image of the 'rational cognitive actor' (see page 65). The individual might be an instrumental goal-seeker, a maximizer of approval, a Goffman-esque performer, or whatever. However, if we are to develop a satisfactory account of collective behaviour, we need also to draw on depth psychology, and explore how unconscious motives and psychic defences are called into play. There is ground for supposing that, in evolutionary terms, it was the human or proto-human group that long antedated any clear sense of individuality, and that conscious awareness is a late offspring of a psyche whose complex workings were oriented to a group existence; its operative realm would now be classed as the unconscious. Moreover, the highly individual 'ego experience' which is prevalent among people in contemporary industrial societies is only a few centuries old. Some of that experience is painful and anxiety-ridden, because it speaks so strongly of isolation and mortality; naturally enough, there is a continuing tendency to try to escape from it, to be submerged again into a group.[1] Thus the collectives of today may be regarded not simply as aggregates of individuals, but as a re-constitution of something that is archaic. Of course, some organizational forms are historically new, and the individuals who are bound together in collectives today do not have the same kind of psychic structure as their remote forebears. In contemporary organizations, then, it may well be the case that social-psychological processes age-old and of great power are in operation, despite a veneer of rationality and control. It must be remembered that the development of moral insight over and against the imperatives of oppressive collectives was a slow process, and hard won. Not surprisingly, it is all too easily extinguished.

ORGANIZATIONS AND SOCIETY

One feature of the collectives that developed with modern society is immediately apparent. Those organizations which have the most social effect, and produce the most highly co-ordinated actions, have a common basic form: they are pyramidal, hierarchical, with a chain of command. Through many variations, their fundamental design is such that orders flow downwards, and information upwards. The simplest of such structures merely have two levels; and the most complex, involving several thousand people, might have ten. Collectives of this kind have often been called bureaucracies, drawing attention, in a double sense, to the existence of an office. There is a position within the structure with precisely defined responsibilities and rewards; and there is a physical place, separate from home, where duties are carried out and documents are kept.

The hierarchical kind of formal organization is of great antiquity. It was a feature, for example, of the imperial rule of Assyria, Persia, and China, and later that of Rome. The Catholic church, and some of the groupings within it such as monastic orders, operated on similar lines, often securing amazing loyalty and self-sacrifice from their members. However, it is only very recently, within the last two centuries, that the hierarchical organization has come to occupy the centre of the stage in working life. Around 1800, in nations such as England or France, by far the greater part of work was carried out informally; only some 10–20 per cent of the working population were employed in formal organizations: in government, the army, the church – and, to a very small extent, the factory. With the growth of capitalist enterprise in industry, the urge towards 'efficiency' in administration and law, and the exigencies of technological war, the hierarchical structure gradually came into pre-eminence in virtually all areas of public life. Now, it has been estimated, some 90 per cent of the working population in contemporary industrial societies are employed in hierarchical organizations,[2] and there are trends in a similar direction in those nations that are now undergoing industrialization. In addition, it is necessary to take account of the 'clients' (pupils at school, patients in hospital, old people in rest-homes, and others) who are subject to imperatives corresponding to those of the employees. Clearly, behaviour in formal organizations is no marginal question; it is certainly something that moral psychology cannot afford to ignore.

One of the main traditions in sociology, that of structural-functionalism, has been particularly effective in putting organizations into a broader context.[3] Every social system is viewed as having four main 'problems', and hence tasks. The first is that of guaranteeing continuity, by making individuals into effective members, and ensuring their long-term commitment. The second is that of adaptation to the social and natural environment in which the system is placed. The third is that of defining overall purposes and goals, and deploying human resources accordingly. The fourth is that of maintaining solidarity and co-operation between members, including carrying out the repair work when social breakdown has occurred. Viewed at this high level of abstraction these problems (commonly termed 'pattern-maintenance', 'adaptation', 'goal-attainment', and 'integration') are claimed to be common to all human groups, whether family, club, church, or nation state; also to all societies, whether 'primitive' or 'modern'.

Within a primal society, such as a band of hunter-gatherers, sub-groupings related to these four functions may be scarcely discernible, although there is, in an obvious sense, some division of labour. A feature of highly industrialized societies, however, is that there are very many collectives, more or less discrete. Each contributes, to some extent, to all four functions, but most of them relate primarily to one. 'Pattern-maintenance' clearly involves families, schools, medical services, recreational facilities, and the media. Adaptation involves, primarily, those organizations that produce goods, and facilities such as roads or electricity; also armed forces and diplomatic services. Goal-attainment is the task of central and regional government, trade unions, and public administration. The function of integration is fulfilled by many kinds of organization; clubs, neighbourhood groups, churches, and the apparatus of law all have a major part. Gross disintegration is ultimately prevented by police and prisons.

Put in this way, there is much that might seem banal. Also, sociology in the structural-functionalist tradition is often markedly uncritical, and can easily provide a bland apologia for western industrial capitalism, using a dense pseudo-scientific jargon. But one feature does stand out from this kind of analysis, so much a part of the taken-for-granted world that it is easy to overlook it. Formal organizations of a hierarchical kind have taken over, to a very considerable degree, the major functions of society, pushing informal action to the margins. They are remarkably effective in moulding people, harnessing their motives, defusing their discontents, drowning out the voice of criticism, dismantling the social movements that would cast the system into disarray. Structural-functionalism does not imply that fundamental social change is impossible, but does suggest that the systemic resistance to it is extremely strong. There is now a vast 'intermediate zone', which stands between individuals, with their close personal ties, on the one hand, and the state on the other.[4] Its presence is, historically, a very recent phenomenon; and in moral terms, this is an extremely problematic way of bringing human beings together.

Another point must be mentioned, and it is one to which attention is hardly ever drawn by organizational theorists. The 'intermediate zone' is overwhelmingly dominated by men. The simplest empirical test of this is to draw a graph showing the distribution of social positions according to status (and hence power) against the frequency of occupation by individuals, both for males and females. In virtually all the major formal organizations of western society, whether of industry, politics, law, medicine, or education, the graph has roughly the form shown in Figure 6.1.

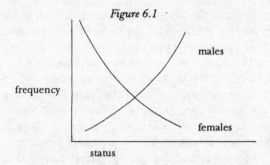

Figure 6.1

In such a distribution the presence of a few female exceptions of high status, such as a chief constable, a senior executive, a judge, or even a prime minister, does not invalidate the general point that the intermediate zone is one dominated by men. Also, for a woman to reach a high position, it is very likely that she will have taken on many of the features of a masculine culture.

In the growth of the intermediate zone, then, we are witnessing much more than part of the process of the 'rationalization' of society: its deliverance from older forms of tradition and the ties of neighbourhood and kinship. In another sense, it is the entrenchment of that social order which had been coming into existence since the sixteenth century: that of the bourgeois class, and specifically of the males within it. The hierarchical mode of organization, which had already proved conspicuously successful in securing compliance in religious and military organizations, and also to some extent in the manufactory, gradually became accepted as the norm; and with it a subtle, yet exceedingly effective, mode of domination.

THE STUDY OF 'MORAL ATMOSPHERE'

Within the psychology of morality, as it presently exists, formal organizations have been given only very scant attention. However, some promising beginnings in this area have been made by Kohlberg and his co-workers, from about 1970 onwards. Here, in attempting to take Piaget's work fully into account, they began to assimilate some of the key ideas of Durkheim; not an easy task, since Kohlberg's approach was strongly liberal and individualistic, whereas Durkheim had given such primacy to understanding how

157

collectives fashion the way in which people both think and act. Thus far, psychological work has focused on two main types of organization: schools and prisons.

One of the early studies was that of Kohlberg, Scharf, and Hickey (1972), working with prison inmates. The prisoners expressed their relationship to the staff primarily in stage 1 terms, focusing on such issues as coercion and punishment; and they tended to see one another largely in terms of stage 2, securing their self-interest mutually, but without any genuine respect for persons. It seemed that the prison was affecting their general outlook, moulding them into a morality that was below their 'private' best. From this and other studies Scharf also showed that organizations might have different types of 'justice structure', more or less independent of the personal morality of the members. The 'lowest' structure would be one where coercion was the norm; and the 'highest', one where a principled morality was, so to speak, built in – roughly corresponding to Rawls' idea of a just society (see page 32). In further work Scharf related different modes of prison treatment to the idea of justice structure; those that used behaviour modification seemed to be of type 2 (instrumental exchange); and those that used some form of psychotherapy approximated to stage 3, in which norms were informally created, and accepted with good will.

Perhaps rather better known than the prison studies is the work of the Kohlberg group on alternatives in schooling.[5] In 1974 a small school, designed to operate as a just community, was set up within the larger framework of an old-established high school in Cambridge, Massachusetts. This was named the Cluster School. Issues within the school were to be settled, not by authority, but by a community meeting in which all could participate and each member, both staff and students, had one vote. Within this experimental project it was possible to observe the gradual growth of a sense of community, and the development of social mores very different from those prevailing in a typical state high school. In due course further alternative schools were set up, based upon similar principles.

In their formal research on alternatives in schooling, Kohlberg and his associates focused specifically upon the emergence of new collective norms, to use a phrase from Durkheim. It was possible to identify, tentatively, both the moral 'stage' of the norm, and the degree to which it had been accepted.[6] For example, during the first year of the Cambridge Cluster School stealing was widespread; by the second year patterns of trust and shared responsibility were clearly developing; during the subsequent three years no episodes of stealing were reported, and evidently most students believed that stealing had been extinguished. It is interesting to note that in this school no norm against drug abuse developed; merely one against being found out. In another alternative school, however, drug abuse was strongly sanctioned. From their studies the researchers tentatively sketched out a developmental process in the formation of new collective norms, from the point where they were first voiced to that at which they were strongly enforced by social control. Also, they marked out the stages in the transformation of a mere organizational aggregate, meeting for instrumental purposes, into what might properly be regarded as a community of persons.

A more detailed methodology for examining 'moral atmosphere' was later developed by Higgins, Power, and Kohlberg (1984). In one study four groups – two from regular schools and two from alternative schools – were compared. It was found that students from the alternative schools showed a closer correspondence between their hypothetical and practical judgements, made more judgements of responsibility, and showed a much greater degree of community valuing. Also, whereas collective norms based on concern for others were clearly held in the alternative schools, this feature was strikingly absent in the regular schools. In educational settings, then, there is some convincing evidence of the importance of 'moral atmosphere'. And the Kohlberg group is surely correct in drawing the Durkheimian implication, that any sound programme of moral education must be concerned about the form of social life in which pupils are involved, not merely with pedagogic methods that focus upon giving theoretical knowledge to individuals.

Research of this kind is but a token of a much-needed shift in moral psychology, away from the extreme individualism and the concern with private choices that have dominated the field in recent years. It might be argued that within the whole subject area, a much more sociological emphasis is required. For example, the focus of the work we have been examining has been on only two out of a large array of organizations, serving different functions in society. Schools and prisons do, of course, have features that are deeply disturbing to anyone with moral sensitivity, and they also have some potential for promoting a genuine respect for persons. There are, however, other organizations that are far more problematic, and perhaps of wider social influence. But there is a more important point. Concepts such as 'justice structure' and 'moral atmosphere' are too vague, and are uncritically grounded in a general liberal humanism. They do not enable us to get to grips with a great deal of what is happening in formal organizations. Moral psychology requires a more incisive analytical frame; one that allows us to speak clearly about differences of power, about class structure and its relation to the broader social structure, about ideology, and about unconscious motivation. This is a vast project; what follows in this chapter is no more than the briefest sketch of how it might proceed.

THE ANATOMY AND PHYSIOLOGY OF FORMAL ORGANIZATIONS

In moving from the sociological to the psychological level of analysis, five features of formal organizations are particularly relevant. To use an analogy: in studying a living organism, we might first look at the large-scale arrangement of the bones, muscles, and organs, and gain some idea of how their functions interrelate; then we might look at in more detail at the cellular metabolism.

Structure

Every formal organization provides a set of social positions: managing director, storekeeper, salesperson, and so on. To each position is attached a status, expectations, and rewards. How, precisely, do these positions cohere together? The 'ideal' structure is shown in official documents, plans, and flow-charts, indicating the chain of command as a naïve senior manager might suppose or desire it to be. The 'actual', or 'extent', structure, as related to the formal tasks, is always somewhat different; intermediaries may be bypassed, individuals may take on responsibilities that lie outside the official requirements, and so on. The real state of affairs is constantly changing, and can only be discovered through detailed empirical enquiry. In addition, members are connected to one another by many ties that do not derive strictly from the organizational task: based on ethnicity, religion, leisure pursuits, areas of residence, and those relationships of friendship and love which arose initially from contact in the workplace. This 'informal' structure is a flexible web of human bonds that crosses over the formal anatomy of the organization at many points. Skilled operators know how to use it. The groundwork for new resource allocation is laid at dinner parties; major industrial disputes have been settled on the golf course.[7]

Weber depicted a pure form of bureaucracy, in which all functions are specialized, all procedures formalized, and all authority centralized; perhaps his real-life model here was the Prussian state. Detailed empirical study of organizations shows that there is, however, a wide structural variety, even though the hierarchical principle is maintained.[8] Those which involve the co-ordination of many different tasks (such as large-scale manufacturing corporations) tend to be fairly decentralized; scientists and innovative engineers, especially, are often allowed wide scope for their personal initiative and creativity. Many organizatons, such as small banks, breweries, and bus companies, have a fairly loose and light-weight authority structure, where formal and informal aspects tend to merge.

The structure of an organization, whether 'ideal', 'extant', or 'informal', is never a totally internal matter. For each member also belongs to society at large, and has a social class position within it: embodied in patterns of ownership, activity, and consumption, and grounded in personal wealth and security. In the organization there is always a reflection of social class, though never a precise replication; and the tensions between different social classes, which are mitigated in times of prosperity but accentuated in times of economic depression, are always present to some degree. One example is that of schooling, which a long tradition of research has shown clearly is primarily a middle-class affair for and by middle-class people.[9] It is a weakness of the Kohlberg work in this field that it never seems to have come to terms with the sociology of education.

Goals

Although there is a strict sense in which only individuals may be said to construct their action in an intentional way, it does make sense to talk about the goals of an organization. Primarily, these are to be inferred by an examination of what the organization actually does, rather than from public apologias; or glossy brochures; or comments made by individual members, who may not understand the true significance of what they are doing. Indeed, a major sociologist has gone so far as to assert, 'One of the advantages of specialization-and-coordination is that it is not necessary for all the participants in a plan of cooperation to have an exact idea of the common goal' (Johnson 1961: 281). To some extent there is an analogy with psychoanalysis. A person may be self-deceived, or have powerful but repressed desires, and mask his or her true intentions by a specious rationalization; it is only when the sense of threat has been vastly lowered that an honest avowal of intention can be made.

One of the crucial examples here is that of technical innovation. The prevailing rationalization is that this is the way that industry meets existing human needs more effectively, brings forth a new range of needs, and creates a more benign and efficient working environment. Like all rationalizations, this has a sufficient basis for it to be plausible. In the 'analytic hour', however, the truth emerges, and it is both crystal clear and chilling. Capitalist industry has two overriding goals, barely meeting even the lowest criteria of morality: survival in a cut-throat world, and the maximizing of profitability. Beyond this, virtually everything is *ad hoc* and unprincipled.

> The challenge, then, is not only one of innovation, but of
> *managing technological innovation for profit.* . . . The only
> justification for devoting scarce financial resources to
> research and development is the belief that they will generate
> innovations which will contribute to the company's survival
> and continued profitability. Furthermore, it must lead to the
> attainment of these objectives more cheaply than if the
> money were spent in some other way.
>
> (Twiss 1980: 2; author's own italics)

162

Evidence that this is the truth abounds in the history of innovation. For example, corporations such as Boeing, General Dynamics, and Chrysler gave massive attention to relatively 'safe' military innovations (such as the cruise missile and the supertank) when they began to face a major crisis of profitability in the 1960s.[10] Lucas rejected a carefully researched plan from its own shop stewards to develop a new range of socially useful products, and remained committed to its heavy involvement with weaponry – purely on grounds of profitability.[11] In the field of innovation, then, any product is acceptable, even though wasteful, shoddy, dangerous, or polluting, provided that a sufficiently lucrative market can be found.

The case of capitalist industry is a striking one, but it illustrates a general point. Some organizations have real goals that are, in moral terms, indefensible. Yet many individuals, with the most acute and sensitive moral capabilities, have little option but to work within them; even in some of the most affluent societies, the alternative is to be in danger of homelessness and near-starvation.

Culture

Broadly speaking, the culture of a social group may be regarded as its shared way of viewing the world, its definitions of what is real and true, of what is important and worth pursuing; its sense of history; its ideas of those personal qualities that are to be esteemed. There is a sense in which a collective (by the classifications it provides, the stories it tells, the records it keeps, and so on), may even be said to 'perceive', to 'remember', and to 'forget'.[12] An individual can only survive, psychologically, within the collective by accepting its shared representations.

Those who occupy high social positions are sometimes inclined to believe that their organization has a single culture, rather like that of a great 'happy family': a culture that is clearly related to the overall goals. The truth usually seems to be that there are several cultures, fairly easy to distinguish from one another. Each one is grounded in the actual conditions of life experienced by its members. Thus, for example, it is often the case that the culture of manual workers is one that involves a good deal of solidarity and co-operation, and with sanctions against anyone who tries to co-operate too much with management or to secure an individual advantage; it has arisen in part as protest and resistance, a way of retaining a sense of personhood over and against the demands of these with power, which would often turn human beings into mere appendages of machines.

The crucial point is that the culture envelops, and even defines, the individual; often there is no place for moral considerations. Again, the case of technical innovation is instructive. Once a person is within the innovator's culture, a whole range of exceedingly complex and fascinating considerations come into the foreground, related to the lived practice of research and development. These include the uncertainty of radical innovations, the difficulty of knowing how far the present state of the art must be surpassed; the prediction of the life-course of products that are already on the market, and those about to be launched; the construction of a sound 'portfolio of innovations', so that those which are risky can be balanced by those which are safe and predictable; and so on. This culture provides great challenges to human creativity; its participants are lured by what is 'technically sweet; anyone who raised moral considerations as valid for technical decision-making would be discounted, ridiculed, or dismissed.[13] With all the major innovations that have shaped the industrialized societies of today – the automobile, chemicalized agriculture, computers, nuclear power, and so on – it is clear that moral thinking had no part in the innovator's decisions. In the case of the Lucas shop stewards, to which we have already referred, where there was a serious proposal to relate innovation in a moral way to human need, the leader soon afterwards lost his job (see notes 11 and 13).

If a person is to sustain a credible identity within an organization, it is absolutely necessary to participate in the culture appropriate to his or her social position. Of course, there is abundant scope for individuality at a first-order level; an analytical chemist might have a perverse preference for NMR above all other techniques, or a psychiatrist might have an aversion to administering ECT. There is, however, no place for deviance at a second-order level. A chemist cannot continue in research while challenging the fundamental epistemology of natural science; a psychiatrist who disbelieved in the existence of mental illness would soon have no professional standing. Those who place themselves outside the culture are, in the literal sense, idiots, utterly alone; and from the standpoint of the cultural adherents they may well be regarded as wicked or insane.

Social Control

This refers to some of the more obvious ways in which organizations encapsulate and constrain their members, binding them by near-religious ties. For those on the path of upward mobility there is, first of all, a selection process, in which a few who appear to have the right aptitudes and personalities are chosen. Once within the organization, a new member's actions and attitudes are moulded suitably through training and supervision. Perhaps here social learning theory is an entirely appropriate theoretical frame; an employee first learns certain behaviours by imitation, and then gradually comes to feel that they are his or her own. Records on performance are kept by superior authority, and provide the basis for consideration for promotion; often the details are kept secret. Desirable behaviour is encouraged by the incentive of privileges and salary increases. Standards are maintained by the threat of various kinds of sanction: the prospect of being passed over for promotion, or relegated to work of low prestige. Ironically, it seems that the highest levels of commitment are achieved when social control operates by means that are apparently gentle and democratic: when people are consulted, when they do not feel coerced or forced into competitive relations with others, when they are given considerable freedom to be creative. There are cases where social control extends even into private life. It has been observed that some corporations, in selecting a male executive, consider his wife's suitability as a social asset; and that some increase the productivity of their employees by putting subtle pressure on their spouses.[14]

At its crudest, social control in the workplace is exercised by the imposition of technology: the assembly line, automation, the programmed lathe, the continual monitoring of productivity by computer. At its most liberal, social control operates by little more than insinuation: that a doctor's knowledge is out of date, that an academic has failed to produce a sufficient number of research papers. Often it is those organizations which are morally most dubious that have to undertake the largest task of deconstruction and reconstruction. A young army or navy officer, for example, is subjected to a thorough re-definition of the world; his self-esteem is first damaged, then recreated; his identity destroyed, and then re-founded; his motives cauterized, and then reorganized towards his 'service' career.[15] There is a sense in which the organization is almost bound to win over the individual. The only effective way of resisting, while remaining within it, is through forming a new collective, such as a trade union. It is a notable feature of the present time that union activity is often seen, from the standpoint of the managerial culture, as dangerous or immoral.

Roles

Anatomically, organizations provide social positions. Physiologically, they provide roles, or patterns of acceptable performance. Roles always exist in the context of what people are requiring from one another, and never in isolation. A nurse expects practical co-operation, but not necessarily emotional support, from other nurses; anticipates certain (mainly technical) instructions from doctors; and assumes that some low-level tasks will be carried out by cleaners or trainees. Often roles are conceptualized in terms of positive and negative prescriptions, related to the various 'role-senders'; but it is also possible to see a role as some kind of definition of the boundary within which organizational behaviour must be constrained. Many roles involve a good deal of contradiction and stress, and activate anxieties that might otherwise lie dormant. From the organization's point of view the crucial thing is that action must be structured in such a way that the overall goals are achieved. Without role-definition the organization would lose direction, and might very soon collapse into a chaos of conflicting desires and fears.

SOME ASPECTS OF ROLE PERFORMANCE

For some purposes there is no objection to referring to organizations almost as if they were human beings, with desires, goals, unconscious motivations, and defences. It need hardly be said that this should not be taken in a literal sense. For organizations consist of individual persons, and ultimately it is their actions which are to be explained. These actions, however, are not precisely similar to those of individuals in their private life, to which moral psychology has given most of its attention. Actions within and for organizations are usually carried out within imposed boundaries, under constraint. The key concept here is that of role.

Role is, of course, no more than a metaphor derived from the theatre, although its application to everyday life has profound significance, and its ancestry is of long standing. Correctly used in social theory, it certainly implies that there is a part to be played; but there is no suggestion that everything is completely pre-set, word for word, gesture for gesture. Even theatrical performance allows considerable scope for individual interpretation of a role, according to the actor's personality and emotional experience. In the most general way the concept of role signifies the existence of patterns of acceptable action, which have some kind of enduring quality, in response to others' expectations. There is a sense in which even breast-feeding, gossiping, or making dinner are examples of role performance. In this broad sense role carries no implication of insincerity, artifice, or self-distancing. The important thing is the wholeness, the flow, and the skilled nature of mutual interaction. When a role has been learned and practised a little, action can proceed with a sense of spontaneity, and attention can be directed towards other matters. Role performance thus defined may be an aid rather than a hindrance to morality. Knowing, in a broad sense, how to behave, a person might be freer to attend to the needs and interests of others. In other words, the presence of a role boundary can, at times, facilitate the creation of moral space. A reciprocal role relationship, then, might be illustrated as in Figure 6.2,[16] using again the idea of the individual's 'total field of experience' as developed in Chapter 3 (especially page 82). The crucial point is that the role boundary, the definition of what is appropriate, does not in itself contribute to individual alienation; and (as in the case of psychotherapy), can even provide conditions in which alienation may, in part, be overcome.

In relation to formal organizations, however, role often has more precise, and less benign, connotations. The crucial point now is that the occupant of a social position is rather firmly 'locked in' to a framework of given expectations, by virtue of the organization's structure, goals, culture, and social control. Here the genuinely interpersonal tends to be curtailed or distorted

Figure 6.2

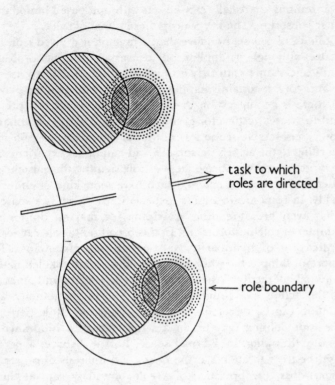

task to which
roles are directed

role boundary

because of more overarching requirements, and some of these are backed by severe sanctions. Ultimately, if the actor will not play the part, he or she must leave the stage. It is role performance in this sense that is so problematic from a moral point of view. In a similar manner to Figure 6.2, the position may be represented as shown in Figure 6.3 on page 169.

The point now is that the constraints embodied in the role relationship are such as to enhance the fragmentation of the psyche, and that role performance by an individual must necessarily involve him or her in a high degree of alienation. The extent to which this is the case depends, of course, on how tightly the role boundary is drawn in real life.

Figure 6.3

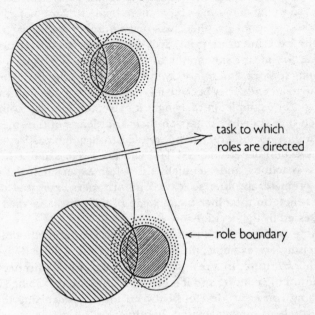

task to which
roles are directed

role boundary

Sometimes it is suggested that formal roles can 'take over' those who occupy them. A classic case in the literature is the prison simulation experiment devised by Haney, Banks, and Zimbardo (1973). Twenty-one male volunteers took part, who had been judged, on the basis of earlier tests, to be stable, mature, and socially well-developed. At the start, they were strangers to one another. By random allocation ten were given the part of prisoners, and eleven that of guards. A realistic prison environment was created in the basement of a building in Stanford University, with cells 6 feet by 9 feet. The experiments went on continuously, day and night, with the guards doing their duty in shifts. The guards had uniforms, and the prisoners a rough tunic; interpersonal differences were thus minimized.

At the start of the experiment the prisoners were realistically 'arrested' by the police, and were taken through the standard procedures at the police station. Each one was then stripped, sprayed with a delousing preparation, made to stand naked in the prison yard, photographed, assigned a number, and incarcerated. As the experiment went forward, it appeared that all participants began to find the situation 'real'. The guards were meticulous in coming to work, and some stayed on duty long after their shift had come to an end. They became increasingly aggressive and authoritarian; for example, in carrying out extremely lengthy 'counts' at which they tested prisoners on their knowledge of the rules. The prisoners, on the other hand, tended to become passive, and to some extent depersonalized. Five had to be released due to acute stress reactions, and eventually the whole experiment was called off, prematurely, after six days. The prisoners expressed delight and relief; on the other hand, some of the guards seemed to be distressed by the decision.

An experiment such as this is open to several methodological criticisms. For example, the environment was no more than a very crude caricature. In a real prison both guards and prisoners have a continuing culture, and it is generally the case that some kind of working consensus develops between them, humanizing the milieu to at least a small degree.[17] In other words, the role boundaries in the experiment were probably tighter than those of real life. But this and similar experiments show remarkably clearly not just that roles take over, but that existing alienation can be dramatically enhanced. Once familiarized to their roles, the participants seem to have lost contact with the greater part of their everyday selves.

At this point we seem to be close to one of the most alarming features of organizational atrocity. It is often the case that people believe that they are doing their duty, even when involved in the most appalling acts. Primo Levi describes this behaviour in Auschwitz, as another batch of Jewish men was being marked out for the gas chambers.

> The officer, followed by the doctor, walks around in silence, nonchalantly, between the bunks. . . . Now he is looking at Schmulek; he brings out the book, checks the number of the bed and the number of the tattoo. I see it all clearly from above: he has drawn a cross besides Schmulek's number. Then he moves on. . . . In this discreet and composed

manner, without display or anger, massacre moves through the huts of Ka-Be every day.

(Levi 1987: 59).

Such acts are rational, in the logical sense of being related to a pro-attitude and a belief; but psychologically, they are most readily explicable as being the consequence of an extreme alienation.

From a managerial standpoint, role performance in an organization is often seen as the easy fitting of individuals into a collective, rather as well-machined cogs into a smoothly running machine. This is part of the ideology that supports the organization's goals, and it is derived from the experience of power. The truth for most individuals and especially, perhaps, for those who are in middle positions (such as foremen or chief clerks) is that role performance is usually a matter of handling contradictions; of achieving a compromise between conflicting demands, and of realizing at some level that no solution is fully satisfactory. Organizational stress may be understood in part as the response of the body to the presence of these contradictions, while they remain largely in the field of 'unacknowledged experience' (cf. page 83).

Theorists often make the point that elements of the role requirement are often unclear, or mutually incompatible. For example, a given 'role-sender' may expect 'good' performance as judged by criteria that cannot be reconciled, such as speed and accuracy. Also, the various role-senders may have different expectations – or at least that is how the occupant of the role perceives it. The academic senses pressure from students for good teaching; from peers for good research; from management for sound administration. The nurse is torn between the needs of the patient for close personal care and attention; the doctors' requirement of technical efficiency; and the demand of the hospital authorities for order, cleanliness, punctuality, and accurate record-keeping. Furthermore, most people occupy several roles, perhaps in different organizations – and to maintain them all convincingly may require considerable skill. To give a typical example from the North of England. A man in his twenties is developing his career in sales for the Electricity Board; here he has to be smooth and deferential to customers. He is also a member of the Rugby League team, which requires extreme

171

machismo, and heavy spending on a Saturday night. He is already married, and becoming a 'traditional' husband and father. Each week he visits his eighty-three-year-old grandmother, now in residential care, to whom he is still a little boy. Across such strongly contrasting roles, he somehow has to 'get his act together'.

There are many conflicts, then, in the area of the role requirements. In addition, the performance of a role may simply be in conflict with desire. Historically, the inculcation of a work orientation that feels 'natural' was no easy matter, and this is still the case in countries that have not had the full impact of industrialization. Finally, there are times when role prescriptions come into direct clash with personally held convictions. A doctor, strongly committed to the task of promoting good medical care, takes on the job of 'unit general manager' in the British National Health Service. Under new policies the role requires the bringing about of major cuts and closures, for which salary incentives are offered. If he refuses to do this, he has failed in the role; if he complies, he has violated his own medical and moral principles.[18]

It is clear, then, that role performance is very far from the straightforward matter that it is often taken to be, especially by managerial theorists and by psychologists with a markedly individualistic orientation. From a moral standpoint that is grounded in depth psychology, there seem to be two crucial problems. One is that the role tends to promote or enhance the condition of alienation; the other that the occupancy of a role almost certainly involves conflict, and that of several kinds. Not surprisingly, successful role performance has been described, in quasi-Freudian terms, as an 'ego achievement'.[19] The Freudian ego had to cope essentially with conflict, and hence anxiety, from 'within'. The organizational member has that, but also a great deal more.

COLLUSIVE DEFENCE IN ORGANIZATIONS

Formal organizations of a hierarchical kind seem to have the potential to arouse four rather different kinds of anxiety. The first is engendered by the structure of authority itself, from the fact that most members are at the behest of one or more figures who are 'superior'. If depth psychology has some truth here, it would imply that for some people, at least, there will be a shadowy recollection of other authority situations, especially those of early life. In other words, however the situation is defined in consciousness, it may also be defined pre-consciously in relation to the predicament of the child, who had neither power nor adequate understanding. The second kind of anxiety derives from the fact of responsibility, of having a task to carry out which it may not be possible to fulfil; there are always uncertainties, not least those deriving from the behaviour of others. The third is related to the task itself. Some organizational tasks are physically dangerous – as, for example, armed combat, traditional mining work, or extracting oil from sources beneath rough seas. Some tasks involve the continual taking of life, like work in poultry farms or abattoirs. Some, like technical innovation, involve the hazards of the unknown. Some require a person to be in close contact with frightening and disturbing human predicaments, such as severe illness, extreme frailty, insanity, and dying. The fourth type of anxiety arises from the several kinds of conflict that may be present in the role situation, such as those touched on in earlier pages of this chapter.

Considering the many grounds for anxiety, it is remarkable how much organizational work is carried out with apparent efficiency. Many soldiers, so it seems, go cheerfully into battle; many executives carry very heavy responsibilities and yet, apparently, leave them aside when their working day is over; many nurses go through long periods of contact with great suffering, and yet, apparently, are undisturbed. One possible explanation, which has been widely taken up by those concerned with the psychoanalysis of organizations,[20] is that besides individual defences against anxiety, there are collusive defences 'built in' to the organizational culture. The suggestion is that there is a kind of tacit, pre-conscious agreement between members, that if they do their work in a particular kind of way, and view the task and themselves from a particular perspective, they will be more secure. Certain facts which are too difficult to bear consciously will be blanked out, and in the sharing of a common, if extremely limited, outlook, there will be a feeling of mutual support. One case that has been studied in some detail is that of nurses. Their routine is such that the division of labour, the shift system, the attitudes inculcated during training, and the prevailingly technical emphasis of hospital care, all serve to prevent a more personal and painful engagement with patients. It seems likely that some of the new approaches, providing a more continuing contact between particular nurses and patients, will in themselves do only little to amend this situation. Without the collusive defences, and psychologically prepared as they now are, many nurses might find the demands of life on the ward impossible to bear.[21]

It seems, then, that Figure 6.3, suggesting a consciously understood role boundary which binds members of an organization together in pursuit of their common task, is very far from the whole story. The truth, for many roles, may be as shown in Figure 6.4.

Figure 6.4

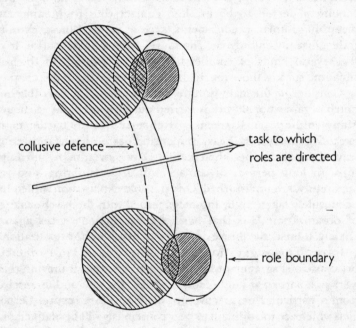

This diagram attempts, very crudely, to suggest that when the collusive defence is high, the individuals are bound together in ways they do not consciously apprehend. It was to something of this kind that Freud was pointing in his monograph on mass psychology of 1922; within his frame, the hypothesis was that individuals 'make over' their superego to an authority figure, thus having something of a collective identity, but at the cost of having lost part of what is truly themselves.

Presumably the collusive defences are highly functional to organizations in achieving their goals. However, they may, over an extended period, have a damaging effect on the individuals involved; so much of what they are undergoing remains unacknowledged. Before coal mining was mechanized, many miners were invalided out with the strange condition known as nystagmus, with its accompaniment of vertigo and psychological malaise; soldiers fall victim to shell-shock or combat neurosis; social workers, apparently without prediction, have episodes of burn-out; executives develop pains in the chest and somehow, unaccountably, find they can no longer go to work. Perhaps these are the individuals for whom collusion no longer provides the additional support needed to contain their anxiety. They are the victims. But the 'intermediate zone' remains in working order by generally keeping the collusive defences intact.

When the conditions for an organization are relatively easy (a secure government bureaucracy, perhaps, or an industrial producer with high profit margins) work within it comes to resemble, to some extent, that of a 'good' traditional family, with a generous and benign patriarch at its head. Anxiety is lowered, and members can carry out sophisticated tasks, with some balance between competition and co-operation, and the sense that senior management is on their side. Perhaps the paradigm case here is the research laboratory, engaged on prestige projects with abundant funding. Such conditions do not necessarily make for personal or moral development, although they may be conducive to highly creative work. Broad (1985) provides a graphic description of some of the young scientists involved in the basic research for the Strategic Defense Initiative. In many respects they are still high-school boys: intellectually precocious as they work on the 'weapons of life', but often emotionally insecure and immature. As one of them described himself, and his involvement with science:

> I loved it. It was a treat. I had emotional problems at home
> with my family life and mother. Science was a world that was

pure and that no longer had emotions. It would never go away and would never leave you. And it was always correct. There was always a right answer. So it had a strong attraction for me emotionally. On top of that I had a knack for it.

(ibid.: 38)

This gives an indication of the way in which science, with its intense objectivity, can form part of the apparatus of collusive defence.

When an organization is under pressure, however, matters are very different. Perhaps there are deep structural changes, with rationalization, closure, and redundancy looming large. In the extreme, the organization's goals are reduced to the single one of naked survival, at virtually any cost to persons. Now the well-established collusive defences may no longer be sufficient, even for the majority. The organization takes on the aspect of an angry, hostile, or vindictive parent, and all manner of archaic anxieties in individuals are aroused. As some Kleinians might put it, 'bad objects' latent in the psyche are revived, and then perhaps externalized, projected on to some seemingly malignant authority figure. There is a disastrous loss of capacity to work creatively, to co-operate with others. Eventually, as new conditions become consolidated, fresh forms of collusive defence are established, and some form of 'efficiency' is restored.

This account of organizational defence has been somewhat sketchy, and it is not well supported by empirical evidence; as yet there has not been much research from this point of view. But if there is some truth here, it may point to a basic reason why so many formal organizations are morally unsatisfactory. Following the argument of page 96, the position seems to be this. For 'moral space' to exist those involved must, of necessity, have free attention available. This is not primarily a matter of time and conscious concentration, but of lowered psychic defences. Organizational roles, however, work powerfully against this. Not only do they bring pressing demands to the conscious self (which are, in principle, not incompatible with the presence of moral space), but they also often create anxieties which must be dealt with by additional defences. Paradoxically, this may be as much the case in some 'caring' roles as in those that are obviously materialistic. If an organizational member were, by some means, to lower his or her defences, there might be a flooding of the psyche with new anxieties; and with no opportunity to 'work them through' (that is, assimilate them into conscious experience with the support of others), role performance might become impossible. If problems of this kind exist in hierarchies, there is no reason to suppose that they would disappear overnight in organizations of a more co-operative kind. There people have to face another set of anxieties, related to mutual trust. But it does seem probable that some of the psychological difficulties, especially those associated with authority, and carrying responsibility in a highly individual way, could be largely avoided.

THE MORALITY OF ORGANIZATIONS

The account given in this chapter might, at first, seem a long way removed from the psychology of morality, especially considering the way this topic has been construed during the last twenty years or so, with its emphasis on the private ought. There is, however, a long tradition of thought, going back at least to Aristotle, which suggests that morality is first and foremost to do with the form of social life, because it is here that individuals acquire their personal way of being. The problem of formal organizations, then, is but part of a very large agenda.

Perhaps the first aspect which requires scrutiny is that of the goals of an organization: not its legitimating ideology, nor its official codes of practice (interesting as these are), but what it actually does in the world, the ends to which its collective action truly points. There is an analogy with the study of the individual; it is his or her lived morality, rather than theoretical statements about what ought to be done, that is the more important. In the case of organizations it is easy to be seduced by common-sensical views about what they are doing, and it may be the case that this has occurred with the Kohlberg group, in their studies of prisons and schools. Sociology, however, invites us to look beyond and behind the 'obvious' to discover more of what is really happening: the latent, as well as the manifest function. Prisons do not simply restrain and rehabilitate offenders. They are part of a social order with great structural injustices, an appendage of a legal system which is subtly biased towards property and privilege. Schools do not simply bring forth the abilities of their pupils. They divert resources and attention to a minority of high achievers, and actually inhibit the development of many. Schooling subtly replicates society, and prepares individuals to accept their place within it with resignation.

When seen in a sociological light, virtually every major organization of contemporary society is highly problematic. Both the latent and the manifest functions can be examined from a moral standpoint. In the case of any organization we may ask two questions. In what way does it, or does it not, meet human need? In what way does it, or does it not, make for social justice? With some organizations, most notably the large industrial corporations, the implications are global. Of course, the identification of human needs and the finding of criteria for social justice, in a way that engages with the contemporary predicament, are major tasks of moral theory, not psychology *per se*. Beyond their external goals, and the effects upon their 'clients', organizations may be evaluated morally with respect to the social relations experienced by their members: in particular, whether or not persons are truly respected within the organizational frame. It was this, primarily, that came under Marx's moral censure, when he saw industrial labourers as deeply alienated and exploited, unable to express their humanity in the workplace, and often condemned to an exceedingly impoverished existence outside it. Those who are forced to sell their labour power as a commodity, waiting to be bought like cattle in a market-place, are bound to be, to some extent, depersonalized. Now, a century later, this is still a major issue, considering the exploitation of industrial labour on a global scale.

The question of the social relations of an organization, however, raises many further issues. Probably some degree of alienation is present in virtually all work within formal organizations. Also, they tend to impose a heteronomous morality; their 'justice structure' is typically that of instrumental exchange. But organizations are never static, and their justice structure fluctuates. When times are good, when there is little external threat, they can ascend to a stage where members can be like 'good' children, trying to please a benevolent parent; when times are bad they rapidly degenerate to something like Hobbes' state of nature, where the prime motivations embodied in the structure are purely selfish, centred on the avoidance of punishment. Perhaps it is significant that Weber, the great theorist of bureaucracy, considered only two main motives for organizational work: status-seeking and conformity.

This, however, is by no means the whole story of the internal morality of organizations; we have simply considered what is strictly required by the hierarchical form. There is another aspect, related more to the informal structure. That is, what place does the organization 'accidentally' provide for the life of its members as sentient beings, and for the growth of a morality of mutual respect, when its strict role requirements have been fulfilled? The truth, surely, is that moral space is continually being created, despite the organizational constraints. Sometimes there are even small enclaves, or groups of workers tied by special bonds, approximating to the idea of moral community. These are potentially subversive of hierarchy, but may well serve to make organizational membership more tolerable in the short term.

Organizations vary greatly in the moral space that they provide. The clearest example of where it was virtually non-existent is that of the concentration camp, where Jews awaited the gas chamber. Here the prisoners were so devastatingly deprived, so monstrously threatened, that all that remained of a common morality was an extreme egocentrism.[22] The people who were generally admired were those who had enough strength and resourcefulness to avoid starvation and illness, to stay their execution for a few more weeks; any signs of altruism were taken as weakness. Only a very few quite exceptional persons could retain a concern for others under such conditions. Towards the other extreme are those organizations which are relatively unpressured, and sufficiently well resourced, for role requirements to be broad, and for the informal structure to pose no obstacle to the overall goals. Privileged universities are a good example, as also are hospitals backed by generous provision. Genuine co-operatives are very much more rare, especially in the area of production. It is here, much more fundamentally, that the hierarchical principle is challenged. A 'liberal' and 'democratic' society is not significantly threatened by the presence of a few alternative organizations; indeed, they provide token evidence of tolerance and pluralism. If, however, organizations which were based on respect for persons, while also having clear social goals, began to flourish, the whole 'intermediate zone' would fall into disarray, and with that the social structure to which it is so strongly connected. The advocates of hierarchy, faced with this possibility, fear that the result might be chaos, or a new hierarchy in which, as in *Animal Farm*, the former subordinates become the bosses. But the co-operative principle, widely applied in organizations, might prove to be one of the harbingers of a different, and in moral terms, much better kind of society, in which the very experience of personhood was different.

We need to consider, finally, the long-term effect of organizational membership on personality or, in moral terms, on character. From a purely cognitive-developmental point of view, those who have had to equilibrate over a long period to a low-level justice structure for the greater part of the day are likely to carry its effects in their whole moral outlook; one who has to be authoritarian at work will probably be authoritarian at home and at play. Depth psychology takes this matter much further. The typical organizational role, with its defensiveness, its selective inattention, its avoidance of responsibility, is the activation of a part-self; it is likely that a person who occupies such a role for a long period will enhance the division and fragmentation of his or her psyche. Perhaps this will especially be the case for one also identifies strongly with the role. The formal organizations of contemporary industrial society, then, create an enormous psychological problem for their members. The years of retirement, restricted in other ways as they are for very many people, do not always make for recovery.

All this implies a vast moral project; it stares us in the face, and yet it is generally ignored. Moral development cannot merely be a matter for individuals, in their private lives. If, as human beings, we do have such strong tendencies to form bonds and associations, to fit in with others' expectations, the crucial task is that of creating collectives that are conducive to moral being, while also fulfilling their instrumental goals. This, however, can not validly be conceived in isolation from deep changes in the structure of society as a whole; and also, by implication, the world-system, with its vast North–South inequities. In the short term, at least one possibility is to increase and cultivate the moral space actually within the hierarchical system. But there is no clear ground, other than prejudice and tradition, for supposing that formal hierarchy provides 'the one best way'.

Chapter Seven

VIRTUE, CHARACTER, AND INTEGRITY

In the western cultural tradition, compounded as it is primarily from Greek and Judaeo-Christian elements, there is a strong commitment to the idea of moral virtue: an enhancement and co-ordination of the natural capabilities, or perhaps something added, from beyond, giving a person special strength and resilience. One of the oldest concepts here, and one that has parallels in the sagas of many neolithic peoples, is summed up in the Greek word *arete*. In the Homeric writings this referred to some kind of all-round excellence: it included certain qualities that might, in our more narrow terms, be considered moral, but also much besides, relating to skill, resourcefulness, physical endurance, and even cunning. Later, the Greeks named four virtues as constituting the core of human goodness. Three had, primarily, an individual reference: wisdom, courage, and temperance. The fourth was social, and is commonly translated as justice. By the time Plato was writing, it seems that these four virtues were common currency, and he tried to show that they corresponded to the natural constitution of the soul. Aristotle, in contrast, claimed that virtue was learned in the course of social life, and added other qualities to the list, most notably generosity or magnanimity. Much later, when Christian thinkers came to deal with the question, they generally retained the original four, and added the three New Testament qualities of faith, hope, and love, highlighted by St Paul in his famous prose poem.[1] Thus western moralism emerged with the idea of seven cardinal virtues, of which four were natural and three supernatural, given by God's grace alone.

This is part of the background, taken into a deeply Christianized common-sense understanding, against which secular moral philosophy emerged in the seventeenth century. It is also the context within which psychologists concerned with the moral life attempted to take up the problem of character. For a long time character was somewhere near the top of the agenda for research, and there was a general hope that certain styles of 'socialization' might be discerned which would generally promote the growth of virtue. Also some workers in the field, influenced by Freudian ideas, held the view that there were certain distinct character types, each with a particular orientation to the world. Character, so it was believed, tended to persist despite maturational changes such as intellectual and physical development, because its roots were so firmly laid down in early life. This gave all the more ground for attending carefully to the socialization process.

Later, as the work of Piaget and then of Kohlberg became widely known, and as naïve trait theory came under severe critical attack, many psychologists came to believe that the search for moral character was near-meaningless; perhaps a better path of understanding would be opened up by trying to 'get inside' a person's moral outlook. In his earlier work Kohlberg was highly dismissive of what he called the 'bag of virtues' approach in psychology and moral education. The concept of character was assailed also from another direction, that of sociology. For here it often seemed that the key to the explanation of behaviour lay not in individuals but in the 'given' features of social situations: a view which, as we have seen in the case of organizations, sometimes contains a good deal of truth, but which never tells anything like the whole story. The idea of moral character, however, is a much richer one than has often been assumed. Even Kohlberg eventually reintroduced it, with his rather simplistic idea of moral types (see page 137).

This chapter falls into two main parts, corresponding, roughly, to the division between 'academic' and 'therapeutic' psychology. In the first part we shall examine some of the evidence which led many psychologists of morality to abandon the idea of character, and then at some of the ways in which it was, nevertheless, retained or reinstated. In the second part we shall look at the process of psychotherapy, as a practical engagement with the problem of character. Seen in a particular light, and idealized to some degree, therapy suggests a path of personal change which is fundamentally moral, although not always recognized as such. All this points to something more profound than virtue, and which provides the missing psychological substratum: it is summed up in the concept of integrity.

I THE SEARCH FOR A PSYCHOLOGY OF CHARACTER

The 'classical' psychology of character may be considered to have reached its zenith in the vast and erudite work of Roback (1927), whose book covered topics as disparate as the theory of humours, Islamic philosophy, the use of character in literature, electrophysiology, and the psychoanalytic theory of Freud. Roback's own conclusion was that in correct psychological usage character should be seen as a subset of personality: it is 'an enduring disposition to inhibit instinctive impulses in accordance with a regulative principle' (third edition, p. 568). True to that liberal tradition which includes theorists as distant in time as Hobbes and Freud, Roback here assumes that the biological inheritance of humankind tends towards chaos and immorality; for social life to continue stably, all that is instinctual must be severely curbed, and brought under the dominion of principles, which are enunciated by the 'higher' faculty of reason. Characters differ, then, according to the instinctual endowment, the nature of the regulative principle, and the extent to which regulation is effective. This view, of course, fits in closely with Christianized and Platonized common sense; but it is one which a great deal of contemporary depth psychology challenges at its very core.

The Character Education Inquiry

In the years 1928–30 three notable volumes were published, the fruit of a large project initiated very much in the spirit of Roback: to find the best conditions under which sound character could be fostered in young Americans. This study, under the direction of Hartshorne *et al.*, involved some 11,000 elementary- and high-school children, who were given a wide range of behavioural tests related to altruism, honesty, and self-control, in such different contexts as classroom, home, church, and play. For example, in what appeared to be ordinary school work, each child in a class was given a box containing a set of puzzles, which 'accidentally' also contained a coin. Later the boxes were to be returned to a central source, without there being (apparently) any way of knowing which box came from whom. In fact, however, the boxes were numbered, so it was possible to find out who had taken the coin. In addition to tests such as these, the subjects were given questionnaires on their moral knowledge and attitudes, and elaborate tests were used to ascertain their 'moral reputation' among teachers and classmates.

The notorious finding from this study was that the inter-correlations between pairs of behavioural measures was of the order of 0.2–0.3, which in each case accounts for less than 10 per cent of the variance. This has commonly been taken as powerful evidence that actions related to morality are situation-specific; and hence that the idea of moral character cannot be sustained. The authors themselves inclined to this view, and came to the conclusion that, rather than attempting to build up character, according to the 'classical' view, moral educators would be better advised to facilitate their pupils' acquisition of specific behaviours through social learning.

The findings of this study do not, however, point so clearly in this direction. For example, when the behavioural measures on altruism are combined together into a battery, the correlation with a single indicator, or with reputation, is of the order of 0.5–0.6; the same applies with honesty and self-control. It has been pointed out by several later commentators that this is a much better index, since there is always a large amount of error variance in simply combining a pair of measures.[2] In other words, when the proper rules of research are followed, the data do give evidence for some degree of consistency, even in an extremely heterogeneous group of subjects, at a point when they are undergoing very rapid developmental change. Nevertheless, the Character Education Inquiry was commonly interpreted as having shown definitively that moral character was largely a fiction, and that traditional views about how to conduct moral education, through the deliberate inculcation of virtue, were misconceived.

Moral character in later studies

In America, at least, it was some time before social scientists recovered from the impact of the Hartshorne inquiry, to pursue again the search for a psychological basis to virtue and good character. One highly influential study was that of Havighurst and Taba (1949), involving all the boys and girls in a small Mid-west community who had entered their eleventh and seventeenth years in 1943. Assessment of character was derived primarily from an attempt to discover the subjects' reputation, on the assumption that this would be validly compounded from a myriad of close observations. Five main character types were identified: self-directive, adaptive, submissive, defiant, and 'unadjusted'. About a third could not be classified clearly. This work suggested a possible way of studying character, rather close to the way in which we attribute traits to people in everyday life. However, it failed to distinguish between what are simply forms of social adjustment and features that are distinctly moral. This work was followed up by the detailed study of Peck and Havighurst (1960) with seventeen boys and seventeen girls from the younger group (cf. page 122). In moral terms the latter was a far more perceptive inquiry, and gave considerable ground for believing that, in some persons at least, there are 'moral' aspects of character that persist despite the maturational changes of adolescence.

During the 1960s and subsequently, the study of moral character as a distinctive topic went into something of a decline. The field of moral psychology was increasingly taken over by cognitive-developmental and social-learning approaches, both of which seemed more able to generate sound research, as well as possible programmes for education. Moreover, moral character tended to be dissolved into the broader field of personality, of which it had generally been considered, in any case, to be a subset. It is only very recently that moral character has been clearly reinstated as a topic in its own right. For example, Knowles (1986) explores the moral implications of the well-known developmental scheme of Erikson (1963). Erikson had viewed the ego as having to pass through a series of crises, the successful resolution of each one being a condition for being ready to undertake the next. Knowles suggests that each crisis might also be associated with the acquisition of a particular virtue. The first, that of trust versus mistrust, is linked with hope; the second, of autonomy versus shame and doubt, with will – and so on. Knowles' scheme is speculative, and it only goes as far as young adulthood. Nevertheless, it could provide a framework for empirical enquiry and restorative work. The crucial question, with a particular individual, might be: at what point was a particular developmental task not undertaken, and therefore what virtues (or added moral competencies) not acquired?

Character and personality

Roughly from 1960 onwards, it often seemed to be the case that when psychologists of morality were speaking about character, they were on virtually the same ground as a much larger group, working on the question of personality. The basic issues in developing a sound theory of moral character appeared to be identical to those for a general theory of personality; also, many of the challenges to the idea of personality were precisely those which could be levelled at the idea of character. This was the context in which Kohlberg and others rejected the study of moral character, ignoring the work of researchers such as Peck and Havighurst. Within the broader frame of personality theory, three approaches are especially significant for the moral field.

(i) *Character as a set of traits* In everyday life it is very common to ascribe traits to others. 'She is generous'; 'He is reliable' – and so on. Presumably what is happening here is that people select, collect, and store a large amount of information from their encounters with others, together with what they learn about their reputation, and then make some very condensed summary descriptions, in the form of ascribed traits. These are useful for prediction, and generally for taking bearings in the social world. Also, people often ascribe traits to themselves, again drawing selectively on a large array of data, covering a variety of social and private situations. Among the trait descriptions in common use, there are many which have a bearing on morality.

It was through an extension of common-sense trait ideas that certain psychologists attempted to develop 'scientific' assessments of personality. There was substantial evidence to support the view that individuals were generally consistent in their cognitive abilities and styles, and perhaps similar methodologies could be applied to the personality field. Three types of data have been used.[3] The first, commonly known as R data, are derived from observers' ratings on behaviour in everyday life or 'naturalistic' settings. The second (S data) are derived from self-report, generally involving standard questionnaires. The third (T data) come from the observation of behaviour in experimental test situations, many of which involve deception or partial information (such as the experiments of Milgram).

Despite the scepticism of psychologists such as Mischel (1969), there seems now to be general agreement among psychologists that there is ground for believing in the existence of fairly enduring traits. Some of the most robust evidence comes from studies using R data, although these are not so common, being very expensive to carry out. The large study by Block (1971), *Lives Through Time*, for example, used 114 personality variables, following a sample of male and female subjects from junior high school through into their mid-thirties. Using rigorous forms of assessment, it was found that some 30 per cent of the variables showed highly significant correlations over the whole period. Some of these, such as those relating to self-control, dependability, and non-conformity, have a clear bearing on morality. To give just one other example, Rushton (1980) has found clear evidence for the existence of the altruistic personality, based to a considerable degree on R data.

S data are easier to obtain, but tend to be rather less robust than those from real-life observation. Nevertheless, there is fairly good evidence here, too, for the existence of certain traits that are related to morality. Emler (1983), for example, reviews a substantial body of work in this field, and adds some of his own primary data. His general conclusion is that a considerable degree of consistency exists in specific forms of moral conduct, and that the evidence for traits is most strong in the case of antisocial, dishonest, and delinquent behaviour.

The case of T data is notoriously controversial, and much has been made of the observation that behaviours in experiments do not correspond too well either to behaviours in everyday life, or to data derived from self-report. Nevertheless Wright (1971) found some ground for using T data in his account of moral character, and the extensive review by Blasi (1980) showed that there were some cases, at least, where findings from experiments correlated with levels of moral judgement. With T data much remains to be resolved, especially concerning the way in which experiments are to be interpreted. However, the crucial evidence concerning traits does not come, and probably never could come, from this source.

It seems, then, that the difficulties in ascribing traits are not so fundamental as some earlier critics had assumed. Even Mischel, in

187

his paper of 1977, reneged to some extent on his earlier position, and suggested that the crucial problem was not so much whether traits existed, as what was done with them. One problematic use of trait theory is that of the psychometricians, such as Cattell (1963), who generally seem to have to assume, for the purposes of measurement, that all persons have the same traits, although to varying degrees. Even greater difficulties arise in those instruments which use ipsative scoring: which implicitly assume that there is a fixed quantity of something, to be distributed over a set number of categories.[4] It seems sounder to follow the methodology of those who work on the assumption that some persons may possess some traits, some of the time.[5] Also, it may be the case that there are individuals who have no clear traits; or, to be a shade reductionistic, their only trait is that of inconsistency.

Much more serious problems arise when psychologists try to move beyond the descriptive level, and use traits in explaining behaviour, whether on a simple model of $B = f(P)$, or a so-called interactionist model of $B = f(P, E)$ (where B = behaviour, P = personality, and E = environment). At the very least, there is the danger of tautology. To explain impulsive behaviour on the assumption of a trait of impulsivity is very much on the same level as Molière's famous case, explaining the action of a soporific drug by the 'fact' that it contained 'dormitive virtue'. But further, when trait theory is used in this way it generally fails to acknowledge that those who are researched upon are agents; a ridiculous antinomy is thus set up between the psychologist and the 'subjects'. The serious challenge is to incorporate the data on traits into a psychology that is genuinely reflexive (cf. page 58).

In summary, then, some trait descriptions stand, and this is a matter for careful empirical enquiry. If all that was meant by moral character was a cluster of traits, psychologists such as Kohlberg were right to regard the topic as unfruitful. But if traits are themselves to be explained by theory which respects the person as an agent, the rejection of the idea of character was premature.

(ii) *Character as self-presentation* There is a very different view of personality, and hence of character, which absolutely refuses to see traits as part of a person's 'real' nature. The emphasis, rather, is on the individual as a social actor: one who wants to make an impression on others within a face-to-face grouping (or possibly several). Much of this derives from the work of Goffman (1969), and from those who have explicated his ideas in a more psychological way. In the field of moral theory two recent examples are Emler (1983) and Hogan and Busch (1984). According to this view, then, consistency does not necessarily lie within the individual; it is, rather, a phenomenon presented to the beholder; and character is a property of persons-in-interaction.

For those who follow Goffman the key motive that underlies all social action, even when other and more obvious ones such as hunger or sexual desire are called into play, is the sustaining of a persona: and thus to be taken seriously, to be recognized, to be distinctive in some way. Putting it in other terms, the suggestion is that every individual has a very great need for approval, attention, and affirmation from others, and will discover or create some strategy to obtain it. This may not necessarily involve straightforward conformity to the prevailing mores; for a person who simply conforms, without also maintaining some kind of distinctiveness, would have no persona and so be lost.

All behaviour, then, whether arriving late at a party, driving a particular kind of car, or helping a frail person to carry a heavy bag of shopping, is to be seen in part as a form of communication, a way of telling others how one wishes to be regarded. Nothing is simply to be taken at its face value. A person's performance in a psychological experiment (providing the researcher with T data) is still the expression of a persona, but in unusual circumstances. Also responses to psychological tests such as those favoured by psychometricians (generating S data), are not to be seen as potentially true and highly condensed reports on patterns of behaviour; but rather, as attempts at presenting a self within the constraints of the questionnaire and its pre-set answers. Moreover, the correlations between responses on different tests, or between tests and other data, then appear not as genuine connections between real entities (such as attitudes and values, or introversion and artistic skill), but simply as the registration of self-presentational consistency. Similarly, the way a person handles a moral judgement interview is to be understood primarily as a statement about how he or she wishes to be taken to be; and the probing questions, designed to test the full competence of moral judgement, are simply pressing certain aspects of the subject's persona towards the limit.

This view, then, provides one way of understanding moral character, and particularly how this idea has become so entrenched in common-sense psychology. Character is to be viewed, not as part of what an individual really is, but as a fairly uniform pattern of self-presentation; however, those who witness it take it to be evidence of a 'true self', and sum it up through the ascription of traits. One person might manage to sustain roughly the same persona in a variety of contexts, and so have a single 'character'; another might have difficulty in so doing, and thus have more than one. The crucial point is that when a person has established a pattern, he or she will be known, affirmed, and talked about, in a particular way, and so will acquire a reputation. Thus it is not, as several theorists have assumed, that reputation gives indirect, but rather reliable, evidence about properties that truly belong to an individual; rather, it is that character amounts to little more than an alternative term for reputation.

Everyone, then, is to be seen as a kind of conformist, seeking esteem from others. The delinquent or hooligan who incurs general censure is none the less pursuing a 'moral career', in which antisocial acts are seen by peers as an expression of prowess. The autonomous and principled moral agents, so much praised by a long tradition of western scholars, are simply those who follow the norms of a reference group that is often invisible to the world outside: that of liberal academics, who enjoy an unusual degree of freedom in the workplace, who travel widely, meet their peers at conferences, and stand somewhat aloof from the concerns of those who are less privileged. Their preference for abstract thought, for formal operations, is not a mark of real superiority, in the moral field or any other, but simply of conformity to mores in which detached intellectualism has a very high place.

This view of character is far from implausible. It highlights the fact that we are social beings, that our self-hood is derived from interaction with others, and the paradoxical need both to belong and yet to be distinctive. Psychologically, however, it is inadequate, or very incomplete, because it seems to bypass certain crucial questions. To what extent do individuals differ in their skill in appraising social situations, in receiving others' messages of approbation or disapproval, in 'impression-management', in holding up their persona in difficult circumstances? Questions such as these come to the fore when Goffman's ideas, formulated

190

within microsociology, are taken to a psychological level. Thus, while the self-presentational theory suggests one important aspect of what character might mean, there are still 'person variables' to consider.

There are moral problems, too, in that a purely self-presentational view verges on cynicism. For it seems to suggest that there is nothing more than 'performance' that is, ultimately, self-regarding; all social skills serve egocentric ends. This seems to rule out, *a priori*, the possibility that some persons, some of the time, might have a concern for others that is valid in its own right, and irreducible to any other motive. Moreover, since actions rarely have a single motive, it is quite possible that a person might be genuinely other-regarding, while also holding up a particular persona. Thus, although much that passes as moral may indeed be little more than self-presentation or conformity, it would be foolish to suppose that all is of the same kind. Also, since this view is generally put forward without any developmental emphasis, it seems to tell us little about how people might (like Goffman himself) move on to recognize much of everyday life as manipulation and deception, and perhaps acquire some feeling for sincerity.

Granted these criticisms, there is one possible way of taking the self-presentational view right into the heart of morality. Someone whose concern for others was well developed might be seen, not as one who conforms to the mores of any existing community, with all its injustice and fraud, but as one who is endeavouring to follow the pattern of life of an ideal moral community in which truth is maintained, promises are kept, and each individual is valued fully as a person. Some human groupings do approximate to this, even if fleetingly and to a small degree. Perhaps it is towards the realization of such a community, not the following of abstract principles, that a moral agent is striving. And, of course, in such a community character as reputation, and character as part of what a person 'really is', would tend to coincide.

(iii) *Character as competence and liability* Both of the views of personality (and hence, of character) that we have looked at clearly contain some truth, but they do not go far enough. Trait theory works well for low-level description; but when used for explanation, soon becomes tautological, and loses the sense of the person as agent. A totally self-presentational theory preserves

191

agency, but it lacks a detailed psychology, and has very little to say about what is distinctively moral. For the understanding of character, there are certain crucial questions. What does each individual bring, *as a person* and *as an agent*, to the social situations of everyday life? What are the main respects here in which people differ? If there is a sense in which the human condition is one of existential freedom, what are the 'inner' constraints upon it? Nothing in the two views we have examined invalidates questions such as these.

Among the various attempts to re-fashion personality theory in a way that goes beyond trait theory, one of the most respected is that of Mischel (1977, 1984). He has suggested that individual differences might be understood in terms of a set of 'cognitive social-learning person variables'. His scheme is still tentative, but seems to have the potential to subsume a range of other concepts in the same domain, such as plans, personal constructs, locus of control, and self-efficacy, and also the various forms of expectancy-value theory. Mischel's approach has also had some appeal to psychologists wishing to move on from a rather static concern with moral judgement, and to get to grips with the problem of moral action.[6]

Mischel's first variable deals with people's ability to generate a range of actions under appropriate conditions; here we might envisage a spectrum from those whose actions are limited, stilted, and sometimes inappropriate, to those who have a wide repertoire and are skilled and flexible in deploying it. The second variable concerns the way in which people attend selectively to information from the general environment, others, and themselves. The third is 'expectancy': the outcomes that are anticipated from particular actions, or from contingencies in the environment. The fourth variable relates to individual values; Mischel here uses the term rather trivially to mean 'desired outcomes', but there is no reason why it should not be used in a more serious sense (cf. page 56). Finally, there is the matter of the rules and plans which people have already internalized, and to which they will tend to adhere even in the face of situational constraint. Through the deployment of a set of variables such as these, the aim is both to preserve the idea of personality, and to deal more subtly with the way in which persons and situations interact.

Each variable, Mischel suggests, is patterned uniquely to the individual, according to his or her 'learning history'; the greater part passes below the level of consciousness, rather as in the acquisition of any sophisticated skill. The cumulative effect of these variables could be transformed into generalized trait descriptions; but if this were done, a great deal of information would be lost, and we would no longer have access to the 'fine structure' of how persons deal, actively, with particular social situations; we would also lose track of the origins of personal consistency. In short, whether or not these particular variables provide the best list, Mischel's claim is that it is along these lines that traits might be illuminated, and actions explained without falling into the snare of tautology. Also, of course, such a scheme could fully subsume a view of personality based on self-presentation.

An account of the kind Mischel has put forward falls very closely within that range of theories that regard the person, in some sense, as a 'rational, cognitive actor' (see page 65). The individual seems to be a cool performer, on the whole; limited at times both in perception and resources for action; but not strongly endowed with feeling or emotion, nor experiencing strong ties or anti-pathies towards others; and certainly showing few symptoms of *Angst*, tragedy, or inner conflict. Thus, valuable as the scheme is, it seems to be lacking something of great significance if we are to understand the moral predicament of today. Depth psychology, on the other hand, often bears witness to what is dark and demonic in human nature, and portrays our state as one of inner division and confusion. Its traditional failure, from the standpoint of social science, has been that it had no account of the anticipatory nature of everyday life. The key question, then, to which an answer was tentatively given in Chapter 3, is whether some kind of coming together is possible.

Mischel does, in fact, himself move a little way in this direction, in his suggestion that a defensive reaction may be understood as 'a failure to adapt to new contingencies because one is still behaving in response to old contingencies that are no longer valid' (1977: 344). This is helpful, but it lacks a developmental insight. The point which is missing is that many patterns of anticipation and response were laid down before a person was capable of making clear and objective appraisals. Some were during the period of pre-operational thought, when the world had an almost magical aspect; some even during the sensori-motor period, when the infant had powerful emotions, and was learning how to relate to others, but had no access at all to the world of conscious-symbolic interaction. These early patterns are so enduring and overarching because they were not available for scrutiny. Generally the developmental reason for their power is neglected by cognitive theories. Thus when it comes to the question of the moral life, it might be fairly easy to develop a frame in which people are seen as well-endowed or lacking in certain 'cognitive social-learning person variables'. It is less familiar, within mainstream psychology, to hold the view that we are inwardly divided, damaged, and, in a sense, deranged. For many people – or perhaps for most of us – there is a task of repair work to be undertaken; it would appear to be more demanding than new social learning, and to involve more of the whole person than a simple move to a higher stage of moral reasoning.

II MORAL RESTORATION

Even the idea of traits, when pressed towards its limits, seems to point in the direction of depth psychology; although, of course, largely in a theoretical sense. But if the psychology of morality is to amount to anything, it requires also a grounding in practical action. Here one of the most promising ventures of today is that of psychotherapy. This, too, is concerned with character, meeting human beings not as objects of scientific enquiry, but in a personal way. The various types of psychotherapy arose, in the first place, in response to patterns of mental distress that verged on the pathological. However, it soon became clear that therapeutic work also implied something more general about the predicament of people in the western industrialized societies. And it is often the case today that individuals become involved in therapy because of vague dissatisfactions: a sense of emptiness, or strain, or imbalance, perhaps, or the knowledge that personal relationships are in disarray. Whatever may be their 'presenting problem', the concern of those who look to psychotherapy often turns out to be to discover some richness of experience and relatedness, some core of goodness, which they feel has eluded them, but which they sense is their birthright as human beings.

Psychotherapy is a prime example of 'the art of inter-subjectivity'. It is not a science, although it is underpinned by some well-tested generalizations. Also, a great deal of attention has been given to the question of its efficacy, employing the orthodox methods of social research. In particular, a technique known as 'meta-analysis' has been used to investigate outcomes. Individual studies are first selected according to criteria relating to their design and rigour, and then their findings are compared on a common metric. Lambert, Shapiro, and Bergin (1986), for example, review fourteen such meta-analyses, which incorporate 1,247 separate studies, and show clearly that (granted the perennial problems of measurement) the positive effects of psychotherapy seem to be large, whether the goals are narrowly or broadly defined. Psychotherapy brings changes much greater than either spontaneous recovery or placebo controls; the greatest effects are achieved within the first six months or so; 'negative outcomes' occur in some 5–10 per cent of all cases. Evidence is far less robust on whether the beneficial effects of therapy are sustained. The general tenor of research findings provides some ground for encouragement to the profesional body of therapists, even if it suggests their work is often incomplete. However, one disconcerting fact emerges strongly from this kind of research. Among those therapies which seek to deal directly with the quality of a person's experience (rather than, say, to carry out operational repairs upon behaviour) about all appear to be equally effective. It is, as Luborsky *et al.* (1975) put it, a race in which to apply the verdict of the Dodo bird in *Alice in Wonderland*: 'Everybody has won and all must have prizes'; and this has been confirmed in more recent work.[7] The most plausible interpretation of this fact is that it is the quality of the interpersonal relationship that really heals; this is worth exploring.

There is a naïve view, perhaps encouraged by superficial ideas of the psychoanalytic process, that therapy is primarily a matter of 'setting in order the contents of the head', by bringing repressed material back into consciousness, and so on. If this were the case, the therapist would be little more than a kind of technician. There is, however, another view, held by some therapists who have looked at the process closely. It is that therapy of almost any kind creates what might be called a 'relational disturbance' in the client's life.[8] If the implicit moral contract of therapy is kept, the client is in a position of a child with a good parent: one who will be totally accepting (even if at times provocative and challenging), and who will provide a safe place for the experience of painful emotion, including the difficulties of being really close to another person. In a sense therapy is a re-creation of the 'holding environment' to which Winnicott so often made reference (cf. page 108). Some people may find that their relationship within it is the first one in which they have ever allowed themselves truly to trust another; and hence, it is the first time they have ever dared to 'let go'.

Bearing this in mind, and deliberately blurring the theoretical technicalities of particular schools or approaches in therapy, we may identify three therapeutic outcomes that are specially relevant to the topic of moral development. If the description is a little idealized, it does not matter; for our concern is, primarily, with what therapy tells us about possibilities for change. It is the moral potential of a particular type of relationship that we are exploring. And if, as seems to be the case, therapy carries enormous potential for corruption, this also speaks in a way of its power to bring about personal change.

Enlargement of the experiential frame

The point here is that the template or frame through which we apprehend the world is often inadequate to what is happening to us. Let us recapitulate, for a moment, the discussion of Chapter 3. The frame is restricted by 'unacknowledged experience', and distorted by 'pseudo-experience'; we are inwardly divided, and our capacity for acting intelligently and lovingly is curtailed. On the one hand, there is much that a person has undergone, as an embodied and sentient being, but which has not been registered or assimilated in consciousness. In so far as this is denied or evaded it remains non-personal, and in the most dire cases it can become demonic. On the other hand, there is much that has been taken in primarily through the medium of language, but which does not correspond to a person's real life; it is taken as true because it comes from others who are respected or feared, and it corresponds to prevalent patterns of self-deception. Along with these two forms of disjuncture, the self becomes fixed, rigidified, reified, locked into the thought-forms and ways of relating that are prevalent in the taken-for-granted world. The situation is summed up diagrammatically as shown in Figure 7.1.

Figure 7.1

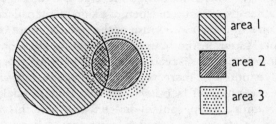

Now, in the warmth of the 'holding environment', the psychological ice-floes begin to melt. Some of what has actually happened is admitted for the first time; not just in verbal propositions, but also in experience. A person who has undergone repeated rejections, while preserving the self-image of one who is special, set apart, acknowledges the truth – and begins to feel the poignancy of rejection. One who has set up life manically, rushing from one activity to another in a way that has imposed colossal stress, stops and relaxes a little – and begins to sense the anxiety which has hitherto been denied. One who has lived over-safely, avoiding serious challenges so as to minimize the risk of failure, sees this life-pattern in a new light – and now begins to deal with deep-seated feelings of inferiority.

Also, elements from that vast set of misleading and damaging half-truths which others imposed on one who was not well-enough resourced to resist, are understood and felt in a new way. Not 'I disapprove of Jews, because they are dishonest', but 'I can see now that a disapproving message was repeatedly given to me that Jews are dishonest'; not 'I ought never to relax and take delight in so doing', but 'I recognize that an injunction against relaxation was laid upon me, and that I often respond to it without awareness'; not 'I am unclean, worthless, useless', but 'I was often treated as if I were unclean, worthless, useless; I accepted this message, and then used it to make sense of my life'.

In Figure 7.1, it is the region where the two circles overlap (area 3) that represents the experiential frame. As unacknowledged experience begins to be assimilated with awareness, and as pseudo-experience is recognized in a more authentic light, the two circles are brought closer together; the frame is enlarged. Out of psychotherapy, then, there emerges a kind of intersubjective truth; a person can make more sense of the past, be more open to the present. Moreover, the boundary between what is conscious and what is pre-conscious is relaxed; a person becomes more willing to attend to intuitions, more aware of bodily states, more sensitive to subtle cues given off by others. Whereas conventional consciousness requires a sharp, content-directed attention, this requires, so to speak, a soft focus, a diffuse awareness, a gentle grasp of a totality. In diagrammatic terms, all this may be summed up as shown in Figure 7.2.

Figure 7.2

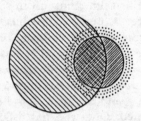

Why is it that the experiential frame is often so restricted? Why do people continue to live in a state of destructive inauthenticity, and perhaps assert in justification 'It's just the way I am'? This is the point at which the so-called defences are most crucially involved. For these are ways that have been learned, perhaps from a very early age, in order to maintain at least some sense of well-being, to make life liveable in difficult times. It seems that there are indeed character traits that endure in some persons, despite maturational and cognitive change. Perhaps these can be linked to the pattern of defences, which become so firmly entrenched as life continues (or, as a learning theorist might say, reinforced by the modest rewards they bring).

On the one hand there are defences against the direct experience of pain or fear that might overwhelm the psyche, against an unbearable sense of powerlessness, emptiness, or abandonment. A process of grief might be completely 'blocked', for example, with a general deadening of feeling. A child might preserve the illusion that a (disastrously inadequate) parent was good by denying the fact of neglect or ill-treatment, or by a strange psycho-logic which makes it all the child's own fault – anything, to preserve the 'good object'. But also, there are defences that are grounded primarily in compliance: a person limits his or her spontaneous, needy, playful, sensuous life, fashions what he or she says, does, thinks – and eventually, *is* – in order to avoid disapproval or rejection. Clearly, then, there are defences against pleasure as well as pain, and certain forms of moralism are highly defensive. Some defences, such as sublimation (roughly, engaging in cultural or physical activity in place of the meeting of emotional need) are relatively superficial. Others are very deep-rooted, possibly going right back into early infancy. The most powerful defences of all seem to be to do with the failure of that environment of nurturant and accepting 'holding' within which it becomes possible to sustain a self. Here, as we have seen, psychoanalysts find the origins of the schizoid disturbance, in which a person subtly withdraws from real engagement, intimacy, and commitment, for fear of being overwhelmed or destroyed. The schizoid state is the last resort of the fragile and threatened self; in another sense, it is also the first.

The enlargement of the experiential frame is no easy matter, and it is a process from which a person may feel constantly tempted to withdraw. It is not comparable to the accommodation that occurs when there is a change from one cognitive level to another, although this may indeed involve some sense of dissonance and temporary confusion. To become more open to experience, to live more truthfully, with less distortion, involves the lowering of those very defences which preserved some kind of emotional and cognitive equilibrium, however limiting it was; radical changes must come about in a pattern of life that did prove functional, at least to some degree. This is rarely something that a person can do on his or her own behalf, in a kind of boot-strap operation, perhaps through reading do-it-yourself books on 'personal growth'. To be one's own therapist, so to speak, is still a with- drawal from trusting others and can easily enhance that very inner division that therapy purports to heal. Therapeutic change requires, rather, the existence of the very kind of relationship that was so notably absent during the period when the defences were first constructed. As defence is lowered, a person may find that it is necessary to pass through layer on layer of psychic pain, as fear, grief, and rage that have been buried for years are allowed to reassert themselves; or severe anxiety, as actions and attitudes that were long ago forbidden, such as assertion of desire, or resistance to authority, are allowed a legitimate place. In short, the lowering of defences involves experiencing that-which-was-defended-against. There is a profound disequilibration of the person, one which may tax the psyche to its limits, before a new and more benign equilibrium is established. It is the security of one or more relationships of outstanding moral quality which allows this to happen.

A deeper self-acceptance

Therapeutic psychology, as we have noted many times, tends to see the person as inwardly divided; as if there is within the psyche more than one self-like structure, each of which can be a centre of intention. This state has arisen because of the difficulties of living in a milieu where one is continually treated as an object-for-others, rather than as a valid subject. Often this inner division is manifested in self-criticism, self-blame, self-sabotage, self-defeat, self-hatred. Sometimes it is almost possible to imagine the psyche containing an angry, hostile, or vindictive parent figure, who is bearing down upon a frightened, powerless, or rebellious child. The child, maybe, is stunted and crippled, lacking in affection and nurture; and yet this is the most truly personal self, the one who is most able to reach out and make bonds with others. Some of the most serious pathologies of the moral life have this division as their psychological substratum. Behind the 'I ought' and the 'I must' there is a parent who is not a parent: one who is callous, blind, and selfish. The child's 'I want' is bullied into silence.

Psychotherapy addresses this inner division; it is a project to make the psyche whole. In Freudian terms, those parts which are id or superego are to become ego, the truly personal 'I'. For a Jungian, it is a matter of accepting and integrating unacknowledged archetypal presences, and so of moving from the ego to the 'true self'. For a Rogerian, it is the gaining of a greater congruence between the perceived and the ideal self. Even behavioural therapists have begun to point in the same direction; for example with the idea that an increased sense of self-efficacy is the crucial change.[9] That is, a person comes to believe that he or she can function successfully in the world, can make an impact upon others, can bring projects to completion.

The explanation of how this comes about is simple, yet profound. It is a direct inference from experience within the therapeutic relationship. If the moral contract is fulfilled, a person is here accepted unconditionally, and so learns that it is possible to drop the pretences and evasions of everyday life, to lower the barriers that ordinarily get in the way of real communications. The discoveries here are alarming and liberating. No feeling of self-hatred or despair, no disgusting fantasy, no murderous desire will be the ground for censure or rejection; they are simply part of the psychological truth.

In this way some of those destructive beliefs and scripts which were taken on during the period of pre-operational thought can be reversed:

> When I express my desires, I am criticized or crushed; therefore my desires are wicked.'
> 'I am male, and therefore strong and decisive.'
> 'I am female, and therefore dependent and stupid.'
> 'I am continually hurt and violated; therefore I will maintain a secret self, immune from all injury through contact with the world.'

It is not just that the false logic of such pseudo-syllogisms is open to exposure. It is that the environment is so markedly different that a person begins to feel 'intuitively' that they are not correct. A new sense of self-hood is acquired, underpinned by different psycho-logic. Its core is a single proposition: 'I am accepted as I am; therefore I am acceptable.' And around this are generated that set of 'good feelings', that sense of inner abundance, which ideally would form a child's pre-conscious moral knowledge (cf. page 118). This restoration of the person is the homely, earthy counterpart to the idea of divine forgiveness; and psychologically it would seem that without it any idea of the grace of God is no more than a theological charade.

The healing of inner division proceeds by a strange dialectic.

The therapist is well aware of the conflict between different self-like structures within the other; can often see the self-defeating knots in which he or she is entangled; senses the struggle between dishonesty and evasion on the one hand, truth and authenticity on the other. And yet the therapist addresses the other as a unity, as if there is already an integrated person, strong and whole. This encounter, then, is not like a typical medical appointment, where the patient is often objectified into a machine with various defects. It is, rather, a meeting between an I and a Thou, and in this context the need for division and masquerade gradually disappears. A sense of inner unity becomes part of the lived experience; and, if all goes well, is taken forward into everyday life.

Paradoxically, this kind of relationship, which so resolutely abstains from all moralizing judgement, is one which is required to meet the most rigorous moral criteria. When it does so, here is the epitome of that respect for persons, fairness, truthfulness, and promise-keeping that make up the stuff of what is commonly meant by morality. But further, if the therapist's own psychological (and moral) work has been properly done, a place is provided where a person can simply *be*, unguarded and unashamed, without having to carry the burdens of imposed projections, without being perceived through the filter of another's unmet needs. How else could the defences be lowered, which gave protection in a hostile and demanding world? How else could the chaos of previously unacknowledged feelings be allowed into the experiential frame? How else would it be possible to acknowledge that new and at first deeply unflattering self-image which comes near to truth; and yet which is, unexpectedly, the starting point for growth and change? A therapeutic relationship, then, in its uncompromising regard for personhood and its resolute pursuit of psychological truth, has moral qualities that are conspicuously lacking in the everyday world. The defences arose, the whole inauthentic way of being developed, precisely because this kind of relationship was absent or in short supply. That is why psychotherapy is sometimes characterized as re-parenting, or as a cure by love.[10]

A shift of identification

This aspect of therapeutic change has been given rather less attention than the first two. It is more subtle, and is less readily grasped within the cultural patterns of the western world, so insistent that the intellect alone is the ultimate source of truth. It is a final rejection of Platonism, with its postulate of a pure, rational soul, separate from the material world, immune from its changes and chances. It is a recovery from the psychology implicit in Descartes' *cogito*. For therapeutic change brings a recovery of many feelings and emotions that were lost; in a sense it is a re-entry into that world of affectivity which for many people faded with the passing of childhood, and the acquisition of the consciousness of the merchant or the scientist. A large new landscape of feelings, parts bleak and desolate, parts wild and tempestuous, parts lush and verdant, gradually becomes familiar. As a result, a person comes increasingly to a self-identification as a sentient, rather than as a purely thinking, being. The psyche is discovered in something of its wholeness, and rational thought is appreciated as only one of its functions.

In a sense, this shift of identification is a return to the body, or a recognition in experience of the unity between mind and body. There is a movement downwards,

> a reduction of stress, particularly in the region of the eyes and mouth and neck (as if one were at last letting them go), a progressive lowering of one's centre of gravity (as if losing one's head were finding one's heart, and guts, and feet, which are now rooted in the Earth), a striking downward shift of one's breathing (as if it were a belly function) and in fact a general come-down (as if the good things one had vainly strived after in the heights were awaiting one in the depths).

> (Harding 1986: 55).

As with the first two aspects of therapeutic change, this shift is no simple matter. It is not, in the sense of a long tradition in social psychology, a mere attitude change; an alteration of content, but within the same modality. It is deeply radical, much more risky and demanding. For when a person remains, tacitly, a Platonist, with assurance being grounded primarily in conscious, rational thought, it is possible to maintain some sense of being in control, and of travelling over well-mapped territory. Everyday life brings conflicts and difficulties, of course, and many fraught decisions, including the resolution of 'moral dilemmas'; but reason gives a kind of mastery, and ultimately (for the cognitively well-developed) there are principles to fall back on. If, however, a person rejects reason as the mature and exclusive guide, and takes a place in the world again as a sentient being, there may at first be a terribly disturbing disorganization. The flattering illusion of control and competence is shattered. It becomes necessary to accept the extent of inner chaos, to acknowledge the truth that we are fragmented, distorted, conflict-ridden, and (even in our most rational and 'principled' moments) deeply unreliable. This was the uncomfortable truth which the founders of the bourgeois era attempted to evade, when they advanced the notion of the unitary subject; when they cleared the streets of all who were mad or vagrant, subjecting abnormality and folly to the 'great confinement'. Therapeutic change requires this admission; this re-admission of the feelings and emotions as the centre of one's being. Perhaps some of the so-called 'negative therapeutic outcomes' arise because this is too difficult, or too threatening, or because at this point the holding environment is not sufficiently secure. Now rational thought is not to be abandoned, but it must take a lower and humbler place. The truth will be grasped after, rather than before or in spite of, the re-integration of bodily and sensuous life. Values emerge from desires that are known and reflected upon by one who is in the process of acquiring a new kind of self-knowledge; but if these values are genuinely personal and not merely second-hand, they still belong to the modality of desire.

Psychotherapy never offered a panacea, a route to instant bliss, or a recipe for a life immune to pain. All Freud held out to those who would receive his 'cathartic treatment' was the replacement of hysterical misery by ordinary unhappiness; his assumption being that some might value this exchange, since they would have more insight and resources for putting their lives to rights. The therapeutic process simply provides a path towards a more sensitive, rich, and honest experience of life, in its wide range of comic and tragic possibilities. In going beyond the rather narrow feeling and expression rules of the culture, a person ultimately cannot pick and choose. Either he or she goes forward to explore this territory, including its dark and terrifying features, or must withdraw. As Blake[11] put it:

Man was made for Joy and Woe
And when this we rightly know
Through the world we safely goe.

So therapy works towards the formation and enhancement of persons as sentient beings. The English language here runs into difficulties, perhaps betraying a cultural deficit. The French have the word *'ressentir'*, which carries a much stronger meaning than mere feeling. It means to feel, not naïvely, but with a knowing and responsible awareness. The shift of identification which we have been examining, then, may be said to be one towards *ressentience.*

Therapeutic change has been characterized here as a process involving an enlargement of the experiential frame, a greater self-acceptance, and a shift in the ground of knowing and being, towards the feelings and the body. Although, as we have seen, it is a move away from simplistic trust in our rational and logical capabilities, it does nevertheless involve the intellect most deeply. The intellect is needed, not to create new abstract theories, but to gain a grasp of what is happening and what has happened: to see beyond the immediate phenomena, to situate them in their broader context. For example, if a person has a general tendency to criticize others, or suffers from an irrational sense of panic, it gives some freedom simply to understand how these dispositions originated. Here concrete thinking is something of a liability; a mode that is more flexible, less context-bound, is required. It does not necessarily require abstractions. But it does involve letting go those defensive and often concrete explanations by which behaviour is sometimes justified: 'I'm naturally critical', 'I'm just a panicky sort of person', and so on. There is some similarity here to formal-operational thought, in the transcendence of the concrete, whether this is expressed in everyday trait theory or even psychiatric jargon. However, there is none of that separation of cognition and affect on which Piaget placed so much emphasis and which, he believed, provided the basis for all truly scientific thought.

Thus there is no question of a flight from reason, or of being subject to the tyranny of raw emotion. We are dealing, rather, with the development of a kind of unity between thought and feeling that scarcely has a recognized place in the life of our major institutions. In moral terms, a person is moving towards a synthesis of love and understanding for which our culture does not even have a concept; the word which comes nearest, when it is used in translation from oriental traditions, is 'enlightenment'. This (with respect to Piaget) would be the true *prise de conscience*, that 'conscious realization' after which nothing can be the same again (cf. page 132). It is indeed an intellectual act, an intellectual process; but paradoxically, this is the very point at which a mere intellectualism is transcended.

Therapy, as we have seen at several points, works at a profoundly moral level. This point now needs a little expansion. Initially the relationship is highly asymmetric; one person is a trained professional, an experienced healer, or whatever, while the other is a needy client or patient. There is an analogy with the parent and the dependent child. Therapy succeeds in so far as this asymmetry is overcome. Through trust and dependence, a person gradually becomes independent; through being knowingly weak and inadequate, becomes strong. Deference, submissiveness, a sense of inferiority in the relationship, even an urge to 'look after' the therapist, are all part of the broader agenda, to be worked on in a mutual project. As transference occurs, the therapist is apprehended through the gross refractions brought about by need; eventually he or she is encountered again more realistically, as a person in his or her own right. There is a sense in which the journey is complete when each party is able to accept the worth, strength, and vulnerability of the other, on an equal basis. The therapeutic process, as characterized here, thus equilibrates into a paradigm case of mutual respect, which Piaget saw as the true desideratum. In short, it may be considered as one of moral restoration.

All this implies not only skill but also a heavy moral responsibility upon the therapist. It is far more than a matter of 'selling love for money'.[12] One who is receiving therapy is disclosing his or her innermost secrets, exposing the points of greatest vulnerability. This means placing enormous trust in the therapist; it may be the first time that such a trust has ever been risked. If the therapist should fail at this point and reject the other, perhaps because of unacknowledged feelings of disgust or anger, or reactions such as envy or fear – and, regrettably, stories of this are not difficult to find – the outcome may be disastrous. One who has been betrayed so deeply may have received the final confirmation that no human being can be trusted: there is no moral world.

Two Types of Moral Stance

Concern for others was drummed into me as a child, so that I was permanently guilty of not doing it, as well as unaware how to, because it was all words and not demonstrated by my parents, who actually endlessly criticized others who were in dire circumstances (typical Tory attitude to blame the poor and sick for being poor and sick). So this sort of concern for others is not only useless but self-destructive. I don't think I really learned to value and truly feel concern for others until I understood my own feelings better and was able to value them and myself.

These words were written by a woman in her fifties, who had gone some way down the therapeutic path. They suggest a kind of change that is not captured within the psychology of morality as we have it at present, but yet which may be crucial. It can be epitomized in terms of two types of moral stance, related to the concept of alienation discussed in Chapter 3.

The first is that of a person who is extremely alienated; whose experiential frame is narrow, whose psyche is divided, who is a stranger to his or her own life as a sentient being. Its essence may be summed up as follows:

I do not know who I am,
I do not know what I want or feel,
But I have some vague and uneasy promptings about what I ought to do.

Some of those who present themselves for counselling or psychotherapy in their late teens or early twenties clearly reveal this stance. Part of their problem is the existential one of discovering and creating their own personal way of life, rather than following the mores of the groups to which they belong, in a very understandable bid for acceptance. Also, their moral outlook depends to a large degree upon precepts and injunctions taken in from others, but without real assimilation. For some, an over-moralization is a central part of the problem. Indeed, as we have seen, it is perfectly possible for a person to become a clever moral judge while remaining in a state of extreme alienation; to recognize moral sophistry as a life-denying game, and an evasion of real encounter with others, might be a definite therapeutic advance.

There is, in contrast to this, a moral stance which entails a much greater degree of awareness, both of self and others. Its fundamental ground is that kind of interpersonal relationship in which a person is accepted, and his or her experience validated: that which is epitomized in therapy. The essence of this stance may be summed up as follows:

I am beginning to know who I am,
I am beginning to know what I want and feel,
And I *choose* (recognizing the validity both of others and myself) the way in which I am going to live.

There is a crucial difference between the two stances. With the first there is certainly a kind of moral concern; indeed, it might even be an obsession. But somehow this concern is not genuine. It does not come 'from the heart', nor does it touch others deeply; it has something of the 'driven creature' about it. In contrast, the second stance might be far less obviously moralistic. However, the person who holds it has become sufficiently in touch with his or her own embodied life, sufficiently integrated, sufficiently free from unacknowledged 'noise' (including the moral cacophony to which so many people are subject), to begin to attend to others with what some therapists call 'free attention', to experience them with less distortion, and so help to create a 'moral space'. At last it might be possible to follow the precept 'Feel the consciousness of each person as your own consciousness. So, leaving aside concern for self, become each being.'

It must be said, however, that much that passes today as therapy falls far short of these ideals. Some of the more naïve and ill-considered practices, which claim to offer an easy road to stress-free living and the achievement of personal goals, are under-written by an ideology of self-seeking individualism that reflects the crudest aspects of bourgeois economics.

I know who I am,

I know what I want and feel,
And now I am going to do my utmost to get it.

Whether or not this is an advance on the alienated stance we
first identified is debatable. Possibly something like it is a necessary
stage that a person must go through, a kind of recapitulation of
early life, in order to 'come home' to a true morality. Desire must
first be recognized, and deprivation taken into account, or they
may become demonic. A person who remains in 'therapeutic
egoism', whether as 'unblocked manager' or as 'assertive woman',
is little more than a needy and greedy infant; but with greater
resources than an infant for gratifying desire, and greater skill in
the manipulation of others. Therapeutic ideology, then, is
disastrously in error when it portrays the naked pursuit of
self-interest as the goal.

Perhaps all this sheds some light on the question of apparent
regression in the level of moral judgement in late adolescence and
early adulthood; a phenomenon which caused great difficulty for
Kohlberg's theory, as we have seen, and out of which came
Gilligan's work on an ethic of care. Furthermore, it is possible to
make some sense of what moral development might mean during
the course of adult life, a topic which has been generally neglected.
Adult morality, or so it seems, is constructed from having to deal
with reality in all its conflicts, limitations, and disappointments; in
the honouring of long-standing ties and obligations; in the
continuing recognition that there are no ideal solutions. For some,
at least, such morality is underpinned by a kind of thinking that
has been termed post-formal, one which allows and accepts
contradiction.[13] In terms of our discussion here, what appears to
be occurring during adult life is some degree of 'therapeutic'
change. Simply through mutual help, some people come to make
greater sense of their experience, and achieve a better integration
between their different selves. In maturity this becomes far more
important than the smooth articulation of theory, or making
abstract moral judgements.

Depth psychology and morality: the confluence

This examination of therapy has pointed in many places towards
its moral implications. The relationship itself meets stringent

moral criteria; the therapist has a heavy responsibility; as a result of therapy, a person may be able to appreciate others with less distortion and projection, and so have a more genuine concern for their well-being. But depth psychology and morality are even more fundamentally related, in a way that does not commonly seem to be understood. Two main concepts concern us here, the one psychological and the other moral: integration and integrity.

What is meant by integrity? In the weakest sense, a person of integrity is said to be one who lives consistently according to some accepted code of behaviour: keeping appointments punctually, being faithful to a partner, being honest in business dealings, and so on. A shade more strongly, integrity is often associated with standing by convictions and principles, even if they are unpopular. These ideas, however, do not go far enough. As Taylor (1981) has suggested, 'the person possessing integrity is one who "keeps the inmost self intact", whose life is "of a piece", whose self is whole and integrated' (p. 144). Integrity involves generally representing oneself to others with truth and sincerity, honouring with real commitment the professions one makes in public. (There may, however, be times when a person 'truly deceives' – for example in resisting oppression.) Integrity also involves giving due respect to one's own biography; a person cannot remain intact and of a piece and yet suddenly cut off all connections with the past, in some attempt to re-fashion life *de novo*. Integrity, then, is not a content-full virtue, like courage or generosity; but it might be regarded as the content-free substratum of all virtue. In her account Taylor is virtually on the ground of depth psychology, although she is dealing purely with concepts, and does not touch on the process whereby integrity might be attained.

Therapy, on its part, is designed to bring about integration in a fragmented psyche, self-deceived and torn apart by rival motivations: that is, there should, ideally, be a single centre of desire and value, a mind and body that are in harmony together, a unity and truthfulness in dealing with the many conflicting demands of a difficult world. As we have seen, it is an exacting and even terrifying process, against which a person may find enormously strong inner resistances. To go through it requires at least one relationship in which a person is taken with the utmost seriousness, and is 'held' with strength while exposing the extremes of vulnerability. If this is to be the case, the therapist, or

210

whoever stands in that position, must be truly and consistently 'available' to the other, open in his or her own communication, free from tendencies to use the situation in working out unfinished private dramas. In other words, the very quality in the therapist that enables the process to go forward is one of integrity, springing from his or her own movement towards integration.

So then, anyone who is sincerely committed, in so far as a divided person can be, to making the therapeutic journey, must also desire integrity on the part of those who are to be the helpers. (He or she may not know it clearly in consciousness, but it follows by an unassailable psycho-logic.) Unless this integrity is present to a considerable degree, the journey will be aborted in its early stages. Further, integration requires a kind of general openness to experience, an awareness and acceptance of others, that must necessarily be accompanied by a greater vulnerability. The psychic defences were a kind of protective armour; anyone who relaxes them is the more liable to violation. How, then, can a person continue to live according to the therapeutic ideal in a world that is often superficial and corrupt, which is constantly pressing the psyche back towards disintegration and defence? In the long term, it would only appear to be possible if everyone with whom there is serious engagement were also moving towards a life that had integrity.

This is as far as argument on psychological grounds seems to lead. However, a further step can be taken, since there is a crucial sense in which all human beings are made of the same stuff, suffer the same kind of anguish, experience similar joys. It is to wish and hope for that same integrity for all persons, within their own particular cultural frame. In short, to seek an inner truth and integration for oneself is of necessity to desire integrity on the part not only of a few close others, but of a much larger circle of friends, colleagues, and acquaintances. But if these, then why not all? At this point psycho-logic and moral argument flow together into a single stream.

Chapter Eight

SOCIAL JUSTICE AND SOCIAL FABRIC

In this book I have tried to spell out some of the consequences of taking depth psychology seriously in moral theory. My own values have, inevitably, coloured my account, and for this I make no apology. I believe that it is better to write from a position of engagement than to remain, supposedly, detached; for detachment itself turns out to be a committed position, albeit a dull and dry one. In this last chapter I want to compare the view I have been putting forward with others that are well known, and to explore briefly what seem to be some of the social implications.

In trying to understand how human beings can have concern for others, the heart of the matter seems to me to be this. If an individual has been generally confirmed and validated as a person, right from the beginning, it is 'natural' to experience a concern for some others, to have some inkling of them as ends in themselves; and it may be possible to extrapolate from that into a broader benevolence. If, however, this is not the case, it is exceedingly difficult to transcend selfishness consistently, to see and value other persons for their own sake. One whose relational experience has been deeply unsatisfactory will be, 'in the depths', too preoccupied to have space for others. He or she will, perhaps, attempt to fill the gaping hole of insecurity by making use of them; or try to find personal affirmation in a disguised way, through the pursuit of prestige, power, or material possessions; or construct an elaborate false self, even one which is, apparently, that of a saint, guru, or hero. For any individual, 'true morality' is a fragile competence. It emerges gradually when there is a climate of respect and acceptance, and when the general sense of threat is lowered. But under conditions of continued privation, or when threat looms large, a person will tend to retreat into that solipsism where his or her own need is overwhelming, and where others are seen through massive projections and distortions. To some extent this may be true of all individuals; perhaps a crucial difference is the threshold at which the threat becomes so great as to induce solipsistic withdrawal. In these terms, 'rational-altruistic' characters, who may be some 10 to 20 per cent in a contemporary industrial-capitalist society, are those for whom that threshold is very high.

Psychotherapy, despite its many failures and corruptions as at present practised, seems to point to a whole dimension of experience into which western moralism has scarcely dared to venture. Piaget, in comparing moralities, had one main bipolar construct, ranging from unilateral to mutual respect. His parameter here is one of structured domination; unilateral respect applies to conditions where this is considerable, but not absolutely crushing; mutual respect applies ideally to conditions where it is zero, where two or more persons meet each other on equal terms (see Figure 8.1).

Figure 8.1

dimension of structured domination

very high ———————————————————— zero

unilateral respect   mutual respect

However, there is also another dimension, with which we have been concerned in different ways throughout this book. A term for it would be 'expressivity'. At one end of this dimension there is extreme inhibition and defence; at the other there is that openness on the basis of which persons may freely express their desires, emotions, and feelings. This can have dire consequences, but is also carries the possibility of a deep understanding and validation of persons. Piaget seems to have been insensitive to this dimension, or unaware of it. Possibly he had reacted against it; for his predecessor in the chair at the Sorbonne was Merleau-Ponty, the apostle of intersubjectivity.

When the two dimensions are combined as orthogonal axes, they map out four different kinds of 'moral situation', as shown in Figure 8.2.

Figure 8.2

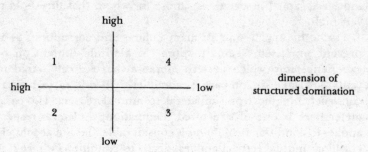

dimension of expressivity

```
                      high
                       |
         1             |            4
                       |
high  -----------------+----------------  low        dimension of
                       |                              structured domination
         2             |            3
                       |
                      low
```

The first quadrant, where structured domination and expressivity are both high, crudely represents situations where those who have power are unrestrained in exploitation, ruthlessness, cruelty, and greed. Of course, it is precisely this kind of situation which almost all that passes in the name of morality is designed to prevent. The second quadrant, of high structured domination and low expressivity, represents the situation commonly found in moderately prosperous feudal societies, in settled hierarchies, in authoritarian families, and the like. There is considerable restraint and inhibition on the part of both of those who do and do not have power. Confrontation is generally avoided, or the possibility of it not even considered; perhaps, pre-consciously, it is known to be too risky. If conflict were brought out into the open, the settled but inequitable situation might be overthrown. Morality here usually takes the form of those 'oughts' and 'rights' which give people general guidance, but avoid real meeting on specific issues. The third quadrant, where both structured domination and expressivity are low, represents the situation towards which almost all egalitarian theories within western moralism aspire, in their different ways. These are the theories that underpin the greater part of our existing psychology of morality, in the succession from Kant to Rawls. As in quadrant 2, individuals are expected to be relatively inhibited and restrained; stating their 'interests', perhaps, or even engaging in moral dialogue, but alienated in a depth-psychological sense. Morality is moulded by the category of 'ought', or occasionally of 'rights'; the scope is different from that in quadrant 2, because it now includes all persons, who are accorded value not because of their social positions, but simply because of being human.

It is the fourth quadrant, however, towards which psycho-therapy points, as the heartland of concern for others: that is, a form of morality which is indeed one of equality and mutual respect, but one where inhibition is greatly lowered, and where persons are free to express themselves as sentient beings. This is not a Utopian fantasy, but a living fact of experience; however, at present not taken up into a broad conception of morality, but confined to miniature and insulated contexts. Many primal societies have tolerated a much lower level of inhibition, a much higher degree of expressivity, than those which claim to be 'civilized'. They cannot easily be fitted on to the map, but perhaps may be viewed as oscillating between quadrants 1 and 4, depending in part on whether or not they were subject to scarcity and external threat.

Why has the fourth quadrant been so little experienced within western society during the last 500 years, and hardly ever been explored conceptually by western moralists? Presumably because it was thought to be far too dangerous. If human beings were allowed to express themselves without restraint, so it was believed, pandemonium would ensue, and social life would not be able to continue. Psychotherapy seems to show, however, that although there are demons (within the therapists, at times, as well as their clients), human nature is not so greatly to be feared; also, that there are ways of possessing 'character' that are not grounded primarily in inhibition. Is it possible that at least since the breakdown of medieval society, and perhaps for longer, there has been a monumental confusion? Is it possible that human nature as manifested under conditions of permanent, and high, structured domination, with all its concomitants of latent hatred and violence, has often been mistakenly assumed to be human nature 'as it is'? The truth, surely, is that human nature manifests itself in many forms; is dialectically constructed (as Piaget might have said)

215

differently according to the social conditions. There has always been a tendency for those who have privilege in societies with deeply structured domination to advance the view that human nature is 'essentially' self-seeking and untrustworthy, and therefore to be curbed. Also, it seems, some egalitarian moralists have inherited similar fears, in views of human nature they have taken for granted.

This is not to argue that the moral situation represented by quadrant 4 would ever be problem-free; nor is it to suggest, like some romantics, that there is an 'essential' human nature that is unambiguously loving, courageous, and truthful. The point is, rather, that in the situation represented by quadrant 4 there is the greatest chance for human nature to manifest itself benignly, for the fears and vulnerabilities that underlie so much of our moral failure to be taken care of. The possibility must be considered, then, that a morally mature person might not be one whose virtue consisted of a well-organized set of inhibitions and defences, but one who, on the ground of his or her relational experience, is singularly open and undefended; and whose integrity does indeed involve 'keeping the inmost self intact'.

Figure 8.2 may be looked at in another way, in terms of 'moral space' (cf. page 98). Quadrant 1 allows virtually none, since it is supremely the domain of oppression and exploitation. Quadrant 2 allows it in only a very limited sense, because of the many vested interests, and all the distortions of subjectivity which are involved in high levels of structured domination. Quadrant 3 allows a good deal more moral space, because it represents situations in which people are (superficially, at least) treated as equals; the problem of alienation, however, has not been adequately dealt with. Quadrant 4 represents a vast enlargement of moral space, because here a much fuller range of experience is opened up. Perhaps one great moral challenge of the present time is to explore this area. We know and understand it only a very little through psycho-therapeutic practice; and this is itself often marred and corrupted through involvement in the cash nexus, or the inadequacies of welfare provision.[1]

There are hints of a historical succession here, which suggests that it is important to look carefully at the societal context. In this we are on the classic ground of Durkheim and Piaget; for they both saw, in their different ways, that the lived morality of individuals

216

was closely connected to their experience of the pattern of social life. We are also on the ground of such thinkers as Marx and Habermas, and their vast project of offering a sociologally based diagnosis of the modern age. Postmodern culture is now coming into the ascendant, with its celebration of a life that is lived in fragments, its abandonment of any concept of society, its flight from any critical understanding of problems of truth and justice in the world-system. The moralism that we have known for the last four centuries now seems ideological; not so much in details of its content, but in its very separation off from a broader range of human concerns. Possibly the larger moral space represented by quadrant 4 points to a way forward; to an enhancement of subjectivity and intersubjectivity, through which even cultural fragmentation may eventually be overcome to some degree.

Immediately, there is a methodological problem. How, when we are ourselves members of a society that seems in some respects to be corrupt and pathological, can we begin to criticize it coherently? As many theorists have realized, the critic's own outlook may be permeated by the thought-forms of the very thing that is to be criticized. Utopias quickly take on a dated character, because they so strongly reflect and replicate the society they were trying to transcend. The tactic of a long succession of liberal scholars has been to attempt to draw up rational criteria for a just society. But the difficulty is always that some arbitrary assumptions are brought in, as can be seen particularly in the case of Rawls (see page 32). A similar move has been made by certain psychologists, taking up Freud's suggestion that whole cultures or civilizations might have malignant tendencies. Fromm, for example, drew up a list of supposedly universal human needs, and on this basis constructed a 'normative humanism' which gave him a standpoint from which to criticize what he called the 'pathology of normalcy' in modern industrial societies.[2] All these approaches are helpful to a degree, and each puts some features of the present predicament into sharp focus. Rawls shows clearly, for example, the moral stupidity of all brash elitism, and Fromm the tragedy of loneliness in the age of mass culture. The problem is that these accounts are more culture-bound than their proponents care to admit, generally reflecting the life-style of a generous-minded and liberal bourgeois. In fact there is no point of Olympian detachment from which to mount a social critique.

217

There is, however, a humbler tactic, one which is much more candid about its limitations. This is simply to spell out the implications of some praxis – some form of committed action – that is already going on within a society, and which points in some way towards its possibilities for transformation. Critique of this kind is knowingly culture-bound. If this is a drawback, it is also, and in another sense, an advantage. For the critique is already grounded in work that is making for change, and beginning to create a different kind of culture. Of all psychological praxis of the present time, it is psychotherapy that looks the most promising in this respect. I recognize that as a lived reality it often falls far short of its own ideals; its moral requirements are most exacting, and it carries the lure of power. Nevertheless, it does uncover deep-rooted disorder not just within individuals but within society. In what follows I have an approach similar to David Smail in some of his recent writings,[3] and to Laing some years ago,[4] although my viewpoint is different from both of theirs.

As Figure 8.2 implies, there is a sense in which the root cause of all the problems which are common to moral theory and to psychotherapy is the abuse of power, generally by those who are blind to what they are doing. The sensibilities, the first moral intuitions, of some infants were ignored or crushed by adults and older children; in such a predicament, it was necessary for the growing person to construct some way of being in order to survive – however destructive its long-term effects. On a larger scale, there are many points within contemporary society where power is imposed; ultimately, although only in exceptional circumstances, it is backed by force. Such power is pervasive, penetrating even to structure of 'normal' experience.[5] Familiarized to oppression and accepting the privileges of others as in some way natural, this is the ground for members of a subordinate group to make their construction of themselves and the world. Conversely, those who are in a dominant position are also damaged; but it is only when circumstances turn disastrously against them that they tend to seek out therapeutic help. In understanding the psychology of domination the paradigm cases of today are colonialism and apartheid. Yet domination is also pervasive within the structure of the liberal democracies, on the basis of class, gender, race, and age. If its gross effects are muted, its psychological consequences are plain to anyone who has been involved in therapeutic work.

This whole question has been dealt with most sensitively by Jean Baker Miller (1976), with many examples from her own work as a depth psychologist. Her particular topic is gender, but the principles of her analysis have a much wider application. The members of a dominant group within society, if they are to retain the position of advantage which came to them simply by privilege, cannot risk the development of their feelings, or they might become sensitive to the pain of those whom they are oppressing. A little cosmetic charity, the occasional co-optation of a subordinate person to their ranks, is all that they can afford. Their proud and assertive self-presentation, however, covers a deeper insecurity, because of a lack of intimate validation by others. The subordinates, accustomed to positions of low status, and identifying with 'inferiors', acquire a low esteem for themselves and others in like position. Continually exploited and denied a voice, they carry a weight of unexpressed resentment. Their own life as sentient beings is often poorly developed, in part because they are bound to give so much attention to messages from others. If they were to allow their feelings to consciousness they would be faced with the colossal task of challenging the whole social order within which they are oppressed. Thus domination both breeds deep psycho-pathology, and creates patterns of defence that work powerfully against therapeutic change. This is the most fundamental obstacle to the long-lasting growth of persons as moral beings.

The existence of endemic patterns of privilege and power in society is, of course, no new phenomenon. We are the inheritors of the injustices of previous eras, and may in certain respects be faring better. At the very least, there is now a widespread respect for the personhood of children, and at least some awareness of racist, sexist, and ageist discrimination. There are also some organizations which work successfully, but without being structured on hierarchical lines. A blind and callous moralism, which tells the powerless that they ought to remain within their 'station', can no longer be recognized widely as valid, although it is still used as a cynical tactic. There is some ground for optimism about the present, but no hint that there was once a golden age.

Therapeutic psychology suggests that the industrial-capitalist societies of today have their own peculiar patterns of psychopathology. Virtually all the major institutions, both in their principles of organization and their preferred forms of practice, work against the development of persons as sentient beings, and provide conditions where moral space is likely to be very restricted. Most formal organizations are run on hierarchical lines; their morality at best, approximates to that of quadrant 2. Technical advance has not only replaced some of the repetitive, boring, and dangerous aspects of production, but also destroyed many of the sensuous and relational aspects of craft work. Currently there seems to be an epidemic of stress-related illness, both physical and psychological, arising from the extreme competitiveness and general dehumanization of the workplace. The greater part of mainstream education is geared to the training of the cognitions, while forcing the sensibilities into a marginal place. Medicine often takes an approach to persons comparable to that of the engineer to a machine; personal encounter is often minimized, and there is little sense of healing. The selection and training of nurses is becoming increasingly intellectualized, while relatively little attention is being given to the skills of care.[6] Even psychiatry, with its present emphasis on technical intervention, shows only superficial interest in the patient's distress, and gives virtually no place for intersubjectivity.

Furthermore, many aspects of everyday life have a strongly schizoid character, so pervasive that it is hard to recognize except through the contrasting experience of a milieu in which person-hood in affirmed.[7] People move quickly from one scene to another, often without being able to make psychological connections. A false sense of agency – derived from action not with persons but upon objects and money – is installed. Compulsive activity in pursuit of entertainment and stimulation, together with an unending acquisition of commodities, is used to compensate for an inner sense of emptiness and deadness. Public life is a kind of charade, conducted on the basis of enormously inflated false selves. The social atmosphere is suffused by a vague militarism, with 'nuclear terror' in the background; the feelings are repressed, but recur in many people's dreams.[8] Capitalism itself, the economic base underpinning all that occurs in culture and psychology, tends to operate by turning all things into commodities, and by treating persons ultimately as mere things, as 'factors of production'. If there is a crisis in capitalism which underlies the postmodern predicament, it is in part that there is so little left to commodify.[9]

This is the social context of the current upsurge in psychotherapy, and the popularity of any activity that purports to engage seriously with the interpersonal. Each of the points that I have mentioned has its reflection in the distresses that are presented in psychotherapy. Thus it is not on the basis of a detached analysis or of Utopian speculation that this dire list of pathological symptoms is brought forward. Is it surprising, then, that so many people, in whom perhaps the foundations of concern for others were securely laid, become 'damaged and derailed' in facing the demands of life today, marred and maimed in their moral capabilities? Of these only a few – and generally from those who are not the most disadvantaged – cross the threshold of the therapist's door. They are but the symptoms of an enormous social pathology, one which is moral at its very core.

The therapeutic process points to an extremely private and sensitive journey, accomplished in a special kind of relationship, and opening up the possibility of a new way of being in the world. That world, however, is profoundly and pervasively in opposition to the therapeutic: not so much deliberately, as through its everyday practices and its massed psychic defences. How, then, is a person who has experienced to some degree the process of moral restoration engendered by therapy to continue along the same path? If he or she returns to the very pattern of life that produced the sense of ill-being, it is likely that there will be a gradual reversion to the former state of affairs; in Freud's terms, there will be a 'return of the repressed'. As yet the evidence for sustained well-being as a result of psychotherapy is not so strong (cf. page 195). On the other hand, a person is likely to consolidate the therapeutic changes if he or she can enter, or possibly create from its beginnings, a social milieu in which the kind of respect that is epitomized in therapy is present. Putting it another way, therapy can do little more than minimal repair work, and that for a minority. Its real social significance is that it could point to a new understanding of morality, and be the harbinger of a different kind of culture.

In contemporary western society such a culture is scarcely to be found, except in fragments: in some families of exceptional quality, perhaps; in a few small communities and co-operatives; in groups of co-workers where the conditions allow the presence of 'moral space'. Generally, it would seem, the main institutions are moving away from this kind of culture, strengthening the structures of domination, and even arrogantly asserting the validity of privilege. Paradoxically, there seem to be two places where something approximating to a therapeutic culture is perfectly acceptable, even if not always actualized to a high degree. One is the playgroup for very young children, who (ideally) are subjected to no pressures to work or to perform for external rewards; they simply have the chance to explore and play with others, with moral space being guaranteed by benevolent parent figures. The other is the hospice for those who are terminally ill and know it. Here there is a vast difference from the conventional hospital, with its typically desperate measures to avoid letting anyone be honest emotionally about the reality of death. There is a kind of gentleness, a relaxation, and even a sense of humour, in the face of suffering and mortality.

The view that I have been suggesting in this book, centring on the idea of 'moral space', is in many respects very different from the kind proposed by those liberal theorists who try to do everything in advance, so to speak, through an achievement of pure reason. It is closer to that of theorists such as Habermas, who place their emphasis on the procedures which might lead to solutions felt to be just by all parties. Also Habermas, in contradicting a superficial celebration of postmodernism, points to the failure of the modern age to achieve its highest aspiration: of bringing the material benefits of industrial technology to all, and of drawing together into one communicative field the discourses of science, morality, and aesthetics.[10] What I have tried to do, however, is to spell out some of the consequences of taking depth psychology seriously; if this is implicit in Habermas' project, it is arguable that he has not done so with any rigour or thoroughness. Some, at least, of the deepest problems of communication are those arising from a dearth of 'moral space'.

Moving back on to more strictly psychological terrain, it seems that there might be a danger in trying to make a fetish of social justice, in the belief that a good society must conform to some logical criterion of fairness. The more serious problem, it might be argued, is the creation of a social fabric that allows an abundance of moral space, a fabric that is based on trust between persons who recognize, despite all their outward differences, the equal value of their personhood. It is simply that pervasive forms of domination, and grossly inequitable distributions of the burdens and benefits of social existence, make a healthy social fabric impossible, because of the distortion and corruption of persons that they entail. Social justice, then, according to some theoretical blueprint, is not an ultimate end; rather, the lack of it is to be avoided, because otherwise a moral world is impossible to sustain.

It is striking that the importance of social fabric has been recognized by a succession of conservative and Catholic social theorists,[11] who have had a genuine worry that radical change might break up organic communities, and destroy bonds formed over a long period. Here there is a strong recognition of the social nature of human life, and the fact that our personhood is guaranteed only by relationship with others. What is almost totally missing, however, is a recognition of the damage caused, both to the dominant and the subordinate, by any structure in which there is permanent inequality. Such naïve conservatism, then, is the very seed-bed of fascism; for people are afraid of the fragmentation of social life, and will collude at almost any cost to regain some kind of solidarity. Liberal theories of social justice came as a reaction to the spurious assertion of community, and insisted in their different ways on taking heed to individuals. In making this vital point, however, they have ignored the importance of social fabric. As I have tried to show in another place, one of the most powerful of these theories, that of utilitarianism, self-destructs when its psychological entailments are considered; it is devoid of any conception of relationship, and takes no account at all of those unique ties which give human beings their personhood and identity.[12]

The truth, psychologically, seems to be that human social life needs a high predictability and continuity for there to be a general sense of well-being. Yet unlike most animals, we do not inherit instinctive patterns of behaviour. Putting it crudely and simplistically, there seem to be two rival possibilities. One corresponds to quadrant 2 of Figure 8.2: the imposition of power and control. As Peregrine Worsthorne has written recently in the British *Sunday Telegraph*:

> Egalitarianism and civilization are incompatible. . . . It will be
> a long haul before the re-civilizing process gets under way

again in this country. But a first condition is to recognize that economic inequality is not enough. It may make capitalism work. But for civilization to prosper, social authority must be added to economic power.[13]

The other possibility is mutual trust: light, delicate, fragile, but creating a moral world in which persons can live freely and enhance their powers in collaboration. It was in the context of the former that the western idea of the 'ought' arose, with its strange psychological adhesions. The possibility suggested by quadrant 4 is of a society which would need to make but very little use of oughts; the norm would be for people to communicate openly (and as far as possible face to face) about their felt needs, their past injuries, their present interests and desires.

Maybe it is no coincidence that some of the closest approximations to moral community, as I have suggested, are in institutions which involve the very young and (generally) the weak or old. These are not in the main current of society, and what happens in them probably has few systemic effects. Perhaps, then, an affluent society can allow this existence of moral space with impunity. If, however, morality in the sense that I have suggested, were to become widespread in our institutions, the structure of society would be shaken to its foundations. There would be enormous resistance, not only because of the threat to naked privilege, but because of the activation of all those psychic defences that keep the status quo in being. To trust other persons is, in a sense, risky even under the best of circumstances, since it carries the threat of betrayal, or even of annihilation. For those who have long learned not to trust, but either to dominate or be dominated, it might be too terrifying to face. Perhaps those archaic terrors, associated with what Kleinians call the paranoid-schizoid position, might be reactivated: it would be a colossal task for these to be worked through, and the defences finally lowered. This would be a therapeutic project comparable, in its own way, to the total abandonment of that other apparatus of defence, the system of nuclear weapons.

So moral progress even at the best of times is likely to encounter enormous psychological difficulties. However, history has shown repeatedly that any oppressive movement within a society tends to generate, in due course, a countervailing force, as people use their skill and ingenuity to fashion new ways of staying human. Change in the direction that I have indicated is unlikely to come from those who are highly privileged, even when they have turned in desperation to the therapists to help to ease their stresses. Nor is it likely to come from those who are so crushed that they are caught up in the sheer struggle for survival. It is more probable that it will come from those who do experience some degree of 'moral space', who have sufficient buoyancy and good feeling to wish to enlarge it. Even if that space is contracting within the main institutions at present, it can still grow in the interstices. Perhaps it is largely there that it will be found during the next few years. Concern for others is fragile, as we have seen; but in its presence and growth there is a kind of strength. The structures of concrete and tarmac, so laboriously created by human will, are eventually broken up by wind and rain, by flowers, weeds, and trees.

This seems to me to be the implication of a moral psychology that takes the 'depth' dimension seriously. Inevitably there are political entailments, if its key ideas are carried through. However, I have not offered here even the rudiments of a political theory: simply a brief statement of what might be a psychological grounding for new political thought and action. The task is the slow but infinitely rewarding one of creating social fabric, and hence the dissolution of those inequities which make social fabric impossible to sustain. The alternative is fragmentation, injustice, and imposed authority, with a continuation of horrendous psychopathology; and in the background, the spectre of the police state. Ultimately, then, the moral project suggested by depth psychology is not something to do merely with individuals – their character, their cognitions, or whatever. It is to do with the form of social life; and the existence of mores that are conducive to the valuing of persons, in the full range of their capacities as sentient beings. Today, although there are many discouraging signs, much more insight is available, and a 'therapeutic' discourse has been generated that is not likely to be extinguished. Those perversions of the modernizing project which are embodied both in industrial capitalism and in massive bureaucratic 'socialism' have been increasingly exposed in their sterility. Perhaps now, gradually, more and more more people will discover the deep satisfaction that rests in the simple fact of their intelligent, aware, and feeling humanity; and a lived morality that corresponds to it will be allowed to grow.

NOTES

CHAPTER 1 THE CONSTRUCTION AND USE OF MORAL DISCOURSE

1 Some sociobiological work, at least, grounds morality in our evolutionary inheritance; but it also suggests that 'naturally' it is limited in scope. See Singer (1976), for an optimistic discussion of this topic.
2 Formalists in ethics, such as Hare (1952), suggest that moral concepts can be identified purely by such characteristics as their being prescriptive and universalizable, regardless of their content.
3 In one of my studies (Kitwood 1980), I found this to be the case with about 20 per cent of the teenagers I interviewed. Recently Matthew Plant has explored this, interviewing about 200 members of 'the public' in Bradford city centre. He claims that most of them seemed not to understand questions of the type 'what ought (or should) you do?', re-framing them as 'what would you do?'. About 20 per cent could not engage with such questions at all (personal communication; Ph.D. forthcoming).
4 Wilson (1975) in *Sociobiology* is a classic case. He simply did not sift the literature on the history of war.
5 Glicksman (1956) deals with this question in relation to some of the societies of Africa. We see something similar in the 'festival of fools' in the European Middle Ages.
6 See, for example, the history by Conze (1980).
7 This is the characteristic message of the prophet or prophets Isaiah. The purely ethical content of the teaching, however, was constantly mixed with the threat of Jahweh's anger, and the dire consequence of disobedience.
8 The literature on this topic is now extensive. See, for example, Fisher (1980). Here the stock-breeding aspect is emphasized.
9 This is the agonized cry of Paul of Tarsus, long after his conversion to the Christian faith (Romans 7: 19).
10 The two volumes recently produced by the American Council for Research in Values and Philosophy are a case in point: McLean *et al.*

227

(1986) (mainly philosophical); and Knowles and McLean (1986) (mainly psychological).

11 It was calamitous for several reasons: a succession of bad harvests, with widespread famine; and ecological crisis; the Black Death; the arrival of firearms; and so on. The atmosphere is captured vividly in Eco's novel *The Name of the Rose.*

12 Estimates of the number vary; some authorities put it as high as 6-8 millions. There are several histories, such as that of Murray (1962).

13 This is a topic which has been taken up, in different ways, especially by Easlea (1981).

14 See Quinton (1973). I discuss some psychological problems associated with utilitarianism in my paper in the MOSAIC volume of 1983.

15 Pettit (1980) presents a very lucid comparison of utilitarianism, the theory of rights, and the conception of justice developed by Rawls. I have drawn on his book here.

16 This specific point was made to me by a Chinese person from Hong Kong, who had been a Buddhist, but who later felt much more drawn to the activism of Christianity.

17 Engels gives a very clear account of this in his essay *Socialism, Utopian and Scientific.* I discuss this question in some detail in my paper on Utopianism (1978).

CHAPTER 2 TOWARDS A PSYCHOLOGY OF THE MORAL LIFE

1 This point was made explicitly by Draper (1976), in her account of the hunter-gatherers of the Kalahari.

2 This is an area of research that was pioneered by Bowlby. It seems now that some of his ideas on 'maternal deprivation' were simplistic, but that his core thesis about early loss still stands. See Rutter's *Maternal Deprivation Reassessed* (1972); also Chapter 4 of this book.

3 I am grateful to Chris Henry for pointing me to some of the work in this field. See her paper with Tuxill (1987); also Abelson (1977) and Carruthers *et al.* (1985).

4 The work of Jane Goodall is especially relevant here. One of the films of the chimpanzees she studied shows this very point.

5 See Lyons (1970), chap. 5.

6 The two anthropologists who are most associated with observations of this kind are Margaret Mead and Ruth Benedict. A more recent work, which moves on to similar terrain, is that of Schweder and Levine (1984).

7 See the articles by Samay and Caputo in the collection *Act and Agent,* edited by McLean *et al.* (1986).

8 The cultural construction of emotion is dealt with, in various ways, in several of the works in which Rom Harré is involved. Katz (1984) has a theory which allows both for cultural specificity and for some cross-cultural universals.

9 This point is touched on in several of Leff's writings.

10 In Blake's play *An Island in the Moon* one character (Inflammable Gas) continually and inanely challenges people 'Your Reason? Your Reason?'. Incidentally, this play is a superb example of 'collective monologue' among adults, and was clearly intended as a parody of polite discourse.

11 Here I am drawing, especially, on an African apprehension, as described for example, by Taylor (1968). In India a similar but 'refined' point comes out in the Upanishadic writings: for example, in the proposition that 'he who sees all living beings in himself, and his self in all living beings, can no longer hate'.

12 This point is made explicitly by Shotter (1975), drawing strongly on the ideas of MacMurray concerning the meaning of personhood. It is also near to the heart of the theory of personal knowledge developed by Polanyi in his many writings; Polanyi was, for many years, a research chemist.

13 There is an alternative way of framing what was happening in this experiment, through recognizing that little Albert was struggling, in his own way, to construe the situation. Watson's original experiment is reported in a paper of 1910.

14 Again, this suggests that personal construal is involved. It was in recognition of this kind of evidence that psychologists such as Walter Mischel moved from straightforward social learning theory to a view that takes a number of person variables into account. This point is taken up in the first part of Chapter 7.

15 Little (1972) shows convincingly that a very considerable part of psychology does not meet the reflexivity test. Both behaviourism and crude Freudianism fail disastrously.

16 This comes out especially in the earlier work of Eysenck, and is summed up in his article in Lickona's collection of 1975.

17 Cattell (1963) worked with sixteen such 'personality factors'.

18 Here I am thinking especially of the work of Harré and his colleagues – for example, *Motives and Mechanisms* (1986). Some of this has been strongly resisted by psychologists. Is it because they think it would leave them with no clear place to stand? I don't believe this is the case, when we view psychology primarily as praxis.

19 Sartre insisted that we all have assumptions, anyway. Naïve empiricism does not avoid this problem, but simply remains 'in bad faith'. See Sartre's introduction to his 'sketch' of 1939.

20 Bettelheim (1983) suggests that English readers cannot fully appreciate Freud. He is more homely, earthy, and nearer to the style of a novelist such as Thomas Mann, when read in German.

21 Shotter has taken up some of the problems of cognitive psychology in his MOSAIC paper of 1987.

CHAPTER 3 SENTIENT BEING, MORAL AGENT

1 This striking quotation comes from a short article on Goebbels in *Time* magazine, by Gibbs (1987).

2 'Unconscious fantasy' has connotations of a space that is occupied by strange images; it seems to be less instinct-ridden than Freud's unconscious. See Juliet Mitchell's introduction to her collection of Klein's papers (1986).

3 The latter is an example from an adult's dream; the image is very like certain figures in Bosch's representations of hell.

4 See, for example, the collection of papers edited by Oakley (1985).

5 Freudians have repression; Piagetians have transformation. The memory question is explored by Casey (1980).

6 When Piaget was nearing the end of his life, he had an extended informal conversation with Jean Bringuer. It is here that he commented on his own experience of psychoanalysis.

7 Some of the evidence is reviewed by Epstein (1985). There is a long tradition of empirical work on this topic, going back at least to the work of McCleary and Lazarus (1949).

8 See, for example, Argyle (1987). Goffman, in his work on the presentation of self, says a great deal about the signals people 'give off', referring to the same topic in a different way.

9 For example, Spitz (1965); Mahler *et al.* (1975).

10 Piagetian cross-cultural study is now massive. See, for example, Cole and Bruner (1971). Cohen (1983) looks at some of the key issues in chap. 8 of his book on Piaget.

11 One of the most accessible general histories is that of Aries (1972).

12 There is a danger in focusing too much on the individuals who do these things. Some child psychologists talk of 'couples at risk' (that is, a child and a care-giver); and the whole phenomenon needs to be understood in a social context. Some psychological aspects are covered in the collection edited by Field (1979).

13 This is well treated by Wegner and Vallacher (1977); their term for the third process is 'direct attribution'.

14 See, for example, the very readable story of 'Sybil', by Schreiber (1973).

15 This point was made strongly by Fairbairn (1952), who made a special study of the schizoid disturbance.

16 See Guntrip (1969) and Laing (1960).

17 Personal communication from a citizen of an east European state.

18 There are several standard works, such as that of Maccoby and Jacklin (1974).

19 This came out strongly in my research of 1980. I was surprised at the conservatism of some adolescent groups, especially in relation to gender.

20 This comes from recent research carried out in association with the Carers' National Association. See their publication *Informal Carers* (1988).

21 The starting point here is Jung's own essay on 'The stages of life' (1930); his point has been substantiated in a great deal of therapeutic work, and not only from a Jungian perspective.

22 My estimate (Kitwood 1987) is that at most some 50 per cent of the variance can be explained through neuropathology. If we exclude very mild dementia, the variance explained by neuropathology is very much less.

23 When beginning my research with adolescents (1980), I thought Harré and Secord's point could be taken almost literally; but I found that indirect methods often facilitated better disclosure, at least to a stranger.

24 See, for example, the many writings of C. L. Cooper, such as his work on cancer (1984).

25 This will be taken up in part 1 of Chapter 7, particularly in looking at Mischel's idea of 'cognitive social learning person variables'.

26 See, for example, the article by Bailey (1980) in the *Journal of Moral Education*, and the later controversy on this topic found in that journal.

27 This theme is developed a little by Rich (1980), and it resonates with a large volume of work on 'tacit knowledge'. See also Philibert (1987).

28 My own 'everyday research'. It must be said that this is not entirely attributable to the personality of individuals concerned; but to (as mainstream psychology might put it) an 'interaction between personality and situation'. In other words, many British academics have been greatly harassed and preoccupied of late.

CHAPTER 4 THE ORIGINS OF CONCERN FOR OTHERS

1 See, for example, the work of Smetana (1981), and especially that of Turiel (1984).

2 Rheingold and Emery (1986) present their own primary data, and also review some of the earlier studies.

3 I am grateful to two babies, Stephanie Ashdown and Chloe Plant (and their parents), for some recent opportunities to observe this.

4 Personal communication from Derek Wright.

5 The archaeological image is pervasive in Freud's work. This particular comment comes from his work on female sexuality, and his ponderings on how most women become heterosexual, given that their first 'love object' is a woman.

6 See, especially, Rutter's comprehensive review of work related in some way to maternal deprivation.

7 Davis and Wallbridge (1981) make this point, in their text on Winnicott.

8 This came out strongly in my own research (1980) on adolescents' values, based on accounts of events in everyday life. It is especially a feature of the so-called 'restricted code' that the context is assumed.

9 Mitchell (1986) summarizes a good deal of this in the introduction to her collection of Klein's key papers.

10 See, for example, the account given by Mahler, Pine, and Bergman (1975). There is a very difficult methodological problem with the Kleinian approach, not least because Klein derived so much of her insight from disturbed children.

11 Winnicott's main papers on this subject are to be found in the collection of 1963, on *The Maturational Process and the Facilitating Environment.*

12 *The Ego Ideal,* by Chasseguet-Smirgel, gives a very thorough account of this part of psychoanalytic theory.

13 Schiff (1974) deals with this in some detail. In her view, based on 'reparenting' work with highly disturbed young people, extreme adaptation is a contributory factor in the development of schizophrenia.

14 Bowlby, among others, describes vividly the 'affectionless' condition. See, for example, his collection of 1979.

15 Schaffer has examined this topic in some detail. A brief summary is to be found in his book on *Mothering* (1977).

16 Some applications of Kleinian theory to moral development are proposed by Money-Kyrle (1951). This author associated morality, virtually by definition, with a sense of guilt; and here I personally disagree with his analysis.

17 Cathie (1987) discusses this question, basing his account primarily on his own therapeutic and pastoral work.

18 This is a very common theme now, both in therapy and in 'assertiveness training'. It has given rise to a number of 'do-it-yourself' books, such as Ann Dickson's *A Woman in Your Own Right.*

19 See, for example, Elshtain's critique of those grand theories which attempt to relate psychoanalysis with gender formation, in *Capitalism and Infancy.*

20 This comes out strongly in recent research in Britain, conducted in association with the Carers' National Association. The association has recently produced a publication on *Informal Carers.*

21 Here is one of the strongest lines of evidence supporting the theses of Chodorow, Dinnerstein, and others. Nancy Friday's *My Mother, Myself,* is a valuable source.

22 Freud's typology of character related to his ideas on psycho-sexual development. Fromm's had a more direct bearing on morality, although at times it looks like a re-description of what is known in common sense, without convincing underlying theory. In his work on destructiveness (1974), Fromm comes dangerously near to the tautology that sometimes presents itself in psychometric trait theories (see Chapter 7, part 1).

CHAPTER 5 THE STUDY OF MORAL JUDGEMENT

1 This is now well-documented in the psychological literature, as some of the references in Chap. 4 make clear. A particularly good recent example is to be found in the fourteenth chapter of the study by Haan, Aerts, and Cooper (1985). It is also abundantly clear in everyday life, for anyone who 'has eyes to see'.

2 Piaget collated his ideas on this topic in one of his later works, *The Principles of Genetic Epistemology* (1972).

3 The book has the title *Biology and Knowledge* (Piaget 1967).

4 A good summary is to be found in Piaget and Inhelder (1969).

5 The question of the proportion who attain formal operations is still controversial, and depends in part on whether or not the concept is limited to its original sense, where it related to scientific thinking. See, for example, Conger (1975), and Shayer *et al.* (1976).

6 Cohen (1983), in his critique and reappraisal of Piaget, gives a striking reinterpretation of a conversation between three young children, which Piaget saw as 'collective monologue'. He shows convincingly that real interpersonal communication was going on (pp. 127ff).

7 See, for example, Loughran (1967) for some early studies, and Modgil and Modgil (1983) for some of the later work.

8 This problem is well explored by Weinreich (1975).

9 This was Kohlberg's doctoral thesis of 1958.

10 An account of the longitudinal work is to be found in Kohlberg's essays of 1981.

11 The re-formulated theory is summarized by Kohlberg, Levine, and Hewer (1983).

12 Gibbs (1979) claims that the sequence goes 'soft' after stage 4, and then relates more to personal than cognitive development.

13 See, for example, Parikh (1980), Nisan and Kohlberg (1982), and Snarey (1982).

14 This is one of the criticisms that has been made most trenchantly. See, especially, Simpson (1974), Sullivan (1977), Schweder (1982), and Vine (1983).

15 Janet Watson has made this point to me in personal communication; it is also reflected in her doctoral thesis of 1988.

16 The key paper here is that of Murphy and Gilligan (1980).

17 This comes out indirectly in the discussion between Smart and Williams in *Utilitarianism: For and Against* (1973); also, directly, in Frankena (1973).

18 Perhaps the best later statement is that of Kohlberg and Candee (1983).

19 Kohlberg, Levine, and Hewer (1983: 48ff).

20 I have discussed this point in some detail in relation to values: Kitwood (1980 chap. 1).

21 Psychometric studies often assume, *a priori*, that all people have a 'personal value system', structured in the same kind of way. If we

look carefully at what 'having values' means, this can be seen as an absurd assumption (Kitwood 1977). Adult development is still poorly explored, but see Malatesta and Izard (1984).

22 There is a useful summary in Kohlberg, Levine and Hewer (1983: 29ff). *The Journal of Moral Education* has recently brought out a special issue in commemoration of the work of Kohlberg. This is vol. 18, no. 2 (1988). It is a valuable resource for appraisal of his work.

CHAPTER 6 ON ORGANIZATIONS: THEIR IMPERATIVES AND CONSTRAINTS

1 This is a point which Fromm reiterated in his many writings. He deals with it in great detail in *The Fear of Freedom* (1942).

2 See Jacques' introduction to this topic, in his *General Theory of Bureaucracy* (1976).

3 A good example of the whole approach, and clear in its treatment of organizations, is the text by Johnson (1961).

4 The term 'intermediate zone' was coined, or at least brought into common use, by Jacques; and as he used it, it referred in part to the way in which unconscious motives are harnessed. Sociologically, Jacques' work tends to side with a rather uncritical structural-functionalism.

5 See, for example, the account by Wasserman (1976).

6 Some of this work is reported by Power and Reimer (1978) see also Power (1988).

7 The latter point was made to me personally by a former trade union official, who felt aggrieved at the deal that had been struck at a high level between his union and management.

8 One valuable empirical study is that of Pugh and Hickson (1968). Although the details have dated now, their principal finding stands.

9 The sociology of education provides alarming news for well-intentioned liberals. See, for example, the collection of articles edited by Dale, Esland, and McDonald (1976).

10 This particular point comes from the economic study by Perlo (1963).

11 The Lucas shop stewards actually produced an alternative corporate plan. For the plan, and its implications for the trade-union movement, see Wainwright and Elliott (1982).

12 For an illuminating recent discussion, see Mary Douglas' book *How Institutions Think* (1987). Here she draws heavily both on Durkheim and the theory of science produced by Otto Fleck, whose ideas were published a long time before the better-known work of Kuhn.

13 This point comes, primarily, from Mike Cooley, one of the main designers of the Lucas Alternative Plan. It is also based in part on my own direct experience, having been involved for a short time in work with those planning and managing technical innovation. See also Davidov (1986).

14 The classic account of this kind of activity is Whyte's *The Organization Man* (1960).
15 A vivid description of this is given by Dornbusch (1958).
16 Here I draw a little on Jacques' ideas, but adapt them considerably. He envisaged the interpersonal as always within the role boundary.
17 This point comes out clearly in the study by Mouledos (1964).
18 The doctor in question found the managerial role extremely stressful, and in fact resigned from his post, returning to his work as a consultant.
19 See the article by Levinson (1959). This was one of the most fruitful of the early attempts to bring about a *rapprochement* between psychology and sociology in understanding organizational behaviour. Levinson, however, had no concept of 'collusive defence'.
20 See de Board (1978)
21 The collusive defence of nurses is examined by Menzies (1970). I touch on this, in relation to dementia, in my paper of 1987.
22 This comes out very strongly in the account given by Primo Levi (1987). Altruism in such contexts, though well documented, is exceedingly rare.

CHAPTER 7 VIRTUE, CHARACTER, AND INTEGRITY

1 His first letter to the Corinthians, chapter 13.
2 For example, Rushton (1980) and Epstein (1985). Both come to the conclusion that the data from this study have been commonly misrepresented.
3 Cattell (1963) refers in this way to the data underlying trait theories. So also does Block (1977), in his critical rebuttal of Mischel's arguments against consistency.
4 A clear example of ipsative scoring is to be found in some of the well-known values questionnaires. It is as if each person has the same amount of 'valuing energy', distributed differently across the different value dimensions (cf. Kitwood 1980).
5 See Bem and Allen (1974)
6 Rest (1983) draws on this scheme in his description of the major components of morality. So also do Musser and Leone (1986), in an even more direct way.
7 See, for example, the extensive handbook edited by Garfield and Bergin (1986).
8 This contrast is drawn out by Symington in his account of *The Analytic Experience*, and he sides with the 'relational disturbance' view.
9 Especially significant here is the work of Bandura (1977).
10 This is a very old idea; but see Schiff (1974) and Laing (1967).
11 From the *Songs of Experience* (1794). But this dialectical theme runs

through Blake's work.

12 Smail (1984) makes this suggestion about psychotherapy, likening it in certain respects to the work of the prostitute. His point is almost cynical. But of course, in a society that was skilled in the art of loving, presumably there would be no need for therapy.

13 One of the very few articles on this topic is that of Roodin, Rybash, and Hoyer (1984).

CHAPTER 8 SOCIAL JUSTICE AND SOCIAL FABRIC

1 This, together with a number of related issues to do with psychotherapy provision, is discussed by Holmes and Lindley (1989).

2 See, especially, his analysis in *The Sane Society* (1956). Fromm would have been on stronger ground if he had linked his idea of needs to some form of lived praxis.

3 In *Illusion and Reality* (1984) Smail has a diagnosis rather similar to mine, but with less emphasis on morality. However, he seems to be more sceptical than I am about therapy, and generally more ambivalent about trust.

4 Social critique is present in almost all Laing's writings of the late 1960s. In chapters 2 and 3 of *The Politics of Experience* (1967), especially, he looks at some social implications of therapy.

5 This point is made by Lukes, in the analysis he gives in his book on *Power* (1974). In effect, he suggests, we cannot understand power fully unless we move on to depth-psychological ground.

6 The concept of care has been relatively little analysed. But see Henry (1989)

7 Richards (1984) analyses skilfully some of the pervasive schizoid tendencies in late capitalist societies.

8 See Kovel's account of 'nuclear terror'. Somehow the fear of annihilation on a large scale resonates with fears of personal annihilation.

9 The history of capitalism may be seen as one of the successive waves of economic activity; in each wave, new items are commodified. I have looked at some aspects of long-wave theory in my paper of 1986.

10 Habermas seems to hold the view that the highest vision of a modern age has not come to pass, and that modernity therefore is an 'incomplete project'. Some postmodern reactions, at any rate, are superficial. See his paper of 1985.

11 This point is drawn out well by Haughey (1977), a Catholic theorist; it is also present, in latent form, in the collection edited by McLean *et al.* (1986).

12 See my paper in the MOSAIC collection of 1983.

13 This quotation comes from an article entitled 'How egalitarianism breeds robbery and yobbery', in the *Sunday Telegraph* of 19 June 1988

(p. 22). The argument seems to be that a good society needs both inequality and authority. The first has been successfully re-established in Britain, but not yet the second.

REFERENCES

Abelson, R. (1977) *Persons*, London: Macmillan.

Argyle, M. (1987) *Bodily Communication*, London: Routledge & Kegan Paul.

Aries, P. (1972) *Centuries of Childhood*, London: Jonathan Cape.

Bailey, C. (1980) 'Morality, reason and feeling', *Journal of Moral Education* 9: 114–21.

Baker Miller, J. (1976) *Toward a New Psychology of Women*, Harmondsworth: Penguin.

Bandura, A. (1977) 'Self-efficacy: toward a unifying theory of behavioural change', *Psychological Review* 84: 191–215.

Becker, E. (1968) *The Birth and Death of Meaning*, Harmondsworth: Penguin.

Bentham, J. (1970): Burns, J.H. and Hart, H.L.A. (eds) (1970) *An Introduction to the Principles of Morals and Legislation*, London: Athlone Press (originally published in 1789).

Bem, D. and Allen, A. (1974) 'On predicting some of the people some of the time', *Psychological Review* 81: 506–20.

Berne, E. (1970) *Games People Play*, Harmondsworth: Penguin.

Bettelheim, B. (1983) *Freud and Man's Soul*, London: Chatto & Windus.

Bion, W. (1986) *Long Week-End: 1887–1919: Part of a Life*, London: Free Associations Books.

Blasi, A. (1980) 'Bridging moral cognition and moral action: a critical review of the literature', *Psychological Bulletin* 88: 1–45.

Block, J. (1971) *Lives Through Time*, Berkeley, CA: Bancroft.

Block, J. (1977) 'Advancing the psychology of personality: paradigmatic shift or improving the quality of research', in D. Magnusson and N.S. Endler (eds) *Personality at the Crossroads*, Hillsdale, NJ: Erlbaum.

Block, J. and Olweus, D. (eds) 1985 *The Development of Antisocial and Prosocial Behaviour: Research, Theories and Issues*, London: Academic Press.

Bowers, K.S. (1977) 'There's more to Iago than meets the eye: a clinical account of personal consistency', in D. Magnusson and N.S. Endler (eds) *Personality at the Crossroads,* Hillsdale, NJ: Erlbaum.

Bowlby, J. (1979) *The Making and Breaking of Affectional Bonds,* London: Tavistock.

Brabeck, M. (1986) 'Moral orientation: alternative perspectives of men and women', in R.T. Knowles and G. McLean (eds) *Psychological Foundations of Moral Education and Character Development,* Lanham, MD: University Press of America.

Bringuer, J. (1977) *Conversations with Jean Piaget,* Chicago: University of Chicago Press.

Broad, W.J. (1985) *Star Warriors,* London: Faber & Faber.

Burns, J.H. and Hart, H.L.A. (eds) (1970) *An Introduction to the Principles of Morals and Legislation,* London: Athlone Press.

Caputo, J.D. (1986) 'A phenomenology of moral sensibility: moral emotion', in G. McLean, F.E. Ellrod, D.L. Schindler, and J.A. Mann *Act and Agent,* Lanham, MD: University Press of America.

Carers National Association (1988) *Informal Carers,* London: CNA Publications.

Carruthers, M., Collins, S., and Lukes, S. (eds) (1985) *The Category of the Person,* Cambridge: Cambridge University Press.

Casey, E.S. (1980) 'Piaget and Freud on childhood memory' in H.J. Silverman (ed.) *Piaget, Philosophy and the Human Sciences,* Brighton: Harvester.

Cathie, S. (1987) 'What does it mean to be a man?' *Free Associations* 8: 7–33.

Cattell, R.B. (1963) *The Scientific Analysis of Personality,* Harmondsworth: Penguin.

Chasseguet-Smirgel, J. (1985) *The Ego Ideal,* London: Free Associations Books.

Chodorow, N. (1976) *The Reproduction of Mothering,* Berkeley, CA: University of California Press.

Cohen, D. (1983) *Piaget: Critique and Reassessment,* London: Croom Helm.

Colby, A., Kohlberg, L., Gibbs, T., Speicher-Dubin, B., and Candee, D. (1983) *The Measurement of Moral Judgment: Standard Issue Manual,* Cambridge, MA: Harvard Centre for Moral Education.

Cole, M. and Bruner J. (1971) 'Cultural differences and inferences about psychological processes', *American Psychologist* 26: 867–7.

Conger, J.J. (ed.) (1975) *Contemporary Issues in Adolescent Development,* New York: Harper & Row.

Conze, E. (1980) *A Short History of Buddhism,* London: Allen & Unwin.

Cooper, C.L. (1984) *Psychosocial Stress and Cancer,* Chichester: Wiley.

Crissman, P. (1942) 'Temporal changes and sexual differences in moral judgements', *Journal of Social Psychology* 16: 29–36.

Dale, R., Esland, G., and McDonald, M. (eds) (1976) *Schooling and Capitalism: a Sociological Reader*, London: Routledge & Kegan Paul.

Damon, W. (ed.) (1978) *New Directions for Child Development*, San Francisco: Jossey Bass.

Davidov, W.H. (1986) *Marketing High Technology*, New York: Macmillan.

Davidson, D. (1962) 'Actions, reasons and causes', *Journal of Philosophy* 60: 685–700.

—— (1970) 'Mental events', in L. Foster, and J.W. Swanson (eds) *Experience and Theory*, Boston: University of Massachusetts Press.

—— (1982) 'Paradoxes of irrationality', in R. Wollheim and J. Hopkins (eds) *Philosophical Essays on Freud*, Cambridge: Cambridge University Press.

Davis, M. and Wallbridge, D. (1981) *Boundary and Space: an Introduction to the Work of D.W. Winnicott*, Harmondsworth: Penguin.

de Board, R. (1978) *The Psychoanalysis of Organizations*, London: Tavistock.

Dickson, A. (1982) *A Woman in Your Own Right*, London: Charlesworth.

Dinnerstein, D. (1976) *The Rocking of the Cradle and the Ruling of the World*, London: Souvenir Press.

Dornbusch, S.M. (1958) 'The military academy as an assimilating institution', *Social Forces* 33: 316–21.

Douglas, M. (1987) *How Institutions Think*, London: Routledge & Kegan Paul.

Draper, P. (1976) *Kalahari Hunter-Gatherers*, Cambridge, MA: Harvard University Press.

Durkheim, E. (1925) *Moral Education: a Study in the Theory and Application in the Sociology of Education*, 1961 edn, New York: Free Press.

Easlea, B. (1981) *Science and Sexual Oppression*, London: Weidenfeld & Nicolson.

Eco, U. (1984) *The Name of the Rose*, London: Pan Books (Picador).

Elshtain, J.B. (1984) 'Symmetry and soporifics: a critique of feminist accounts of gender development', in B. Richards (ed.) *Capitalism and Infancy*, London: Free Associations Books.

Emler, N. (1983) 'Moral character', in D. Locke and H. Weinreich-Haste (eds) *Morality in the Making*, Chichester: Wiley.

Engels, F. (1892) Socialism, Utopian and Scientific, in *The Essential Left*, 1971, London: Unwin Press.

Epstein, S. (1985) 'Some implications of cognitive-experiential self theory for research in social psychology and personality', *Journal of Theory of Social Behaviour*, 15: 283–309.

Erikson, E.H. (1963) *Childhood and Society*, New York: Norton.

Eysenck, H.J. (1975) 'The biology of morality', in T. Lickona (ed.) *Moral Development and Behavioural Theory: Research and Social Issues*,

New York: Holt, Rinehart & Winston.

Fairbairn, W.R.D. (1952) *Psychoanalytic Studies of the Personality*, London: Routledge & Kegan Paul.

Field, T.M. (ed.) (1979) *High-Risk Infants and Children*, New York: Academic Press.

Fisher, E. (1980) *Woman's Creation*, London: Wildwood House.

Foucault, M. (1976) *Madness and Civilization*, London: Tavistock.

Frankena, W.K. (1973) *Ethics*, Englewood Cliffs, NJ: Prentice-Hall.

Freud, S. (1922) *Group Psychology and the Analysis of the Ego*, London: International Psycho-analytic Press.

—— (1927) 'Some psychological consequences of the anatomical distinction between the sexes', *International Journal of Psychoanalysis* 8: 133–42.

—— (1962) *The Ego and the Id*, rev. edn, London: Hogarth Press, trans. J. Riviere.

Friday, N. (1977) *My Mother, Myself*, New York: Delacorte.

Fromm, E. (1942) *The Fear of Freedom*, London: Routledge & Kegan Paul.

—— (1956) *The Sane Society*, London: Routledge & Kegan Paul.

—— (1974) *Anatomy of Human Destructiveness*, London: Jonathan Cape.

Garfield, S.L. and Bergin, A.E. (1986) *Handbook of Psychotherapy and Behaviour Change*, New York: Wiley.

Gellner, E. (1985) *The Psychoanalytic Movement*, London: Paladin.

Gibbs, J.C. (1979) 'Kohlberg's moral stage theory: a Piagetian revision', *Human Development* 22: 89–112.

Gibbs, N.R. (1987) 'Inside the Third Reich', *Time*, 14 Sept. p. 11.

Gilligan, C. (1982) *In a Different Voice*, Cambridge, MA: Harvard University Press.

Gilligan, J. (1975) 'Beyond morality: psychological reflections on shame, guilt and love', in T. Lickona (ed.) *Moral Development and Behaviour: Theory, Research and Social Issues*, New York: Holt, Rinehart & Winston.

Glicksman, M. (1956) *Custom and Conflict in Africa*, Oxford: Blackwell.

Goffman, E. (1969) *The Presentation of Self in Everyday Life*, London: Allen Lane.

Goodall, J. (1986) *The Chimpanzees of Gombe*, Cambridge, MA: Harvard University Press.

Gosling, D.W. (1984) 'Emotions in moral education – an analysis of Rich's "constitutive emotions"', *Journal of Moral Education*, 13: 22–4.

Guntrip, H. (1969) *Schizoid Phenomena, Object Relations and the Self*, New York: International Universities Press.

Haan, N., Aerts, E., and Cooper, B.A.B. (1985) *On Moral Grounds*, New York: New York University Press.

Haan, N., Smith, M.B., and Block, J. (1968), 'Moral reasoning of young

241

adults: political-social behaviour, family background and personality correlates', *Journal of Personality and Social Psychology* 10: 183–201.

Habermas, J. (1968) *Knowledge and Human Interests*, London: Heinemann.

—— (1985) 'Modernity: an incomplete project', in H. Miller (ed.) *Postmodern Culture*, London: Pluto Press.

Haney, C., Banks, C., and Zimbardo, P. (1973) 'Interpersonal dynamics in a simulated prison', *International Journal of Criminology and Penology* 1: 69–97.

Harding, D.E. (1986) *On Having No Head*, London: Arkana.

Hare, R.M. (1952) *The Language of Morals*, New York: Oxford University Press.

Harré, R., Clarke, D., and de Carlo, N. (1986) *Motives and Mechanisms*, London: Methuen.

Harré, R. and Secord, P.F. (1972) *The Explanation of Social Behaviour*, Oxford: Blackwell.

Hartshorne, H., May, M.A., and Maller, J.B. (1928-30) *Studies in the Nature of Character*, New York: Macmillan, vol. 1, *Studies in Deceit*; vol. 2, *Studies in Service and Self-control*; vol. 3, *Studies in the Organization of Character*.

Haughey, J.C. (1977) *The Faith That Does Justice*, New York: Paulist Press.

Havighurst, R.J. and Taba, H. (1949) *Adolescent Character and Personality*, New York: Wiley.

Henry, C. and Tuxill, A.C. (1987) 'Persons and humans', *Journal of Advanced Nursing* 12: 33–9.

Henry, I.C. (1969) 'The concept of care', *Journal of Community Care* 1:27–39.

Higgins, A., Power, C., and Kohlberg, L. (1984) 'The relationship of moral atmosphere to judgments of responsibility', in W.M. Kurtines and J.L. Gewirtz (eds) *Morality, Moral Behaviour and Moral Development*, New York: Wiley.

Hochschild, A. (1975) 'The sociology of feeling and emotion: selected possibilities', in M. Millman and R.M. Kanter (eds) *Another Voice*, New York: Octagon Books.

Hogan, R. and Busch, C. (1984) 'Moral action as autointerpretation', in W.M. Kurtines and J.L. Gewirtz (eds) *Morality, Moral Behaviour and Moral Development*, New York: Wiley.

Holmes, J. and Lindley, R. (1989) *The Values of Psychotherapy*, Oxford: Oxford University Press.

Horney, K. (1946) *Our Inner Conflicts*, Henley: Routledge & Kegan Paul.

Hsu, F.L.K. (1985) 'The self in cross-cultural perspective', in A.J. Marsella, C. Devos, and F.L.K. Hsu (eds) *Culture and Self*, London: Tavistock.

Jacques, E. (1970) *Work: Creativity and Social Justice*, London:

Heinemann.

—— (1976) *A General Theory of Bureaucracy*, London: Heinemann.

Johnson, H.M. (1961) *Sociology: a Systematic Introduction*, London: Routledge & Kegan Paul.

Jung, C.G. (1930) 'The stages of life', in D. Storr (ed.) (1983) *Jung, Selected Writings*, London: Fontana.

Katz, J.O. (1984) 'Personal construct theory and the emotions: an interpretation in terms of primitive constructs', *British Journal of Psychology* 75: 315–22.

Kitwood, T.M. (1977) 'What does "having values" mean?' *Journal of Moral Education* 6: 81–9.

—— (1978) '"Utopia" and "science" in the anticipation of social change', *Alternative Futures* 1: 24–45

—— (1980) *Disclosures to a Stranger*, London: Routledge & Kegan Paul.

—— (1983) 'Personal identity and personal integrity', in D. Locke and H. Weinreich-Haste *Morality in the Making*, London: Wiley.

——(1986) 'Long waves in economic life: an image without a method', *Journal of Interdisciplinary Economics*: 1: 107–25.

—— (1987) 'Explaining senile dementia: the limits of neuropathological research', *Free Associations* 10: 117–40.

—— (1988) 'Researching moral interaction', *Journal of Moral Education* 17: 71–4.

Knowles R.T. (1986) 'The acting person as moral agent', in R.T. Knowles and G.F. McLean (eds) *Psychological Foundations of Moral Education and Character Development*, Lanham, MD: University Press of America.

Kohlberg, L. (1958) 'The development of modes of thinking and choices in years 10 to 16', University of Chicago, Ph.D. dissertation (unpublished).

—— (1981) *Essays in Moral Development*, New York: Harper & Row.

Kohlberg, L. and Candee D. (1983) 'The relation of moral judgment to moral action', in W.M. Kurtines and J.L. Gewirtz (eds) *Morality, Moral Behaviour and Moral Development*, New York: Wiley Interscience.

Kohlberg, L., Levine, C., and Hewer, A. (1983) *Moral Stages: a Current Formulation and a Response to Critics*, Basel: Karber.

Kohlberg, L., Scharf, P., and Hickey, J. (1972) 'The justice structure of the prison: a theory and intervention', *Prison Journal* 51: 3–14.

Kovel, J. (1982) *Against the State of Nuclear Terror*, London: Free Associations Press.

Kurtines, W. and Greif, E.B. (1974) 'The development of moral thought: review and evaluation of Kohlberg's approach', *Psychological Bulletin* 8: 453–70.

Kurtines, W.M. and Gewirtz, J.L. (eds) (1983) *Morality, Moral Behaviour and Moral Development*, New York: Wiley Interscience.

Laing, R.D. (1960) *The Divided Self,* Harmondsworth: Penguin.
—— (1967) *The Politics of Experience,* Harmondsworth: Penguin.
—— (1969) *Self and Others,* Harmondsworth: Penguin.
Lambert, M.J., Shapiro, D.A., and Bergin, A.E. (1986) 'The effectiveness of psychotherapy', in S.L. Garfield and A.E. Bergin (eds) *Handbook of Psychotherapy and Behaviour Change,* New York: Wiley.
Leff, J.P. (1973) 'Culture and the differentiation of emotional states', *British Journal of Psychiatry* 123: 299–306.
Leming, J.S. (1976) 'An exploratory inquiry into the multi-factor theory of moral behaviour', *Journal of Moral Education* 5: 179–88.
Levi, P. (1987) *If This is a Man,* London: Abacus.
Levinson, D. (1959) 'Role, personality and social structure in the organizational setting', *Journal of Abnormal and Social Psychology* 58: 170–81.
Lickona, T. (ed.) (1975) *Moral Development and Behavioural Theory: Research and Social Issues,* New York: Holt, Rinehart & Winston.
Little, B.R. (1972) 'Psychological man as humanist, scientist and specialist' *Journal of Experimental Research in Personality* 6: 95–118.
Locke, D. and Weinreich-Haste, H. (eds) (1983) *Morality in the Making,* Chichester: Wiley.
Loughran, R. (1967) 'A pattern of development in moral judgments made by adolescents, derived from Piaget's scheme of its development in childhood', *Educational Review* 19: 79–96.
Luborsky, L., Singer, B., and Luborsky, L. (1975) 'Comparative studies of psychotherapies', *Archives of General Psychiatry* 32: 995–1007.
Lukes, S. (1974) *Power,* London: Macmillan.
Lyons, J. (1970) *Chomsky,* London: Fontana.
Maccoby, E. and Jacklin, C. (1974) *The Psychology of Sex Differences,* Stanford, CA: Stanford University Press.
MacIntyre, A. (1967) *A Short History of Ethics,* London: Routledge & Kegan Paul.
——(1981) *After Virtue,* London: Duckworth.
Mackie, J. (1977) *Ethics,* Harmondsworth: Penguin.
McCleary, R.A. and Lazarus, R.S. (1949) 'Autonomic discrimination without awareness', *Journal of Personality* 18: 171–9.
McLean, G.F., Ellrod, F.E., Schindler, D.L., and Mann, J.A. (1986) *Act and Agent: Philosophical Foundations for Moral Education and Character Development,* Lanham, MD: University Press of America.
MacMurray, J. (1957) *The Self as Agent,* London: Faber.
McNamee, S. (1978) 'Moral behaviour, moral development and motivation', *Journal of Moral Education* 7: 27–32.
Magnusson, D. and Endler, N.S. (eds) (1977) *Personality at the Crossroads,* Hillsdale, NJ: Erlbaum.

Mahler, M.S., Pine, F., and Bergman, A. (1975) *The Psychological Birth of the Human Infant: Symbiosis and Individuation*, New York: Basic Books.

Malatesta, C.Z. and Izard, C.E. (eds) (1984) *Emotion in Adult Development*, Beverly Hills, CA: Sage.

Malerstein, A.J. and Ahern, M. (1982) *A Piagetian Model of Character Structure*, New York: Human Sciences Press.

Menzies, I.E.P. (1970) *The Functioning of Social Systems as a Defence Against Anxiety*, London: Tavistock.

Milgram, S. (1974) *Obedience to Authority*, London: Tavistock.

Miller, H. (ed.) (1985) *Postmodern Culture*, London: Pluto Press.

Millman, M. and Kanter, R.M. (1975) *Another Voice*, New York: Octagon Books.

Mischel, T. (ed.) (1977) *The Self*, Oxford: Blackwell.

Mischel, W. (1969) *Personality and Assessment*, New York: Wiley.

—— (1977) 'The interaction of person and situation', in D. Magnusson and N.S. Endler (eds) *Personality at the Crossroads*, Hillsdale, NJ: Erlbaum.

—— (1984) 'Convergences and challenges in the search for consistency', *American Psychologist* 39: 351–64

Mitchell, J. (ed.) (1986) *The Selected Melanie Klein*, Harmondsworth: Penguin.

Modgil, S. and Modgil, C. (eds) (1983) *Lawrence Kohlberg: Consensus and Controversy*, London: Falmer.

Money-Kyrle, R.E. (1951) *Psychoanalysis and Politics*, London: Duckworth.

Mouledos, J.C. (1964) 'Organizational goals and structural change: a study of the organization of a prison social system', *Social Forces* 42: 283–90.

Murphy, J.M. and Gilligan, C. (1980) 'Moral development in late adolescence and adulthood: a critique and reconstruction of Kohlberg's theory', *Human Development* 23: 77–104.

Murray, M. (1962) *The Witch-cult in Western Europe*, Oxford: Clarendon.

Musser, L.M. and Leone, C. (1986) 'Moral character: a social learning perspective', in R.T. Knowles and G.F. McLean (eds.) *Psychological Foundations of Moral Education and Character Development*, Lanham, MD: University Press of America.

Nagel, T. (1970) *The Possibility of Altruism*, Oxford: Clarendon Press.

Nisan, M. and Kohlberg, L. (1982) 'Universality and variation in moral judgment: a longitudinal and cross-sectional study in Turkey', *Child Development* 53: 865–77.

Nozick, R. (1974) *Anarchy, State and Utopia*, Oxford: Blackwell.

Oakley, D.A. (ed.) (1985) *Brain and Mind*, London: Methuen.

Olweus, D., Block, J., and Radke-Yarrow, M. (eds) (1986) *Development of Antisocial and Prosocial Behaviour*, New York: Academic Press.

Orbach, S. and Eichenbaum, L. (1986) *Understanding Women,*

Harmondsworth: Penguin.

Parikh, B. (1980) 'Moral judgment development and its relation to family environmental factors in Indian and American families', *Child Development* 51: 1030–39.

Peck, R.F. and Havighurst, R.J. (1960) *The Psychology of Character Development,* New York: Wiley.

Perlo, M. (1963) *Militarism and Industry,* London: Lawrence & Wishart.

Perls, F. (1969) *Gestalt Therapy Verbatim,* Moab, Utah: Real People Press.

Perry, W. (1968) *Forms of Intellectual and Ethical Development in the College Years,* New York: Holt, Rinehart & Winston.

Pettit, P. (1980) *Judging Justice,* London: Routledge & Kegan Paul.

Pfeiffer, J.E. (1978) *The Emergence of Man,* New York: Harper & Row.

Philibert, P.J. (1987) 'Relation, consensus and commitment as foundations for moral growth', *New Ideas in Psychology* 5: 183–95.

Piaget, J. (1932) *The Moral Judgment of the Child,* London: Routledge & Kegan Paul (Penguin edn, 1977).

—— (1967) *Biology and Knowledge,* Edinburgh: Edinburgh University Press.

—— (1972) *The Principles of Genetic Epistemology,* London: Routledge & Kegan Paul.

Piaget, J. and Inhelder, B. (1969) *The Psychology of the Child,* London: Routledge & Kegan Paul.

Polanyi, M. (1946) *Science, Faith and Society,* London: Oxford University Press.

Power, C. and Reimer, J. (1978) 'Moral atmosphere: an educational bridge between moral judgment and action', in W. Damon, (ed.) *New Directions for Child Development,* San Francisco: Jossey Bass.

Power, C. (1979) 'The moral atmosphere of the school', *Moral Education Forum* 4: 9–25.

Power, C. (1988) 'The just community approach to moral education', *Journal of Moral Education* 17: 195–209.

Pugh, D.S. and Hickson, D.J. (1968) 'The comparative study of organizations', in D. Pym (ed.) *Industrial Society,* Harmondsworth: Penguin.

Quinton, A. (1973) *Utilitarian Ethics,* London: Macmillan.

Rawls, J. (1972) *A Theory of Justice,* Oxford: Oxford University Press.

Reps, P. (ed.) (1957) *Zen Flesh, Zen Bones,* Harmondsworth: Penguin.

Rest, J.R. (1979) *Development in Judging Moral Issues,* Minneapolis, MN: University Press.

Rest, J.R. (1983) 'The major components of morality', in W.M. Kurtines and J.L. Gewirtz (eds) *Morality, Moral Behaviour and Moral Development,* New York: Wiley.

Rheingold, H.L. and Emery, G.N. (1986) 'The nurturant acts of very young children', in D. Olweus, J. Block, and M. Radke-Yarrow (eds)

246

Development of Antisocial and Prosocial Behavior, New York: Academic Press.

Rich, J.M. (1980) 'Moral education and the emotions', *Journal of Moral Education* 9: 81–7.

—— (1985) 'Emotions, commitment and moral education – a rejoinder to Gosling', *Journal of Moral Education*, 14: 170–2.

Richards, B. (ed.) (1984) *Capitalism and Infancy*, London: Free Associations Books.

Roback, A.A. (1927) *The Psychology of Character*, New York: Arno Press (3rd edn, 1973).

Rogers, C.R. (1961) *On Becoming a Person*, London: Constable.

—— (1965) *Client-centred Therapy*, London: Constable.

Roodin, P.A., Rybash, J.M., and Hoyer, W.J. (1984) 'Affect in adult cognition', in C.Z. Malatesta and C.E. Izard (eds) *Emotion in Adult Development*, Beverly Hills, CA: Sage.

Rushton, J.P. (1980) *Altruism, Socialization and Society*, Englewood Cliffs, NJ: Prentice-Hall.

Rutter, M. (1972) *Maternal Deprivation Reassessed*, Harmondsworth: Penguin.

Samay, S. (1986) 'Affectivity: the power base of moral behaviour', in G.F. McLean, F.E. Ellrod, D.L. Schindler, and J.A. Mann *Act and Agent*, Lanham, MD: University Press of America.

Sartre, J.P. (1939) *Equisse d'une Théorie des Emotions*, Paris: Herman.

Schaffer, H.R. (ed.) (1971) *The Growth of Sociability*, Harmondsworth: Penguin.

Schaffer, R. (1977) *Mothering*, London: Fontana.

Schiff, J. (1974) *Cathexis Reader*, New York: Harper & Row.

Schon, D. (1983) *The Reflective Practitioner*, London: Temple Smith.

Schreiber, F.R. (1973) *Sybil*, Harmondsworth: Penguin.

Schweder, R. (1982) 'Review of Lawrence Kohlberg's essays on moral development, vol. 1, *The Philosophy of Moral Development*', *Contemporary Psychology* (June 1982), 421–4.

Schweder, R. and Levine R.A. (1984) *Culture Theory*, Cambridge: Cambridge University Press.

Selman, R.L. (1980) *The Growth of Interpersonal Understanding*, New York: Academic Press.

Shayer, M., Kuchemann, D.E., and Wylan, H. (1976) 'The distribution of Piagettian stages in British middle and secondary school children', *British Journal of Educational Psychology* 44: 266–74.

Shotter, J. (1975) *Images of Man in Psychological Research*, London: Methuen.

—— (1987) 'Cognitive psychology: its lack of social accountability', paper delivered at MOSAIC, Brighton, July 1987.

Silverman, H.J. (ed.) (1980) *Piaget, Philosophy and the Human Sciences*,

Brighton: Harvester.

Simpson, E.L. (1974) 'Moral development research', *Human Development* 17: 81–106.

Singer, P. (1976) *The Expanding Circle: Ethics and Sociobiology*, Oxford: Clarendon.

Smail, D. (1984) *Illusion and Reality*, London: Dent.

—— (1987) *Taking Care*, London: Dent.

Smart, J.J.C. and Williams, B. (1973) *Utilitarianism: For and Against*, Cambridge: Cambridge University Press.

Smetana, J. (1981) 'Preschool children's conceptions of moral and social rules', *Child Development* 52: 1333–6.

Snarey, J.R. (1982) 'The social and moral development of Kibbutz founders and sabras: a cross-sectional and longitudinal study', Harvard University dissertation (unpublished).

Spitz, R. (1965) *The First Year of Life*, New York: International Universities Press.

Stiles, W.B., Shapiro, D.A., and Elliott, R. (1986) 'Are all psychotherapies equivalent?', *American Psychologist* 41: 165–80.

Straughan, R. (1983) 'Why act on Kohlberg's moral judgments?' in S. Modgil and C. Modgil (eds) *Lawrence Kohlberg: Consensus and Controversy*, London: Falmer.

Sullivan, E.V. (1977) 'A critique of Kohlberg's structural theory of moral development: a critique of liberal social science ideology', *Human Development* 20: 352–76.

Symington, N. *The Analytic Experience*, London: Free Associations Books.

Taylor, C. (1977) 'What is human agency?', in T. Mischel (ed.) *The Self* Oxford: Blackwell.

—— (1986) 'The person', in M. Carruthers, S. Collins, and S. Lukes (eds) *The Category of the Person*, Cambridge: Cambridge University Press.

Taylor, G. (1981) 'Integrity', *Proceedings of the Aristotelian Society*: LV, 144–59.

Taylor, J.V. (1968) *The Primal Vision*, London: SCM Press.

Turiel, E. (1984) *The Development of Social Knowledge: Morality and Convention*, New York: Cambridge University Press.

Turnbull, C. (1961) *The Forest People*, London: Paladin.

Twiss, B. (1980) *Managing Technological Innovation*, 2nd edn, London: Longman.

Vine, I. (1983) 'Moral maturity in socio-cultural perspective: are Kohlberg's stages universal?', in S. Modgil and C. Modgil (eds) *Lawrence Kohlberg: Consensus and Controversy*, London: Falmer.

Wainwright, H. and Elliott, D. (1982) *The Lucas Plan: a New Trade Unionism in the Making?*, London: Allison & Busby.

Walker, L. (1984) 'Sex differences in the development of moral reasoning: a critical review of the literature', *Child Development* 55: 677–91.

Wasserman, E.R. (1976) 'Implementing Kohlberg's "Just community concept" in an alternative high school', *Social Education* 14: 203–7.

Watson, J. (1988) 'Teacher's conceptions of morality and moral education', University of Leicester, Ph.D. dissertation (unpublished).

Watson, J.B. and Rayner, R. (1920) 'Conditioned emotional reactions', *Journal of Experimental Psychology* 3: 1–14.

Wegner, D.M. and Vallacher, R.R. (1977) *Implicit Psychology,* New York: Oxford University Press.

Weinreich, H. (1975) 'Kohlberg and Piaget: aspects of their relationship in the field of moral development', *Journal of Moral Education* 4: 201–13.

Whyte, L.L. (1962) *The Unconscious Before Freud,* London: Tavistock.

Whyte, W.H. (1960) *The Organization Man,* Harmondsworth: Penguin.

Wilson, E.O. (1975) *Sociobiology: the New Synthesis,* Cambridge, MA: Harvard University Press.

Winnicott, D.W. (1949) *Through Pediatrics to Psychoanalysis,* London: Hogarth Press.

—— (1963) *The Maturational Process and the Facilitating Environment,* London: Hogarth Press.

Woods,). (1979) *Biko,* Harmondsworth: Penguin.

Worsthorne, P. (1988) 'How egalitarianism breeds robbery and yobbery', London: *Sunday Telegraph* 19 June.

Wright, D. (1971) *The Psychology of Moral Behaviour,* Harmondsworth: Penguin.

—— (1983) The moral judgment of the child revisited', in D. Locke and H. Weinreich-Haste (eds) *Morality in the Making,* Chichester: Wiley.

—— (1986) 'An outline of an approach to moral education in schools', *Westminster Studies in Education* 9: 45–55.

NAME INDEX

SUBJECT INDEX

(Page numbers in italics refer to entries in the Notes)